THEY NEVER THREW
ANYTHING AWAY

Memories of the Great Depression by Americans Who Lived It

Ed Linz

Published by Exchange Publishing
Cover and Formatting: Streetlight Graphics

ISBN: 978-1-7367348-0-3

Also by Ed Linz

Non-fiction
Life Row (1997)
Team Teaching Science (2011)
Weekly Opinion Columns (1978-present) written under the pen
name, *Eyes Right*, and archived at eyesright.us and edlinz.com

Fiction
Hurtling to the Edge (2015)

In memory of my Mom
who taught me to listen

About the Front Cover

THE PHOTOGRAPH ON THE FRONT cover, *Bud Fields and His Family at Home*, was taken by Walker Evans in the summer of 1936 in Hale County, Alabama. Evans was working for the Farm Security Administration, one of the government organizations established during the Roosevelt administration to combat rural poverty, but he was on leave while doing an assignment for *Fortune* magazine with the writer, James Agee. Because their goal was to document Depression-era poverty, he and Agee spent eight weeks living with three sharecropping families near the town of Akron in southern Alabama. Although *Fortune* opted not to run the finished product, their work gained national acclaim in 1941 when published as a book, *Let Us Now Praise Famous Men*. Several of Evans' photographs from his experience with the Temple, Fields, and Burroughs families featured in that book became iconic reminders of the poverty and hardship experienced by so many Americans during the Great Depression. In their book, Evans and Agee used pseudonyms to protect the identity of the three families, but, interestingly, Evans' photos, which are archived in the Library of Congress, have the actual names displayed.

Evans was quite a character. Originally from a privileged background in St. Louis, he studied at private boarding schools in the Northeast before spending a year in Paris. Upon his return to the U.S., he attempted writing while living amongst the bohemian crowd in Greenwich Village, but soon developed an interest in photography. In the summer of 1933 Evans traveled to Cuba for a photographic assignment. There he became a nightly drinking buddy of Ernest Hemingway with whom he developed a strong friendship. Following WW II Evans worked for both *Time* and *Fortune* magazines for the next 20 years. His Depression photographs are readily available for order at the Library of Congress and were cataloged in the 1973 book, *Walker Evans, Photographs for the Farm Security Administration, 1935-1938*.

Table of Contents

Introduction

THIS BOOK IS A COLLECTION of remembrances of the Great Depression, that difficult period of American life between the end of 1929 and the early years of World War II. Each of these stories was gathered as I traveled the United States in the late 1990's talking to "average" citizens who lived during that time frame. Everyone I interviewed was eager to tell their story, whether filled with happy thoughts, or memories of exceptionally challenging days. I received recommendations from several friends and relatives as to who would have "good stories" to tell, while other interviews came serendipitously from chance encounters on the street. All the interviews were preserved using a cassette recorder; I also took notes as the speaker answered my questions. Many folks showed me photographs and memorabilia gathered during the Depression, including newspaper clippings and magazine articles. Although many of the stories relate misery, some were filled with joyful memories, such as the African-American who worked in the turpentine forests of rural Georgia, the granddaughter of the chief engineer of the Panama Canal who took her on an ocean liner to Panama, and a barnstorming bi-plane aviator in the Northwest.

I sat on these interviews for over 20 years, primarily because I found myself fully occupied with classroom teaching and family responsibilities. Those notes and taped interviews would probably have stayed in my basement, but for the emergence of the corona virus in early 2019. As the economic conditions in the U.S. worsened, I began to worry that this vicious virus (and governmental reaction to it) might lead to another deep recession, or even a Depression. Out came my research notes, tapes, and photos from those late 1990's interviews. It is my objective that this collection of remembrances can provide context and hope during our current era. The generation of Americans described in this book lived through incredibly challenging, personally difficult times. Hopefully, we will not be faced with that scenario, but if it happens, their memories can give us a blueprint of what to do and how to survive.

The exact dates bracketing the Great Depression are difficult to pinpoint, and the causes are too vague to identify a prime event with certainty. Many, for example, argue that the stock market crash which occurred over several days in October 1929 was more of an overdue reaction to economic forces which had been brewing for years than a single causative event. Many historians and economists now agree that there were other contributing factors to the economic collapse, such as farming losses, poor political leadership, and ineffective action by the Federal Reserve - all contributed to the disastrous results which buffeted our nation for the following decade.

What is not arguable is that the human misery which engulfed America during the 1930's was widespread and severe. The economic and social tragedy was not short-lived. Despite numerous federal efforts to mitigate unemployment with government programs, such as the Civilian Conservation Corps (CCC) and the Tennessee Valley Authority (TVA), a second sharp recession in the summer of 1937 erased most earlier gains, plunging the nation deeper into economic chaos. It was not until the middle years of World War II when 15 million Americans were in uniform that employment reached pre-Depression levels. The stock market took even longer to recover.

For an entire generation of Americans, the Great Depression was the defining experience which shaped their lives during this difficult period and their outlook on life during the better days which followed after the end of WW II. My introduction to this hectic period of American history came from talks with my mother when I was a child in Kentucky. She had vivid memories of that era and was determined to be prepared if another such calamity were to occur. The trait which defined my parents, particularly my mother, was frugality. She never assumed that prosperity would continue indefinitely and was fully prepared for harsh economic times. Her daily activities were to use, conserve, and re-use. The title of this book, *They Never Threw Anything Away*, is an apt descriptor of her approach to life and that of many of her friends and family. I have since learned from discussions with my peers that this grandly frugal trait also defined their parents and relatives.

When the Great Depression began my mother was 15 years old. She was living in extreme poverty with seven siblings in what was essentially a shack outside Cleaton, Kentucky. Her mother had passed away leaving her and an older sister responsible for raising the younger children. Her description of early family life was always, "We were poor, but clean." Mom's father worked in the coal mines in western Kentucky on the other side of the state from the more well-known mining region in Appalachia. She was able to complete high school (only one brother or sister did so) and, with essentially no money, boarded a train for a 12-hour ride to begin nursing training at Speers Hospital in Dayton, Kentucky.

Nearly all nursing programs at that time were associated with hospitals, and the nursing students were basically indentured servants working for room and board. She graduated and passed the licensing examination to become a Registered Nurse (R.N.) in 1936. She had met my father while she was in nursing school, and they were married by a Justice of the Peace in late 1939. An only child, I was born in 1943 in the midst of WW II and shared a bedroom with them in a 4-room house until I was 12. We later moved to a farm in a rural area until I left Kentucky for a career in nuclear submarines.

I provide this brief background to explain that my mother experienced the trials of the Great Depression up close and personal. It was truly the defining period of her life. The survival techniques she mastered during this difficult period stayed with her throughout the remainder of her days. As a child in a small working-class town, I watched with curiosity how she maintained these same patterns of behavior as our family gradually became more affluent. Both of my parents had continuous employment during WW II and in the following years, although neither had high-paying jobs. My father's education had ended after the third grade when his family's poverty forced him to work on a horse-drawn milk wagon. All his subsequent work involved hard labor. My mother worked as a nurse in local hospitals or doing private duty nursing in patients' homes (this was a common practice at the time).

Mom was not alone in her frugality. Essentially all her friends exhibited this same awareness of the temporary nature of good times. Most of our entertainment consisted of interacting with families of relatives and friends. I never had a babysitter, and none of my childhood friends had one either, unless it was an older sibling. Even as a child I noticed that many of my mother's traits were also exhibited by other families around us. They were all survivors of the Great Depression. Once Mom confided to me that she actually hoped for a severe economic downturn because "I've been there, I know what to do."

After Mom passed away in 1991 following a car accident, I began to reflect on the defining characteristics of her group of Depression survivors and became determined to begin interviewing that generation. Unfortunately, I was then diagnosed with an unusual disease, cardiac sarcoidosis, and given two years to live. However, I survived, thanks to a life-saving heart transplant operation in 1994. During my extended recovery period I traveled throughout the U.S. gathering stories from other survivors of the Great Depression about how Americans, from different backgrounds, coped with those drastic economic times of the 1930's. After doing local interviews in the mid-Atlantic, I traveled to the West Coast, to the mid-West, the Northeast, and to the deep South. All the wonderful people I interviewed were eager to share their stories and were uniformly proud of their survival. Their eyes would often dance with joy as they recounted their experiences, although many involved challenging and difficult days.

I have not attempted to edit the words or grammar used in the interviews – what you read is what was told to me, sometimes in colorful terms. Background information is interspersed throughout each chapter to explain or expand on persons, places, or things mentioned (e.g., a Hupmobile). Much of this was gathered from open-source materials, and I have not listed sources or provided footnotes. This book is strictly an oral history of the Great Depression, told by 22 Americans as they recalled it.

Each chapter is titled with the name of the person I interviewed, along with a phrase describing their situation, the date of the interview, and the location where they lived during the Depression years. The final chapter includes a discussion of common threads from their memories of that era.

At the end of the book there is a brief chronology of major events which took place during the Great Depression.

None of the individuals I interviewed was "famous," but all were special individuals. Their grit, determination, and wisdom set a high standard for all who follow in their footsteps. It is my goal that the remembrances presented here can provide context, hope, and a pathway to relief if, God forbid, we are faced with comparable troubles ahead.

"Dust Bowl to Rice Bowl"
Vorda Mae Honnold

Wood River, Nebraska
Interviewed February 8, 1999

V ORDA CAUGHT MY ATTENTION AT a monthly luncheon in Washington, D.C. held by the George Washington University Hospital Women's Board. At the time I was the only active male member of the organization which proudly describes itself as "a philanthropic powerhouse." It was founded in 1898 by "prominent Washington women" and had just celebrated its centenary. After speaking to the Board about some medically-related issues on several occasions, I was invited to become a member because, as they liked to describe it, I "had a woman's heart." This was literally true because I had been the extremely grateful recipient of a 33-year-old woman's heart five years earlier during a transplant operation.

Vorda was sitting next to me at the luncheon and was an exceptionally outgoing conversationalist. When she learned that I was interviewing people who had memories of the Great Depression, she insisted that we meet so that she could tell me about her experiences while growing up in rural Nebraska. Two weeks later I visited at her apartment located midway between the infamous Watergate complex and George Washington University hospital. Her apartment was decorated with numerous Chinese paintings and sculptures. Several books about China were displayed on tables. Vorda was wearing a long-sleeved blouse in a black and white print pattered in what appeared to be repeating animal tracks. The blouse was fastened at the collar with a small broach. Large black earrings matched her black trousers. Her elegant white hair was obviously styled and looked terrific. In short, she exuded casual elegance.

Before beginning our conversation, Vorda insisted that we have hot tea. She also placed a large dish of what proved to be irresistible homemade cookies in front of me. We spent the next 2+ hours discussing her life, beginning with her pioneer grandparents.

My grandparents on my mother's side were very wealthy. My grandfather, William Johnson, had come from Virginia. He and his two brothers were students at VMI [Virginia Military Institute, in Lexington, Virginia] when the Civil War began. His two older brothers both fought as officers for the Confederates and were quickly killed in battles. Grandfather Johnson chose to leave Virginia rather than end up dead like his brothers. He headed west to Texas and then up to Wyoming where he became an explorer, trader and trapper for large East Coast companies. While he was there, he married an Indian woman. I was always told, that during this phase of his life, he lived just like an Indian. He had two boys with that woman, then left her....I don't know why, but he always took care of those boys financially. One of them became a professor.

Grandfather Johnson went into ranching near Green River, Wyoming. He became wealthy and was appointed the county sheriff. After that he served one term in the state legislature. At one time he had one of the largest herds of cattle in the west. I'm not sure exactly when, but he met and soon married my grandmother, Sophia Larson, who was 16. Her family had come from a shipping company in Norway and had money. She and grandfather had three sons and one daughter, who was my mother. The boys all became highly successful. One, my Uncle Bryan, went to Harvard and later ran for governor of New Mexico, but lost. Both he and his brother, my Uncle Fred, became prominent members of the Democratic Party and were closely tied to President Roosevelt. My mother, her name was Ellen Johnson, was born in Wyoming, but was sent to a girl's school in Lincoln, Nebraska. She was an exceptional pianist and had her own grand piano.

At this point, Vorda went into a long discussion about some of the conversations which she had with her grandfather Johnson concerning his relationship with Chinese workers who had been employed to build the Union Pacific railroad. From the tone of her voice and the twinkle in her eyes, I could tell how much she cherished these memories. When the railroad was completed in 1869, there was little work for the over 12,000 Chinese who had been imported as labor for the Union Pacific. Most had no option other than to remain in the western U.S. while trying to survive on whatever work they might find from local settlers. Vorda explained their predicament:

Those remaining Chinese were treated very badly. Some of the cowboys thought it was great sport to hunt them down like rabbits to cut off their long black pigtail hair....I think that those were called queues. Every Chinese man who had this happen to him was devastated by this cruel action because he believed that without his queue, he was not a complete person and would not be accepted by his ancestors when he died. Several years later, around 1900, during the Boxer Rebellion, China tried to expel all foreigners; this led to even more discrimination of the Chinese in America. My grandmother, Sophia, made it known throughout her Wyoming community that any Chinese coming to the Johnson home would be protected. She and my grandfather, William, saved the lives of many Chinese men; two that he mentioned were "China Joe" and Yu Yi-tom. Grandfather helped these two start a Chinese restaurant in Green River, known as "The Shanghai." Yu was very grateful, and later in his life, he gave my grandmother many beautiful gifts which he had imported from China. These stories generated an urge in me to someday visit, or even live in, China....I will tell you how that came about later.

Vorda now returned to her grandparents coming to Nebraska:

My grandfather Johnson had a home built in Wood River, Nebraska [about 160 miles southwest of Omaha] as a base for his cattle business. It was a central location where they could bring the cattle to be fattened before sending them to the stock yards in Omaha. My parents, Perley and Ellen Honnold, had met there via mutual friends who played baseball with my father. Papa - that's what I always called my father - came from a large family: 11 brothers and sisters. Papa was next to the youngest. His father, John Honnold, was from Ohio. He had fought for the Union Army but was captured and spent most of the war in a Confederate prison camp. After the war he came to Nebraska as a homesteader and became a successful farmer. John built a log cabin in front of a cave that he dug in the side of a hill about four miles south of Wood River. He did well as a farmer and when he died in 1915, each of his children received $1500 - a large amount in those days!

I was born at home in Wood River on March 10, 1910. It is close to the exact center of Nebraska; the nearest large town was Grand Island, about 16 miles away. My parents had been married in 1905 and moved into a home which Papa had built a block north of the Catholic Church. I did not really get to know my mother because right after I was born, she went into what I was always told was post-partum depression. Papa, whose name was Harman P. Honnold, was a rural mail carrier and had a route out of Wood River. He never went by Harman - ever - and was always called by his middle name, "Perley" or "HP." My mother, whom I do not like to talk about, was put into institutions for the rest of her life. I only saw her a couple of times. The first time I was 12 years old and she was in a hospital in Hastings, Nebraska. She could still play the piano beautifully. I saw her again when I was 20, and I remember her telling one of her nurses, "See, I told you I had a daughter." Papa always made sure she had good clothing and whatever she needed there. I'm not sure who paid for the nursing home...it may have been the Johnson family because they were so wealthy....but Papa never saw her again. She died in a nursing home in St. Paul, Nebraska in 1974 at over 90 years of age.

Once she left, Papa hired "nurses" to take care of me. They were usually what were called "sleep-in types." They took care of me, but they also took care of Papa, if you know what I mean. One wanted real bad to marry him, but that was impossible in Nebraska at the time because you could not get a divorce if your spouse was in an institution. In 1917 Papa bought a house about a mile north of Wood River on 4 acres. When he wasn't doing the mail route, he did some farming.

Initially Papa did the mail route with two horses, "Old Ves" and "Old Billy." He was really attached to those horses but sold them to a farmer when he got a Model T [Ford] to do the route. He cried quite a bit when he sold those horses, because neither of them was used to pulling a plow. After we got the new house, two of my aunts, Papa's sisters, took turns coming to live with us. When the Spanish flu epidemic hit in 1918-19, I was not yet 10, and I am pretty certain that I got it because my aunt made me live by myself for a month in just one part of the house. I was really sick for that whole time. Papa was terribly worried then because at least 25 people on his mail route died from the flu. It really hit the local Mennonite population hard, especially healthy men who were the bread earners. It was so bad no one went to any of the funerals because they were afraid of catching it.

As I now listen to Vorda's taped comments about funerals during the Spanish flu epidemic, I was struck by how fear of an unseen, and deadly, disease has always run through the human condition. A century later we still are just as much at the mercy of such viruses. Several friends who passed away during the COVID-19 pandemic (due to other causes) were not able to have traditional funerals with family and friends in attendance. Vorda continued memories of her childhood:

I went to grade school in Wood River - I always walked, even when we lived outside of town. When the weather was real bad, Papa would take me. When I was 16, and in high school, he bought me a car, a second-hand Ford coupe, so then I drove. All during high school I was keeping house and fixing all the meals for Papa. I liked doing this. My father was extremely strict - no dates, no boyfriends, until I graduated from high school. So....I had my first date on the night I graduated! I had seen this fellow around town because he was an older brother of one of my girlfriends. He was what we now call a "hunk." As soon as I first saw him, I told his sister, "That's the man I'm gonna marry." His name was Malcolm, but everyone called him Nick. He was my first date, and the only fellow I dated. We went to dances or the movies and played a lot of cards. I always loved to play cards, and everyone said, "She was born with a deck of cards in her hands." Sometimes we would play until 2 A.M. but we never played for money. Papa was so strict that he not only wouldn't allow any cursing, but not even much slang. He got upset if you said, "Gee whiz!" He was very strait-laced, but he always had a "housekeeper" because, as he put it, "He needed a companion."

Things quickly got bad in Wood River after the stock market crashed in late 1929. We were mostly okay because Papa had a monthly government check from the mail carrier job, and we had no debt. I think that he lost $40 when the bank closed, but others lost a lot more. Many local families started to suffer because they had no cash for basic necessities or for services of dentists and doctors. Houses started to get run down, and many of the farm fields were going to waste. Homes and outbuildings went unpainted for years and even the countryside took on a dilapidated appearance. The barter system was frequently used. Instead of paying cash, people often settled bills with fruits, vegetables, chickens, eggs, meats, and other farm products. Sometimes lifetime personal possessions were used instead of cash. Papa was able to acquire a large number of antique firearms from local folks who sold them to him at low prices so that they could eat. He was immensely proud of the number and quality of those guns. He also assembled a large collection of Indian artifacts which he had found in local fields. In addition, we had another collection of African spears, bows, arrows, and other items sent to him by a nephew living in what was the Belgian Congo. Whenever anyone would visit our home, Papa would proudly give them a tour of each of his collections. After he passed away, I donated all of these to the "House of Yesterday" historical museum in Hastings,

Nebraska where it is displayed as the "H.P. Honnold Collection." I am certain that Papa would be proud of me for doing this.

One time Papa loaned $10 to one of the men who lived on his mail route. The farmer promised to re-pay with a quarter of beef the next time he butchered. The meat was delivered to our house on a very cold winter day....I think it was in 1931. We were surprised by how large a piece of meat this was, so we had to keep it on our outside porch overnight. I had some canning jars and borrowed as many others as I could from friends. We got up at 5 in the morning and sterilized the jars. I cooked the meat in batches for nearly 10 hours. When we got finished, we had 87 quart jars filled with delicious, tender beef, which came in handy over the next year. I kept them in the cellar where it was cool. We never had electricity in that house....just used kerosene lamps for lighting. We heated with a furnace in the basement that could use coal, wood, or even corn cobs from the nearby farms. What we did have was a form of indoor plumbing. We had an outhouse originally, but Papa put a gasoline engine in the basement which pumped water upstairs from our well. The toilet was interesting in that when you pulled down the seat to sit, it pumped water into an overhead tank which flushed when you put the seat up.

We started to notice a lack of rain in our area in 1931. Over the next several years, it got worse - real worse. The summers were blisteringly hot, and farmers began to lose whatever crops they had planted in the spring. Sometimes the dust from the fields blew steadily and densely for days on end. Keeping your house free from the dust was impossible. The outside of the windows was a separate problem because the covering of dust there would be converted to sticky mud whenever there was the occasional sprinkle. Sometimes I could not drive - no one could - because in those dust storms you couldn't see more than a few feet ahead. Sometimes you just had to stop your car and wait several minutes until the road was visible. Papa had a bad accident and was injured because he didn't stop during one of these dust storms.

The "Dust Bowl era" occurred during much of the 1930's throughout the American High Plains. Vorda's region was not hit the hardest but probably received much of the dust generated out of the southwest cluster of Texas, New Mexico, Oklahoma, Colorado, and Kansas. In addition to the severe drought, farming practices of deep plowing of topsoil used at the time led to the elimination of much native grassland which had previously trapped moisture and blowing soil. The huge clouds of dust often blackened the skies (as Vorda recounted to me) and traveled east and north across the U.S. even reaching East Coast cities, including Washington, D.C. and New York City. These "black blizzards," as they were often called, reduced visibility to less than three feet. Tens of thousands of farmers were forced to abandon their farms when their crops failed, and they could not pay their mortgages. In current money terms, the losses exceeded $500 million a day. John Steinbeck's 1939 classic novel, *The Grapes of Wrath*, dramatically captured the misery of these days.

Vorda now shifted to her love life....

Nick and I dated for just over 4 years, and when Papa and one of his girlfriends went on a vacation up to the Badlands in South Dakota in 1932, Nick and I secretly went up to South Dakota ourselves and got married by a minister up there. I don't remember his name. We gave him 10 bucks, and he seemed happy to do it. We didn't tell anyone, including Papa. When we came back, I lived at home and Nick lived at the family farm. Nick did give me a wedding ring, but I never wore it except in bed with him. We spent many nights together at my home. Papa knew we were sleeping together, but what could he do? I was 22, and in view of what he had been doing for the past 20 years, what could he say? Nick and Papa got along fine and even went hunting together. Nick couldn't find any work, so to bring in some money, I was doing substitute work for the postal service, but I wasn't allowed to sub for Papa because two people from the same family could not do the same route.

My marriage didn't last long. I say "my" marriage because Nick never really gave up other women. I loved him with all my heart, and I still believe that he loved me, but I just made a bad choice. Whenever I learned of one of his "escapades," I would confront him. He always told me that the other girl "didn't mean a thing." Even some of my girlfriends slept with him! He always told me that he didn't want children, but later

I think that he did have some....not sure. Even though our own sex life was great, I had too much pride to continue on. When I told him that I was going to divorce him, he didn't say much. I went up to Grand Island and got a lawyer and sued him for non-support. Nick didn't contest it, and, by 1934, I was divorced. Unfortunately, the news of the divorce was in the paper, so everyone found out at the same time that I was married and divorced! I will say this about Nick: he taught me to dance and I had my first drink with him. After our divorce I stayed home for nearly a year and was losing my mind. I didn't even want to have coffee!

I ran into Nick a year later when I was having dinner with a man I was dating. Nick came over to our table and asked me to dance. I never hesitated and said, "No thanks." I knew that if I danced with him and he was touching me I would go to pieces. Many years later I heard that Nick had married three more times, including twice to the same woman - one that had lived just around the block from us. The last I heard, he was still living in Nebraska and worked for the railroad.

After Vorda had shared with me all these intimate details of her marriage, I asked her if there were any parts of her story that she did not want me to write. She laughed with a few giggles, "You can print all of it - every bit, even the sex stuff. Just don't use his last name in case he did have children. I have no regrets because if we had been married for 50 years, I would have missed so much of the experiences and excitement that those years have given me."

I forgot to tell you; my real name is not Vorda. My mother named me Vodra, but once she was gone, Papa changed it to Vorda. He never told me this nor why he changed it. I learned when I later had to get a passport. I found out that I had no birth certificate and had to get an affidavit from the doctor who delivered me. One day while I was sitting around home feeling sorry for myself, my Uncle Fred Johnson, the one who worked as Land Commissioner for Roosevelt, stopped by and said that he was appalled that I had not been to college. This was now the mid-30's. He gave me money to go business school up in Grand Island. I rented a room there and learned typing, dictation, and shorthand. Uncle Fred had a lot of connections and knew Senator Norris [powerful 5-term

U.S. senator from Nebraska] real well. Norris wrote a letter to the WPA asking them to hire me. So right away I got a job as the secretary to the County Engineer of Hall County there in Grand Island. I was paid $65 a month and was living in the Hotel for Professional Women in town. I had no car, but quickly learned to entertain myself.

One day I decided on a whim to go to a fortune teller in Grand Island. I remember her words exactly, "One day soon you will get a call and will be offered a job far away." One week later, it was now 1938, I got a call from Washington and was offered a government job at Social Security in Baltimore. I never knew for sure, but I am pretty certain that Uncle Fred was behind this. The next week I was on the train to Baltimore and a new life. I worked from 4 in the afternoon to 11 at night at an office on Pratt Street. They started me as a GS-1 getting $1005 a year. I had a room on Charles Street in a boarding house with other girls working there. I could walk to work, but it was through some rough neighborhoods with strip clubs. Not too long later I was offered a better job with Social Security as a GS-2 in D.C. That was a simple decision for me because I got a raise to $1440 a year, and I knew that there were clubs and nightlife in D.C. so I could have a social life. So, I moved to D.C. and started living in a small apartment in what had been, at one time, the French Embassy. I had 7 typists working for me, but I was not long for the job. Shortly before the war began, I saw an opening for a GS-4 job with a new federal agency, the Office of Price Administration. I immediately applied and got it. I really liked what I was doing, especially the $1800/year that I was being paid. I was now a "Corresponding Secretary" and was working with a lot of "Dollar a Year Men." This was an entirely different environment for me, and I didn't just like it, I loved it.

The concept of "Dollar a Year Men" began sometime in the early 1900's in the U.S. when experienced leaders of industry volunteered to serve in government positions, but without pay. However, for legal reasons at the time, it was mandatory that they be on salary, so they accepted pay of one dollar a year (many still retained pay from their corporations). The practice began in the early 1900's when Gifford Pinchot, a wealthy forester, did work for his close friend, President Teddy Roosevelt. During WW I there were nearly 1000 such "employees" of the federal government. The financier, Bernard Baruch, was one of the more famous.

The Office of Price Administration (OPA) had been set up within another federal agency in early 1941 to control prices and rents in anticipation of the U.S. entering WW II. In January 1942, it became an independent agency with the power to place ceilings on all prices (except agricultural) and to ration other scarce commodities, such as gasoline, sugar, coffee, meats, processed foods, and nylon stockings to name only a few items. The program lasted throughout the war. I recall my family and their friends still having ration booklets for various items. Those women's nylon stockings, which had been invented by DuPont Chemical Company in the late 1930's, had become a craze. According to the Smithsonian, when Dupont recognized the apparently insatiable need of American women for their new products, they cleverly set May 16, 1940 as "Nylon Day" and put four million pairs of brown nylons in department stores. They sold out in two days! But when the war came, DuPont was directed to channel all nylon into the making of parachutes, mosquito netting, and other military uses. Following the war, there were actually "nylon riots" where women fought over nylon stockings which were being slowly returned to department stores! Rationing of various items continued for many months after the war, but the OPA was officially abolished in May 1947. Vorda continued....

One day a very wealthy man visiting OPA asked me to have breakfast with him. While we ate, he asked me if I could take dictation. By the time we finished breakfast he offered me a job as his secretary. He was with the Office of Strategic Services, that was the OSS. I was promoted from GS-4 to GS-5 and moved to a great office by the Reflecting Pool near all the monuments between the Lincoln Memorial and the Washington Monument. Professionally this was a great situation. It was still during the war and I was working for the top intelligence agency. I had plenty of time to do volunteer work for the Red Cross and to have a date whenever I wanted one.

Less than a year after I had begun there, I was approached by another wealthy man who took me to dinner and then said, "I'm asking you to be my secretary. What kind of legs do you have?"

Here Vorda paused to catch my reaction....then she had a big laugh and continued:

He said, "In this job you may have to do a lot of walking." Apparently, he wanted me to go to London to work with him there. He told me that it would be dangerous because the Germans might soon use buzz bombs on the city. Before deciding, I went home to see Papa. He told me, "I'm not going to be here when you come home next time." Shortly after I returned to D.C. I received a long-distance call from Nebraska telling me that Papa had dropped dead from a heart attack.

Papa's death devastated me. When I came home for the funeral, I found that he had burned all my letters and photos. I was a wreck and decided that I couldn't return to Washington because I was the only one who could settle the estate. I wanted the most dangerous job I could find and went to work at a bomb plant in Hastings, Nebraska. I was the medical secretary, and each day went with doctors who inspected the workers on the bomb-making assembly line. Dynamite is extremely dangerous because exposure all day to the ingredients can be very harmful. I saw blue lips, yellow eyes, and very gray skin among the workers. Most were having respiratory problems. I stayed there in that job for nearly a year until the estate was settled. Then I returned to Washington and was able to get my job back at OSS at the same desk.

Vorda went on to tell me about many of her subsequent adventures with the OSS. She met and worked with several men who were famous at the time, such as Alfred DuPont, "one of the Mellons," and Richard Helms who later became Director of the follow-on intelligence agency, the CIA (Central Intelligence Agency). Because of her maternal grandfather's interest in China, Vorda began taking Mandarin classes in 1946, and when friends at the CIA learned of this, she was asked, "Can you be in San Francisco in 30 days to go to an assignment in China?"

"I got to there in 15 days and was waiting for the ship to take me to China!" After more tea and cookies, Vorda spent the next hour regaling me with her post-war CIA adventures in Shanghai, China prior to the Communists taking over in 1949. She obviously had great love for the Chinese people, many with whom she established close friendships. But she had an equally intense contempt for Generalissimo Chiang Kai-shek, the leader of the Nationalist (Kuomintang) Party who was defeated by the communists under Mao Zedong. Vorda regarded Chiang as one of the most corrupt and evil men she had encountered.

Vorda's gave me a copy of 45-page typed essay, "Memories of Shanghai," in which she detailed her time there with the CIA from June 1947 to April 1949. In addition to discussing the work environment and the social life of the large expatriate community in Shanghai, she recounted in great detail the overwhelming poverty, particularly among the continuous flow of refugees arriving daily from war torn regions of the country. "Of course, each of us had a driver, a boy, and a woman working for us, whether we needed them or not. Each had a rice bowl." I learned many years earlier while watching the 1966 Steve McQueen movie, *The Sand Pebbles*, that this last phrase was widely used in China to describe how each person's job, however menial, was the only thing keeping that person and his family alive. If, out of kindness, you insisted on doing their work yourself, you were not only insulting that person, but taking away their livelihood. Vorda's written descriptions of widespread hunger, rampant opium addiction, and prostitution by desperate women and children was heart-wrenching. "People were tearing bark off trees to boil, hoping for some possible nutrition to allow them to live yet another day. Others would throw themselves onto moving cars in the belief that, if they were sufficiently injured to be taken to hospital, they would be fed." Unfortunately, there were even worse times ahead for many Chinese during several periods of rule by the CCP (Chinese Communist Party).

Over the next 12 years Vorda worked for the CIA in 9 different countries, including Japan, Bangkok, and Switzerland before retiring in February 1969. Subsequently she did stints with two major U.S. corporations but did not return overseas.

Vorda was very proud of her family history and insisted to me, "You know, people say that those who fought World War II were the 'Greatest Generation.' I disagree. Our pioneer families were the greatest American generation." Vorda's closing comment to me as I was leaving her apartment was, "You know, life in that Dust Bowl was a very depressing time for almost everyone. But I survived and went on to a wonderful life."

I would have to agree.

"The Music Man"
John Michael Toran

Huntington, New York
Interviewed March 11, 1999

John Toran (center)

WHENEVER THE MERITS OF IMMIGRATION to the United States are discussed, I would offer the life of John Toran as Exhibit A in support of immigration. I came to know John during a visit to his modest home in an upscale section of McLean, Virginia after a mutual friend recommended that we chat. Because I explained in a previous telephone conversation with John that I was collecting personal stories about life during the Great Depression for a future book, he had collected several documents and photographs to share during our conversation. After warmly greeting me at the door, he took a seat in his living room in front of several paintings which he had recently created. He spoke with a firm voice, and throughout our talk kept saying that he wanted to "keep things in sequence." I tried to oblige, but, because he had so many interesting asides, we kept bouncing around chronologically. He began with his early life:

I was born at home in Bayonne, New Jersey on January 24, 1911. My mother always told me that I was delivered by a midwife. My parents, Anthony and Pauline Tworzyanski, were from Poland. They came here through Ellis Island in about 1900 - not sure of the exact day or year. Neither spoke any English then. My father had been a blacksmith in Poland, but there wasn't much need in their new neighborhood, so he started up a little butcher shop. You know, at that time, most people would pay the shopkeeper what they owed them at the end of the month. Dad found out the hard way that many couldn't, or wouldn't pay, and, after two years of not making any money, he closed the shop. We moved to Huntington over on Long Island [New York] when I was four years old. It was about halfway out on the island. The family that had sponsored us to come over from Poland lived there and found a place for us to live. My father was initially able to get a job as a laborer working on one of the rich estates....not sure which one....I think it may have been Mellon's. We were living on Pigeon Hill Road in Huntington Station. Some fella, I don't remember who, had 50 acres of farmland sitting empty and offered it to my dad on the stipulation that if he would till it, he could use it. So, we got a "free" farm, although we did not own it!

When I was seven, I started going to school at South Huntington Elementary. It was just over a mile away and I could walk there. Eventually Dad got some dairy cows, about 20 of them. My mom never worked outside our home because there were four of us kids. My younger brother, Tony, was born in 1915 - I'll be telling you a lot more about him later. The only problem with our having a dairy farm was that we didn't have a pond for water, so we had to take barrels to a pond in the town to bring back water for the cows. When I was 15, I started driving our Model T delivering the milk all over Long Island. I was always short for my age, and I had to use a cushion under my rear end to see enough to be able to drive. It was during our 4th year of having the dairy that we had to stop because the town would no longer let us get that water. My father still kept farming and we had plenty to eat. There was never any scarcity of food for us. Mom would can everything, and we had pigs and plenty of meats and vegetables. All of us kids had jobs to do....I always said, "There's no inactivity in the Tworzyanski household."

I went to high school from 1925-29. It was Huntington High School. The only activity that I remember from high school was that I ran track....not long distance....mostly the quarter mile, and usually on a relay team. From reading the Daily News, I got real interested in Golden Gloves - you know, the amateur boxing competition. A professional boxer, Dodo Jackson, used to train at one of the local estates, and I would go over there and spar with him. I really wanted to enter the Golden Gloves, but I was 16 and my mother would not sign to allow me to do it, so I never got to compete.

I finished high school in 1929, but I couldn't find a decent job, so I went to work on the nearby estate of Otto Kahn over in Cold Spring Harbor. He was a Wall Street money man who I was told was a buddy of J.P. Morgan - the really rich guy everyone knew about. Mr. Kahn's place was enormous and had a 9-hole golf course on it. My job was to cut the grass on the greens. One of his sons - I think it was Roger - had an orchestra and was a pilot, so Kahn had an airstrip put in that they could use. I did this job for a year, but it didn't pay much. Through an employment agency I found a job in New York as a runner for an export company, Menley & James, at 70 West 40th Street - I remember that address exactly! They paid me $17 a week to run documents downtown to be certified for shipment to South America. I also did some typing and filing for them. I was living at the YMCA on the West Side near Madison Square Garden where I used to go watch the fights [boxing matches]. I had most of my meals there at the "Y" but occasionally I would get a meal at Horn & Hardart, you know, those cafeteria places that had coin-operated machines that dispensed food. My favorite was the mac and cheese. It was cheap and filled me up. Living at the "Y" was not that expensive, $10/week, but there were some real disadvantages. Whenever a large Navy ship would come into port, you would get kicked out so that they could accommodate the sailors. When that happened, I would have to get a furnished room at one of the places on 14th Street. All of this meant that I couldn't save much money. I did help myself *sometimes by walking the 8 blocks to the Custom House instead of taking the subway, then putting in a voucher with Menley & James for the subway fare. I never felt bad about doing that.*

One of the advantages of living in New York around 1930 was that I could go to those fights at Madison Square Garden to see some really good boxers, like Fritzie Zivic and Jack Starkey. I'm not sure how much you follow boxing, but Starkey went on to be the Heavyweight World Champ a few years later. The Starkey fight I saw, when he beat Tommy Loughran, cost me $5 for a seat up in the bleachers, but it was worth it. Jack put him on the floor in the second round and he didn't get up. It was great!

During the summers I went to a lot of baseball games. I could see the Giants at the Polo Grounds or the Dodgers over at Ebbets Field. I was not a Yankee fan, so I never went to Yankee Stadium. It cost $2.75 to see the Giants, and I got to see Carl Hubbell pitch, Mel Ott in right field, and when the Cardinals came to town, there was Dizzy Dean and the Gas House Gang.

Boxing was a very popular sport in the 1930's. John told me many stories about fights he attended at Madison Square Garden during his time in New York City. He spun a good yarn about Fritzie Zivic (a.k.a., The Croat Comet), "out of Pittsburgh," who later held the world welterweight championship for six months in the early 1940's. Boxing was considerably "rougher" during this period. It was not unusual for head-butting, thumbs to the eyes, and punches to the groin. John laughed when he recalled one of Zivic's fights in the Garden against Al "Bummy" Davis. Davis was a legitimate title contender and became annoyed by Zivic's usual "rough" tactics of eye gouging and rubbing the laces on his gloves on his opponent's eyes when the fighters were in a clinch. Davis, according to press accounts, "went bezerk," firing at least 10 punches below the belt before kicking Zivic in the groin. The referee immediately stopped the fight, and then he was kicked by Davis! Zivic was awarded the win. According to John, the following year in a bar fight in Brooklyn, Davis was killed. When I later checked on this, I learned that Davis served in the Army from 1941-43, and after being discharged, continued boxing until he retired in 1945. He used money he had earned to buy a bar in Brooklyn, but in late November that year, four robbers entered the bar. In the ensuing melee, Davis was shot three times, but was still chasing the robbers when he received a fourth shot which was fatal. John told me more stories about boxing matches that he saw at Madison Square Garden, including the one he mentioned, the very memorable 1929 fight when Jack Starkey, a heavyweight, knocked out Tommy Loughran (a.k.a., The Phantom of Philly), the light heavyweight champion, in the second round. Starkey went on to become the world heavyweight champion for a year in 1932 but faded quickly as a boxer and lost to Loughran in 1933.

The fellow with whom John sparred in boxing, Dodo (Charles) Jackson, was a bantamweight (115-118 lbs.) boxer from Jersey City, NJ. He had 35 bouts from 1923-37. Based on the records I was able to find, he won only 11 of these matches, including a streak of losing 6 of his last 7 bouts. Although he scored 5 knockouts, he was knocked out himself twice. Because of his small size, John would have been an ideal sparring partner for Jackson, particularly since he was not being paid to get in the ring with the professional. I did not ask John how he fared during those practice rounds, but it obviously provided many good memories.

As a teenager, I developed a feel for the prime role which boxing played in sports during the 20's and 30's when John was watching these prize fights. In the 1950's my father had a small convenience store in rural Kentucky and several former boxers would come in to buy beer and talk with Dad. Most of these fellows were still living their glory days in the ring with memories which always began with a proud claim of the sort, "I went five rounds with _____" (always a highly ranked boxing legend with it left unsaid that he had made it that far before being knocked out). My father always described most of these fellows as "punch drunk" due to the obvious neurological damage they exhibited (a la Muhammad Ali). As John was talking about his youthful fixation on boxing, I found myself agreeing with his mother's decision not to allow him to box in the Golden Gloves.

John's baseball stories also brought back memories. As a youngster I was a baseball fanatic and was very familiar with all the players he mentioned. Dizzy Dean was a particularly memorable character. Even though he was one of only three Major League Baseball pitchers to win 30 games in a season in the past 90 years (Denny McLain and Lefty Grove were the others), he is remembered more for his brash personality and memorable quotes. His real name was Jay Hanna Dean, but he embraced the nickname "Dizzy." His brother, Paul, was also a pitcher for the St. Louis Cardinals at the same time but was quite the opposite of Dizzy in personality and hated being called "Daffy." In early 1934, Dizzy predicted, "Me and Paul, we're gonna win 45 games this year." No one took him seriously, because it was rare for one pitcher to win 20 games in a season. But they not only won 45, but between them, 49, and the National League pennant, and the World Series. This led to one of Dean's famous quotes, "If you've done it, it ain't braggin'." The Dean brothers were just two of the Gashouse Gang that John mentioned. The name was given to the Cardinal team of that era not only because of their antics, but their style of play which was fun-loving and aggressive. Most of the players uniforms would be covered in dirt by the end of games leading some sports writers to compare them to the uniforms of car mechanics. When "Gashouse Gang" was used a few times to describe them, it stuck and they embraced it.

John now resumed how he continued his education while working in New York for the export company:

I wanted to go to college full-time but couldn't afford to do that. My uncle, who ran the golf course at Otto Kahn's estate, told me that he would help me some if I would do school while I was working in New York. So, I applied and got into NYU [New York University]. I wanted to be a surveyor, so I took classes during evenings and on Saturdays. Because the Saturday classes were on the campus near Yankee Stadium, I took the subway up there; the evening classes were in some building downtown on Chambers Street. I took engineering classes on things like stress and some math classes. But I had to quit school in June of '31 when I got laid off by Menley and James. I had no money, so I went back to live at home on Long Island. The only job I could find was working for Huntington Cleaners and Dryers. I wasn't making much at all doing this and finally got on with a job working on the dairy farm on Otto Hahn's estate. That paid $75 a month but was terrible work. I lived in quarters on the estate and had to get up every day at 4 A.M. to milk the cows, *then work all day on the golf course, then do the milking again between 5 and 6 P.M. I did this for nearly two years but quit in early '35. I took a year off doing whatever I could to survive and was living again with my parents. In 1936 I got a job as a gas station attendant pumping gas. I saved up enough money and bought a Model A Ford. I had always been shy around girls. Whenever I went to a social in high school, the girls would have to ask me to dance. But I met this girl who was the daughter of Mr. Hahn's chauffeur, and we started dating. We would just go to movies and then head to a diner on Jericho Turnpike for a hamburger.*

I was unemployed again around Christmas of 1938 and was looking for any type of work. I saw a poster in the Post Office advertising a position at the VA Hospital [Veterans Administration] in Northport, Long Island. I applied immediately and got the job there as a hospital attendant making $1020 a year. I also got free room and board in quarters near the facility. This is how I began my career in government jobs for the next 33 years.

The VA job was not easy, but it was a lot better than the dairy farm. In addition to all the jobs I was expected to do, like taking care of patients and helping them with baths and spoon feeding some, I often had to restrain some patients who had psych issues. Then I got assigned to the physical therapy department and, being a little guy, I developed a hernia trying to do some lifting of patients. The VA never admitted that I got the hernia on the job, but when I went to enlist, the Army wouldn't take me because of the hernia and made me 4-F for the draft.

I got married early during my time at the VA. I met her on a blind date, and her name was Evelyn Demery. She was a lot younger than me. I was 25 and she was only 17. She had been commuting to a clerical job in New York. We were married on September 22, 1940 at St. Hugh's Catholic Church in Huntington Station. We had four kids....all of them were good. One is a lawyer, one does social work, one is in the car business, and one is an actor. We were married 50 years, but Evelyn had a ruptured aorta and passed away nine years ago. It was a great marriage.

As John paused, perhaps reflecting good memories of his marriage to Evelyn,

I took the opportunity to ask a question which had been puzzling me since early in our conversation, "John, you were born Tworzyanski. When, and why, did you change your name to Toran?

We did it for "business reasons." We kept having to explain to people how to pronounce our Polish name, so in September 1933, we changed it. My brother, Tony, and I had become musicians in our teens. Some guy came through selling secondhand instruments, so my parents bought some for us. I started playing trumpet at 16; Tony did the sax. He was four years younger than me but was always a better musician. Not too long later, I switched to sax too. We took lessons from a professional instructor, and soon I got into a band with three local guys: Tom Cross, John Rupp, and Artie Smith. As we got better, we would buy new instruments on time at one of the shops in Times Square. My first sax cost $175 and I paid it off in a year. Our group was called Tommy Cross and his Orchestra. I remember it well, our first gig was on November 28, 1933. We started getting a lot of jobs around Long Island and the New York area, like at the Westbury Inn. They wouldn't let us play in the City because we weren't union. One night I remember we were playing at the Nine Acres and it was the first night after Prohibition was lifted earlier in the day - that was the 5th of December 1933. Everyone was drinking heavy and a lot of the women were passing out because they were not used to the booze. Some nights we played louder to distract people from fist fights that were going on after some drunk guy tried to hit on another guy's blonde. Those were wild nights.

Not too long later, Tommy "faded out" and my brother, Tony, took over the orchestra. Now we were called, The Tony Toran Orchestra. I was 22, but Tony, who was our leader, was only 18. We played mostly old standards, you know, Let Me Call You Sweetheart, Who's Sorry Now, Sweet Georgia Brown, Stardust, My Blue Heaven. We would drive into Manny's, a music store off Times Square on 48th Street to get our sheet music. I was driving my own car, a Model A; Artie, the drummer, had a Chevy. Several times each show I switched back and forth between the sax and the clarinet, depending on the song. At that time, we were playing mostly on Friday and Saturday nights, usually from 9 to 1. They would fill up most of those gin mills when we played, usually

75-100 people. We were paid pretty good when they had those crowds. Occasionally we would do a wedding on a Sunday. We had pretty good outfits; I called them "fake tuxes," because we had white bibs and black ties which made it look like we were wearing a tux. We got to these gigs using two cars; Artie always had the drums in the rumble seat.

In 1936 we hit it big and had our own show at the Hillsdale Tavern in Jamaica, New York. We played there five nights a week for over a year and a half. By that time John Rupp was on keyboard, Artie Smith played drums, I did clarinet, and Tony played sax. We had a complete floor show, with comedians, a female vocalist, and some girls who would do a "semi-strip." All of them had to audition for Tony. So, there I was pumping gas during the day, and leading this other life at night. By the late 30's we had grown to 12 pieces, still called the Tony Toran Orchestra. We had a real following on the island [Long Island], and played often at the Huntington Theater, but a lot of the gin mills there couldn't afford us. Most of the clubs we played at, there was always a lot of booze flowing, but I never drank much myself and I never smoked. We played pretty much up to when the war broke out, and basically everyone in our orchestra either got drafted or got married, like me. I often wonder what would have happened to our orchestra if the war had not come.

John paused here and began to show me photographs of The Tony Toran Orchestra along with other memorabilia. He even gave me several professionally photographed shots of him and his brother in their musician's outfits. John then proceeded to tell me details about his subsequent life in a variety of government jobs. In 1943 John transferred to a position with the Department of Agriculture in Chicago where he worked in the stock yards as a meat inspector. This lasted less than a year, because Evelyn became homesick for the East Coast, and, as he phrased it, "I didn't mind the blood, but I hated the smells."

John and Evelyn soon headed to Washington, D.C. after he had seen an opening posted for a position as a statistician for the Agriculture Department. He stayed in Washington for the next 30 years while furthering his government career in various agencies, including the General Accounting Office and the Department of Defense. He mentioned that he had learned accounting "during the war," but never explained this in detail. Following his retirement in 1973, John did work for Bloomingdale's and Nordstrom, usually in the Public Relations sector. He also became an artist and proudly showed me several pieces hanging in his living room which he had recently completed. Before I took his photograph, he proudly proclaimed, "I'll be 88 in June. I've had six operations and a triple bypass, but I feel great and am continually active." As I drove home my only regret was that I did not ask John to play one of those "old standards" for me.

Several times during our conversation John mentioned his family's work connection with the estate of Otto Kahn. His only description of Kahn was that he was a "Wall Street money man." When I later did some research on Kahn, I learned that John's description was something of an understatement. Otto Kahn was one of the wealthiest men in the United States in the early 1900's. Although he did not come to the U.S. until 1893, he quickly amassed a fortune through marriage and an uncanny skill of re-organizing most of the American railroads. Through astute financial maneuvers while working for the Wall Street firm, Kuhn Loeb (now renamed Lehman Brothers), he saved a litany of failing railroads from bankruptcy, such as the B&O, the Missouri Pacific, and the Union Pacific. Kahn is often credited with personally helping the country from suffering at least three banking panics. He was also active in international banking, arranging $50 million in City of Paris bonds. After becoming a U.S. citizen in 1917, Kahn became a confidante of local, state, and national politicians. In 1919 he purchased

443 acres in Cold Spring, Long Island and had a 109,000 square feet, 127-room estate constructed. At the time it was the second largest residence in America, behind only Vanderbilt's Biltmore estate in Asheville, North Carolina. Within the next few years he added a 9-hole golf course, and a private landing strip for airplanes belonging to one of his sons. This estate, which Kahn named "Oheka" (apparently based on his name, **Ot**to **He**rbert **Ka**hn) was where several members of John Toran's family secured work to begin their own American success stories.

Those talking about income disparity now might benefit from studying the history of this era 100 years ago. It could be argued that it was far worse then. Kahn's wealth and influence were beyond enormous. In addition to his Long Island estate, he also owned the largest private home in Manhattan (directly across the street from Andrew Carnegie's NYC home), and a large home in Florida. It is said that Kahn and fellow banker, J.P Morgan, were the inspiration for the mascot, "Rich Uncle Pennybags" of Parker Brother's popular board game, Monopoly. Based on the photos I have seen of Kahn, the resemblance of the caricature is remarkable. He was, of course, like most tycoons of his era, a provider of countless jobs for less affluent Americans, including many immigrants such as the Tworzyanski family. John, for example, always seemed to be able to find a job when he needed it at "Oheka." Kahn was also a very generous patron of the arts. His love of opera was legendary; he counted many of the major performers as personal friends. In fact, two of the most famous opera stars of the time, Enrico Caruso and Anna Pavlova, performed at Kahn's daughters' coming out party. He was also the consummate politician, if not by choice, then by necessity, as Congress frequently called him to testify regarding what they regarded as "Wall Street thievery." One political opponent lamented, "Kahn was always immaculately dressed and irresistibly charming....we couldn't win."

In his own way, John Toran was equally as successful as Kahn, Morgan, and all the others who had amassed early 20th century fortunes. John and Kahn, for example, were both immigrants to the U.S., but Kahn had the good fortune to come from infinitely more wealth and education than John. I would suggest that John, by the time I interviewed him, had made a greater financial percentage gain. What is certain is that despite Kahn's wealth and connections, John had the last laugh: Kahn died of a heart attack in 1934 at age 67; John was still going strong at 88!

In retrospect, I now realize why John kept admonishing me about "sequencing" while we were discussing his life. I still cannot determine exactly how he was getting by during the 30's with several different jobs and periods of unemployment intermingled with his nighttime musical activities. What is apparent is that he was continuously scrambling to earn a living while also indulging in his passion for music and the obvious excitement of being a performer in the "gin mills" of the era.

"The Pie Lady"
Tillie Flipse

Grinnell, Kansas
Interviewed June 20, 1996

W HEN I WAS VISITING A submarine buddy, Charlie, in Salem, Oregon, I mentioned that I had been interviewing folks who lived during the Great Depression. "You have to talk to Tillie. She's my sister-in-law's mother and lives near here. She's got great stories from growing up in Kansas before she came here to Oregon." We telephoned her, and Tillie immediately invited Charlie and me to come over for a visit. Within a few minutes we were at her home, a very well kept up mobile home where she lived independently. It was surrounded by flowers which she proudly told me she tended to herself. Two of her three daughters, Debbie and Beverly, had come over to listen to my interview.

Tillie, whose full name was Mathilda Catherine Flipse, was a youthful-looking octogenarian with sparkling eyes and an infectious smile. Her pure white hair had a nice-looking perm. She was wearing a white, tunic style blouse buttoned to the neck. Her trousers were neatly creased, and to complete the outfit, she was wearing small hoop earrings. Basically, she had the look of a successful retired executive. I quickly learned that Tillie had excellent recall of her childhood, and for the few details she could not remember, the answers were provided by her daughters. Charlie stayed with me during the visit and assisted me in locating some small cities in Oregon when those became topics of discussion. Tillie began by telling me about her parents:

Both of my parents were German Catholics. Everyone where I was born, in Grinnell, Kansas, was the same religion. The only church in town was Angelus Catholic Church - that's where we all went to Mass. I was born at home on our farm on September 3, 1915. My parents' names were Anthony and Amelia Baalman; they had 9 children - 6 girls and 3 boys. I was the second oldest, so I ended up spending a lot of time helping to take care of the younger ones. We had about 50 acres of farmland in Gove County, maybe 9 miles out of town. There were probably less than 200 folks in Grinnell at that time. When I went back there in the 50's, it was not much bigger....maybe a hundred more.

You have to understand, we were always very poor. My father raised wheat, corn, and cattle, but it was always a struggle. From about 9 years old on, I had to get up at 5 A.M. to help to milk the dairy cows - we had about ten of them. We only drank skim milk because my mom always saved the cream to sell. After milking those cows, I had breakfast and then walked two miles to school. As far as I know, that school didn't even have a name - we just called it "the country school." I got to go to school only until 8th grade, because I was expected to help take care of my sisters and brothers. One of my chores each day was to take the cattle and the cows two miles up to some grasslands that were part of the farm. One of my brothers had to bring them back. I actually started working outside our home when I was 10 doing baby sitting and helping other farmers with cleaning and cooking during harvest time. Those babysitting jobs didn't pay much, usually 10 to 20 cents an hour.

Sometimes all I got was a quarter for the whole evening! Everything I earned came home to Mom to help with the family expenses. I don't remember our own family ever using a babysitter ourselves. When I was young, all of us children went wherever my parents went. I remember that once FDR [President Franklin Delano Roosevelt] came in my father received payments from the federal government during a few years not to grow wheat or corn. That helped some, but we were still real poor.

We lived a quite simple life. I didn't have any dress that wasn't homemade until I was 17. I learned to sew by watching Mom using her "pedal Singer." She never used patterns - she just knew how to make things. No one on farms there had any electricity, so at night we used kerosene lanterns. There also weren't any phones, but there was good daily mail service. Of course, we had an outhouse and, just like everyone says, we used catalog pages for toilet paper. I didn't know what toilet paper was until I moved away after I got married.

The payments not to grow crops which Tillie mentioned were the result of one of Roosevelt's first "New Deal" programs. It was put into operation in early 1933 to help low income farmers (such as Tillie's dad) and was called the Agricultural Adjustment Administration (AAA). The goal was to balance the supply and demand of certain agricultural products by reducing surpluses. It was funded by a tax on companies which processed farm products. By 1936, when the AAA was ruled unconstitutional by the U.S. Supreme Court, nearly $1.5 billion payments had been made to farmers. Similar programs had been proposed in earlier American administrations, but this was the first which had been signed into law. Its effects have received mixed reviews, generally following political viewpoints.

The "pedal sewing machine" described by Tillie was made by Singer Company. It was nearly ubiquitous in American homes in the first part of the 20th century. The first American patent for a sewing "machine" was granted in 1846 to Elias Howe, but five years later Isaac M. Singer and a New York lawyer, Edward C. Clark, began the first successful commercial production of these machines. A legal battle over patent rights quickly followed. Howe won this battle and received not only a lump sum payment, but also a $1.15 royalty for every Singer machine subsequently sold. Singer and Clark set up their first large factory for production in Elizabeth, New York. Their machine used the basic concept of lockstitch developed by Howe, but they devised techniques to make the machines heavier and more powerful.

Singer was not only an inventor, but, among many other skills, a theater manager who understood marketing. He and Clark were particularly adept at obtaining new patents, leading them to engage in large-scale production prior to the outbreak of the Civil War. Singer understood sales techniques and directed much of his advertising toward women; he also was among the first to introduce installment payments and rent-to-own options. By 1876 Singer had sold two million of his machines, and in a marketing ploy, put Number Two Million on public display in Philadelphia. By 1900 he had captured most of the world-wide market and sold more machines annually than all other makers combined. The original Singer sewing machines were operated by having to constantly turn a handle. It was quickly replaced by a foot-driven treadle, which through gearing, generated the sewing motion. This treadle was the "pedal" mentioned by Tillie.

As a child I watched my own mother sew on a Singer powered by the treadle. It can be argued that the invention of the mass-produced sewing machine contributed more to American lifestyle in the 19th century than any other device. Because it did not require electricity, women living in rural farms and ranches were now able to make essentially all of their family clothing at low cost. If there were no local sources of sewing materials, that Sears & Roebuck catalog sitting in the outhouse was the *Amazon* of its day. Homemakers could browse the new one received each year to order whatever was required, not only for sewing, but for all other household needs. You could even order a house! Tillie continued describing her home life as a child on the farm:

For washing clothes Mom used a washboard with one of those wringer gadgets that was turned by a hand crank. We did have a good well...I assume it was hand-dug, but it never ran out of water, even during the droughts. The water was pumped by a windmill....the wind always seemed to be blowing, maybe because it was so flat in our part of Kansas. For heating water and cooking, we had a "cook stove" that burned wood, coal, or "cow chips." Now you might not believe this, but those cow chips burned real good because of the straw that was in them. They made a hot fire, and this you really won't believe, they had no bad smell. One of my other jobs was to go around the pasture with a wagon and pick up those chips and bring them back. We dried them outside, of course. When we used that cook stove in the summer, it made that kitchen real hot! We used cast iron kettles and skillets on that cook stove, and you had to be careful because they were heavy. If you were not careful, it was easy to get burned.

We had another stove to heat the house. It was a "Mize Hot Blast." I know that name for sure because one time when it was real cold in the house, I stood too close to it. I accidentally bumped into it and got those letters in burn marks on my butt. My sister always teased me that I had branded myself.

Many cultures around the world still use cow dung as a fuel source for heating. The "cow chips" described by Tillie were what those of us on Kentucky farms called "cow patties." No matter the name (and there were many regional versions), there is considerable energy in this organic material, and, as Tillie mentioned, when dried and burned, those chips produce considerable heat. In essentially every farming village I visited in India a few years ago, each home had rows of cow chips carefully positioned to dry in the sun....and there was no discernible odor!

I did not understand how Tillie could have "branded" herself if she had been wearing clothing. I chose not to quiz her on this topic because she was racing on to tell me more about her farm life:

We always ate well because of our garden and all the animals. My mom did a lot of canning, but we just never seemed to eat that much meat. We had a lot of fried potatoes and pickles - sounds crazy, but I liked it. I mean, we ate meat occasionally, but just not that much.

There was one doctor in town. We needed him to come out when Mom had two miscarriages. She almost died during one of them. That one happened during her second miscarriage which was between the last two children. I remember the doctor coming outside our home and saying to us, "It's looking like your mother is going to die." But somehow, she didn't and still had one more child after this. I myself had all the usual childhood illnesses: scarlet fever, measles, mumps, chicken pox, and whooping cough - I got 'em all - but I never went to a doctor. I was told that my dad got real sick during the flu epidemic when I was about four. He developed a bad case of pneumonia, but he made it through okay. I was young then and don't know how many others in our area got that flu or died from it.

Like I said, I didn't get to go to high school because I was needed to help there on the farm. I started dating when I was 16. I went to a lot of dances, but no movies....there wasn't a movie theater near....so it was mostly dances. When I was younger, we always had to take a buggy or a wagon when we went anywhere, but when the Fords came out, my Dad bought a Model T. Whenever he was gone, us teens would take it out onto the prairie and drive it around - you know, joy rides. We also did a lot of horse riding....I never got threw off. The Christmas holidays were big for us Catholics, but I never received many gifts. Usually, we would get a lot of oranges and some new homemade clothes. Sometimes when I was young, I would get a new doll.

When I turned 18, I got a waitress job over in Oakley, not too far west of us. Both it und Grinnell are on Interstate I-70 now. The reason I got the job was that I was dating Harvey Flipse, and he was the youngest brother of the restaurant owner, Julia. She offered me a job waiting tables. No tips were allowed. I don't remember exactly what salary I was making, but it wasn't much. I would get a ride over there and back with an older woman who was also working there. This was the first job I had where I didn't have to bring everything home for our family. I kept a little of what I made, but still gave most of it to my parents.

Harvey and I dated for two years. We got married on November 25, 1935, not too long after I turned 20. It was a real nice wedding with friends and family in the Catholic Church. Afterwards Harvey and I took his old Plymouth and went on our honeymoon. We drove down to his mother's farm outside a small town in Missouri - I don't remember the name. This was the first time I was outside 30 miles from my home. Now this sounds real strange, but we took his brother and four nieces and nephews with us in that Plymouth on our honeymoon. Those four kids were from his older brother who had died. So, there were seven of us in the car. Believe it or not, we had a real good time.

I laughed (along with the rest of her family listening to us) when Tillie told me about having her honeymoon with her mother-in-law. I explained to her that she was the only other woman I had met besides my wife who had been in this situation. Mine was a complicated situation, but my wife has never forgiven me. Now I plan to tell her that she did not have it so bad.... we did not have a brother-in-law and 4 kids along!

We came back to Kansas and started living with Harvey's brother on his farm. He was not married, and we had those 4 kids with us, so I was doing all the cooking and housework for 7 and taking care of the cows. The farming was going well, and Harvey was able to trade in the Plymouth and buy a new pickup truck. In addition to the cows, we were doing some wheat farming, but then the drought came, and practically everyone, including us, was going broke. In early 1937 we got a letter from Harvey's sister, Julia, who was now in Oregon where she and her husband, Fred, had started a new restaurant. She said that there was logging work out there. She owned a small restaurant and told us to come out. Things were so bad in Kansas, the two of us decided to put our stuff in Harvey's pickup and head to Oregon. I was real pregnant with our first child, and I remember that we stopped only one night on our way there....it was in Wyoming. The rest of the time we were driving.

The restaurant, Fred's Cafe, was in Lakeview, Oregon, and we rented a little one-bedroom apartment there. Our son was born shortly after we arrived, on April 27, 1937. Harvey went to work right away driving a logging truck. I had a newborn baby so I couldn't work at the restaurant, but I made some money by baking 30 pies every day. They were mostly berry and apple pies, but sometimes I would make a few cream ones. One of Julia's employees from the restaurant would come by in a van before noon each day and pick them up. They would sell pieces of pie for 25 cents each. After a year or so, one of the guys Harvey worked with helped him to buy his own logging truck, so he became an independent logger. There was a mill in town and that's where you sold the logs. Most of the men in town worked for that mill. Pretty soon Harvey had three trucks and a Caterpillar and four guys working for him. His company was called Flipse Logging Company. Meanwhile I went to work in the restaurant.

I asked Tillie where Harvey did the logging and what, if any, financial arrangements were involved. Did he have to pay for rights to the logs? Was his work in national forests? Who owned those forests? Unfortunately, neither Tillie nor her family who were with us knew the answers. I got the impression that Harvey kept most of his business dealings to himself while Tillie concentrated on raising their children and taking care of all the household issues. This was not an unusual arrangement during this era. Tillie continued to describe the area of Oregon where they lived:

Lakeview is way up in the mountains close to the California border. There is high desert to the east.... I think that it's the highest city in Oregon. What I know for sure is that it is real cold there in the winter with lots of snow. One time my little boy, David, was waist deep in snow. I always thought it was interesting that with all that timber around, everyone heated with oil. It was a small town, but the restaurant always did well because it was on Route 395 which was a major road north out of Reno. As a matter of fact, that road was the only way in and out of Lakeview. Because the winters were so bad, no one did logging during the winter, so we started to go back to Kansas every December in that same pickup truck. We would stay with family and come back in early March. One year we moved up to Burns [Oregon] so Harvey could do some work up there for a different logging outfit, but we came back to Lakeview after a year or so. Our first daughter, Barbara, was born up there in neighboring Prineville, and then the next daughter back in Lakeview. I always seemed to be pregnant when we were on the road in that pickup. Eventually we got homesick for Kansas and moved back there after the war to do farming. Our last two daughters were born in Kansas.

Because it was getting close to dinner time for Tillie's family, and I still had to drive several hundred miles that evening, we stopped our interview at this point. Fortunately, I was able many years later to contact her daughter,

Beverly, to learn how Tillie and Harvey ended up back in Oregon. When they arrived in Kansas, they took over the Baalman family farm (Tillie's parents) and worked that for many years, with Tillie fully occupied raising their five young children. Before leaving Oregon, Harvey had given power of attorney for his logging company to his business partner. Several years later Harvey learned from a friend in Oregon that all his logging equipment and trucks had been sold by the partner. Harvey returned to Oregon, and finding that the business was gone, was forced to declare bankruptcy, which, according to Beverly "broke Dad's heart." Harvey and Tillie returned to Oregon for good in 1956 and lived in several different logging communities, such as Ashland, Glendale, and Grant's Pass where Harvey drove logging trucks. After he was seriously injured in a logging accident, Harvey was forced to retire, and they moved to Salem to be near their children. He passed away in 1993 just prior to their 58th wedding anniversary.

As I departed Tillie's home, my friend and I had a lengthy conversation about the grit exhibited by so many American women during the Great Depression. Not having the benefit of access to a formal education beyond grade school, Tillie gained a Ph.D. in the "School of Hard Knocks" by taking every opportunity to learn useful life skills from both of her parents. These lessons, and strong personal courage, enabled Tillie, and millions in her generation, to forge successful lives - a legacy to be proud of.

"The Stonemason"
Clair William Peechatka

Scotrun, PA
Interviewed May 5, 1997

D EBBIE, A FRIEND IN OUR northern Virginia church, told me about her great uncle Clair. "I'm certain that you will find his life very interesting. He spent most of his years in Pennsylvania and much of his life working with stone. He's visiting his son, Farley, who lives in a wonderful stone home west of here near the West Virginia border." After Debbie's phone call arranging an interview, the next morning I was in my pickup truck with our Australian cattle dog, Sydney, who came along to assist. After a several hour drive, I found Farley's home near the end of a dirt road high in the Appalachian Mountains. Although it was a mild day in early May, there were no signs of spring; every deciduous tree was bare. The house was a beautiful structure faced with flat stones of various colors and shapes held in place with mortar. Near the entrance was a rectangular concrete insert with the words:

ROCKY TOP
P P & P 1987

A tall, white-haired gentleman greeted Sydney and me as we exited my truck, "Hi! I'm Clair Peechatka. Welcome to Rocky Top!" He was wearing a long sleeve flannel shirt open at the neck and used a cane for walking. He invited both of us inside and introduced me to his son and daughter-in-law, Farley and LaVerne. After ensuring that I was comfortable, he began telling me about his early life in Pennsylvania:

I came from a large family. My mother had 13 children; 11 of us survived. Three were older than me. My full name is Clair William Peechatka...it's Polish-American. Both of my parents were born in Pennsylvania in the 1870's. Mother was Sarah Anna Heckman, and my dad's first name was Oscar. They were married on May 30, 1895. I came along on April 5, 1905 and was born at home in Scotrun, Pennsylvania. That's in the Poconos [mountains] about ten miles northwest of Stroudsburg. My father was a stonemason, and from an early age I helped him doing this type of work. He did everything stone, from building bridges to doing houses. In terms of school, I went only to the 8th grade....that's as far as you could go there at that time....the school was Scotrun Elementary. So, at 13 years old, I went to work for my dad full time. We would build not only whole bridges, but also the parapets. I lived at home until I got married.

I met my wife at a Sunday School picnic at her church, which was Methodist. They always had big picnics over there. I was Lutheran and eventually persuaded her to go to my church. She lived about 12 miles away from my home, and I got to her place in a Model T car which I bought new in 1923 for $865 when I turned 18. Of course, I had to buy it on time; no banks were involved....the car dealer held the note. I had that car for years; later I built a body on the back to convert it into a truck to haul rocks, and even later, my boys converted it into a tractor. I guess we got our money's worth out of that Ford! Other than my car payment, most of the money I earned outside of working for my dad went straight to our family.

Fern and I got married on January 23, 1929 when I was still 23. Fern was just 19; her full name was Fern Evelyn Keltz. I will always remember our wedding day because it was really cold that night. The wedding itself was funny. We went to the St. John's Lutheran parsonage to get married. The pastor had a pretty bad speech impediment. There was a carpenter working upstairs pounding nails or something and my older brother, Carl, who was with us as best man, complained to the pastor that he couldn't hear anything because of the noise. So, the pastor yells real loud in his funny voice, "Hey up there, hold that hammering for a few minutes until I marry this young fellow!" Well, it never bothered me, and we ended up married for 67 years.

Although Clair had no problems with his wedding, I suspect strongly that the ceremony was not exactly what his young bride, Fern, had envisioned. I did not have an opportunity to talk to her because she passed away two years prior to my interview with Clair. During our talk he showed me with pride a 1929 family photo of him and Fern. She was indeed a beautiful young woman. What he did tell me several times was that "Fern helped tremendously during those hard years....I don't know how I would have made it without her."

Clair now began a lengthy explanation of stonemasonry:

When I first started working for my dad, my job was to mix the mortar - that's what you use between the stones to set them. It was just a mixture of sand, cement, and water. We bought the sand and cement at a lumber yard. How I got to do some stone laying started accidentally. We were building a house for a railroad man. He would come home at something like two in the afternoon and he said to my father, "Does your boy lay stones?" Dad paused and told him a fib, "Yes." There was an extra trowel and hammer there, and the man said, "I'll mix the mortar if you're willing to let the boy lay stones." So that's how I became a stone mason! It was a veneer job and I worked next to Dad. He kept a close eye on me and made sure that I was doing it right. The stone was what we called "creek stone." They were not really cobble stone, which is smaller, but a large "natural" stone. These rocks had been in moving water so long that all the sharp edges went away. They came from nearby streams and were hauled away by a horse and wagon. Often the customer building a house, or some other structure, would buy the stone and have it there for us to use. You could mix the mortar as long as it was above freezing. You see, a load of concrete or mortar generates a lot of heat as it sets due to the chemicals in there. When they pour a lot of concrete to build those large dams, they have to run water in cooling pipes through it to make sure it doesn't overheat. They just leave the pipes in there as part of the dam. Bet you didn't know this!

Small cabin built by Peechatka family in early 1900's

At this point Clair took me outside to show me some stones which had been used in the exterior wall of his son's home. He explained how the size and shape were evaluated by the stonemason before inserting it in the mortar on the wall, "Basically you find a good-shaped stone and it goes where it fits best." As I looked closely at the exterior walls of the house, I began to appreciate the artistry in stonemasonry. It is certainly one of the most ancient professions. I have been fortunate to see many of the more famous stoneworks such as the Egyptian pyramids, the Incan walls in Cusco, the Taj Mahal, Stonehenge, and Roman stone structures in England and Africa. The creative part of stonemasonry is to find which stone in the pile fits best in the available opening. It is art.

Clair mentioned using a trowel and a hammer when doing stonework.

These have been the traditional tools of stonemasons for thousands of years. Usually there are also several hammers with chisels on one end to help shape the stone to ensure that it is a good fit. The trowel is used to apply mortar between stones to set them into place. Sometimes this use of the trowel is called "pointing" (although Clair did not use this term). Thinking how artists often place their names on a finished canvas, I wondered if he and his father ever etched their initials or some personal mark somewhere in the mortar to signify their work, but I never asked Clair directly about this. However, the question was in my mind while we were outside, so I asked Clair about the "P P & P" near the front door of his son's house. With obvious pride he laughed, "Oh, that's the boys who built this. Two Peechatkas and a Phoebus...my son and grandson and Farley's son-in-law. Stonework runs in the family!"

I later learned that the Peechatka name was synonymous with quality stonework in the entire region of eastern Pennsylvania around Stroudsburg. Several churches, homes, and businesses were built by Peechatkas, including some of the larger structures at Pocono Manor Resort. It is my understanding that many of these remain standing today.

We then returned inside "Rocky Top" where Clair changed the subject.

When I was growing up, I also did a lot of caddying on local golf courses starting when I was nine years old. The Poconos were always a major resort area, and there were several places for me to caddy. They had a 9-hole course at Pocono Manor Resort which was a 5-mile walk from our home. I would be paid 25 cents for carrying a golf bag 18 holes; they would go around twice. Usually I would also get a tip. The best I ever had came from a fellow who gave me a dollar...that was the 25 cents plus 75 more. That guy was interesting because we started off with some "differences." His first shot went into the woods and I couldn't find it, so he had a lost ball penalty. Then on the next hole he did the same thing. On the third hole he again put it deep in the woods and that ball was lost. So, he's angry at me for not finding his balls and says, "You lose one more ball, son, and you're going straight to the caddy shack." I looked at him, threw down his clubs and started walking back. He yelled, "Where are you going?" I told him, "You don't have to worry about me no more.

I ain't waiting for you to lose another one." He cooled down and when we finished the 18, he gave me the big tip.

I got in good with the Caddy Master, so I would usually get out every day and do several rounds. Sometimes he would let me clean people's clubs and I could get an extra dollar for doing this. One summer day my brother, Carl, and I were caddying all day, and when we counted our change from several days, we found that we had just over ten dollars. We went to the clubhouse and asked to exchange it for a ten-dollar bill because neither of us had ever seen one. When we took it home, we put it on the ironing board where Mom was working. She nearly fainted and said, "My God, boys, where did you get that?" This was huge money for the family because Dad was only making $3.40 a day laying stone.

I really liked the caddying. That's how I met my best friend, John Casella. I didn't know him then, but he showed up one day at the caddy shack and asked me how to caddy. I got permission from the Caddy Master to take him along with me for a few rounds. It turned out that he had the exact same day of birth as me, even the year! Do you believe it? Exact! We were just two "chummie kids" then and remained great buddies for the rest of our lives. I never had trouble remembering his birthday!

All of us kids in my family began work at young ages. The boys would caddy or pick weeds out on the golf course greens....that sometimes paid better than caddying....and the girls would pluck chickens. My mother also worked various jobs at home to make money for the family. In the summer she raised flowers, especially sweet peas, and would take them up to Pocono Manor and the other resorts and sell them to the folks who were staying there. In our family, everybody worked.

Having spent my teen years living on a farm, I was familiar with chicken "plucking." After a chicken has been killed for eating, the body is dipped in hot water allowing the feathers to be pulled out easily - I have done this, and it is not a fun job - and I assure you that you will not like the smell. Pulling out those feathers is called "plucking."

When Fern and I were married in 1929, I took out a $3000 loan from a local bank called Keystone Building Association. I did not realize it at *the time, but it was a real bad loan. I had a wooded lot, so we cut down most of the trees except for those to block the north wind. We planned the location so that the house was facing south to get as much sun as possible. Three of my brothers and I built the house, but we had help with frolics. We had two of them; one to dig the basement, and one for the rest of the house. All I had to do was to offer hot dogs and sauerkraut and more than a dozen men came over. We dug out that basement with nothing but picks and shovels. There was one really big rock there, so we just built the house around it. It had 3 bedrooms, a bath, kitchen, and a living room. Many of the houses and barns up there in that part of Pennsylvania got built by frolics. We would also do frolics lasting late into the night on moonlight evenings when it was time to pick corn.*

I had not heard the term "frolic." The word is derived from Dutch and German, so it is not surprising that this predominantly German community adopted the term to describe a "cheerful" party of volunteers from the neighborhood who show up to assist a neighbor in a large building project or a harvest. The Amish from nearby Pennsylvania have almost made this an art form in which large groups of men (and boys) come together as a "fun" social activity to accomplish a large task, such as a barn raising, that one or two could not do alone. To do a frolic, the host, in this case, Clair, provided a game plan for the project, food and beverages, and invited everyone in the local community to come for the day to "make it happen." Clair's mood now quickly changed from the fond memories of the frolics to the beginning of the Depression era:

Things began to get real bad for us in late 1929. All the work dried up and pretty soon I was behind the 8-ball. I couldn't make payments on the house and in the next spring I put up a FOR SALE sign on the house. Some guy came by and offered me $6000 for it, but that was an insult in view of everything we had put into it. The bank wasn't pushing me or threatening to take the house away because they already had so many that they had foreclosed on that were sitting empty. I was getting desperate and started doing some labor for farmers at $5 a day. Fern was cleaning rooms up at the Manor and she had a good garden. During the fall she also made cider for $5 a day. This is when I first got into the habit of drinking a lot of warm water in the morning before I *went to work. I found that it took away my hunger and that the food I ate went further. We had a lot of potato soup, but we also had pretty much fish and wild meat. I could catch brookies [brook trout] in Scotrun Creek and did a lot of lake fishing for bass, pike, perch, and bullheads [catfish]. For hunting I used two guns, a 12-gauge shotgun and a 32 Special Winchester rifle. I could get shells from a gun club nearby - they were 50 cents cheaper there. A box of 25 cost $1.25, and I didn't waste any of them. I shot pretty many deer, grouse, and rabbits those years. We didn't buy hardly any meat, but we always ate what I shot. I had a lot of notches on that rifle.*

At this point Farley's wife interjected, "He was a real sharpshooter. Each of those notches on that rifle meant a deer. And he still drinks that warm water." Clair smiled and answered my next question about grouse. "Well, some people call them pheasants. All I know is that it is more like a chunky chicken than a pheasant. It is really good eatin'." When I later looked up the difference between a grouse and a pheasant, I found that Clair's description was accurate. One source said that the grouse has a "substantial" body and is similar to the domestic chicken. Pheasants are smaller, but more colorful. I am certain that Clair would have remarked, "You can't eat colorful."

In late 1931 I heard that there was an opening with the Highway Department over in Taylorsville where they were building some roads. I went to work there full time for 45 cents an hour for a ten-hour day. They did it this way: they had 3 shifts of workers, Monday to Saturday. Each shift would get to work two days. This way they could give work to more people. We were building new roads, cracking field stones by hand down to a small size so that it could be used for the base of the road. I was only making $10 a week, and this was about the time Fern had our first son. I often wondered how we were going to make it. Thank God that Fern could stretch a dollar better than anyone. One year during this time we made some money by renting out our house to a schoolteacher who had a good job. He paid me $25 a month for our house, and we moved into a real small furnished place that we got for $10 a month. It had no insulation, just weather board on studs and we nearly froze that winter. We heated it with two wood stoves; one was a cooking stove, and the other was a room stove. That extra $15 a month was real *helpful, but we were glad to move back into our warm home after a year. It was heated with a coal furnace.*

We didn't have any extra money for entertainment, but we did have a radio. I remember listening mostly to KDKA and WLS. There was a movie theater in Stroudsburg, but it cost a nickel to see a show. We just couldn't afford to go out much, so we mostly entertained ourselves. One time we were at my aunt's place and I had gone over to see a movie; when I came back, she had me tell her everything about it....everything. I talked to her for at least an hour. When Prohibition ended, there were several saloons which opened, but I never was a drinker. I smoked "Velvet" in a corn cob pipe but never had any cigarettes. Every one of my older friends who smoked cigarettes had a terrible morning cough, so I was never interested.

Velvet tobacco was one of the popular brands during the early 1900's. It came in a 4-inch tall distinctive red tin (can) which contained 1 1/2 ounces of "pipe and cigarette tobacco." "Velvet" was spelled in white script letters at an upward slanting angle with a large V. It was advertised as being made "from the best sun-ripened Kentucky burley tobacco aged to mellow perfection in natures [sic] slow, sure way. It features a mild-medium strength with a sweet, classic note." Although a modern knock-off can be purchased online today, most of the current ads are for the old cans which have become a collector's item. They range in price from $12 up. One thing which Clair emphasized to me was that he did not smoke the popular Prince Albert brand. As with cigarettes, there was strong brand loyalty among pipe smokers!

Several of the early radio stations in large midwestern cities, such as Pittsburgh (KDKA), Cincinnati (WLW), and Chicago (WLS), were allowed to originate their AM (amplitude modulation) signals at 50,000 watts of power so that listeners in distant rural areas could pick up the signals at night. Radio signals travel in straight lines, but in the AM range (kilohertz), often reflect at night off the ionosphere, a layer of the atmosphere 50-600 miles above Earth. This layer is constantly ionized by solar and cosmic radiation; the density shifts at night when the sun is not shining at that location, creating a specific layer of electrons which vibrate at AM radio frequencies. These vibrating electrons essentially re-transmit the signal at that same frequency back to Earth. In this manner the signal travels up and down over great distances, allowing listeners to hear the powerful stations, although the reception varies by the minute. Local AM stations were mandated to reduce power at sunset to avoid interfering with these "super stations." There were no FM (frequency modulation) stations at the time; the first commercial FM station did not go into operation until 1941 at a station in Nashville. Due to the frequencies now assigned to FM stations, their signals do not travel long distances due to the nature of the electromagnetic waves at the higher megahertz frequencies. If you are traveling at night and listening to AM radio, you can still hear these same stations at great distance.

Clair now shifted from tobacco to finance:

I was now still trying to pay that bank loan, but I was struggling on just working two days a week for the state. It was tight living, I mean tight! My brother, Carl, had a lawyer friend who turned out to be a life saver for me. His name was Alva Mervine. He asked me to show him my loan and told me that the Keystone Bank was actually charging me 28% interest because even though I was making payments, they were not reducing the principle. Mr. Mervine told me, "I'll take on your mortgage for you, and you can pay me whenever you can." I said to him, "You know I won't be able to do anything much until I get better work. Anytime I get five or ten dollars, I'll give it to you." We did a handshake on it, and I got rid of that bad loan and replaced it with one at 6%. I finally paid it off after the war when things got a lot better.

I did the two days a week work with the Highway Department for nearly three years, but in the mid-30's I got steady work with them and became a foreman. I had about 30 men working for me doing road work. Things began to get better for me and Fern. I worked for the Highway Department for 38 years and retired on April 8, 1970. Then I got a job as the Superintendent of a nearby 9-hole golf course. Even though I had a few clubs from my caddying days, I thought during those dark days of the 30's that I would never play again. When World War II ended, I got myself some new clubs and began playing quite a bit, mostly "twilight golf" after I was home from work and the green fees were cheaper. Fern wasn't a fan of this because I wasn't at home to eat dinner with the family....I ate a lot of cold dinners on those nights.

I learned that you had to be careful with your politics when working for the Highway Department, especially as you rose in the ranks. Early on I was warned by my co-workers about "being on the wrong side." Some of those highway jobs were political, depending on who was in and who was out. Over the years I went through a lot of different governors with different political persuasions, but I never changed my party registration. I never told anyone what I was. I generally voted Republican, but I did vote for Roosevelt each time.

Working for the Highway Department never paid much during the '30's. We would be laying stone on weekends and nights. We never got paid overtime, but we did get paid for any extra hours over our regular time. Once, following a storm, I worked 40 hours straight with no sleep. There was no end to the work then. Sometimes I would come home and be raking leaves in the dark. I was also laying stone on weekends and nights, and often made more doing that for two days than working for the state for five days.

I had a couple of funny stories from my working for the Highway Department. When I became an Assistant Superintendent for our area, I got a state car to use. One day while mine was in the shop getting repairs, I used one of the others. As I was out inspecting roads, I saw that someone had thrown some beer bottles on the median, so I picked them up. The next day, after I had turned that car in to get mine back, I got a call from the Superintendent saying that the motor pool guy told him that there was a smell of beer in the car that I turned in. It took me a long time to have him understand that it must have come from those beer bottles I picked up. He knew that I didn't drink and laughed because he was certain that I thought that I was gonna get fired. Another time I was in the state car and started feeling funny. I got out and walked around and felt okay. But the next day the same thing happened and before I could stop, I passed out and hit a concrete abutment at 42 mph. I learned the speed because they found the speedometer stuck at that *number when they looked at the wreck. We had no seatbelts then and I got a broken leg and some kidney damage. It turned out that there had been a leak in the exhaust system on that car and I had carbon monoxide poisoning!*

Following these stories, my dog, Sydney, discovered my hosts' cat and was creating quite a disturbance with her barking. When I realized how long Clair and I had been talking, I took photos of Clair and "Rocky Top" before thanking everyone for their hospitality. On the way home, I reflected on the remarkable lives of so many of the Depression-era folks that I had interviewed. They endured extremely difficult financial challenges, yet continued living in a civilized manner, asking little from others, and even sharing in "the troubles." Many of this generation, such as Clair, sacrificed dreams of what they *wanted* to do, in order to do what they *had* to do for a living. I wonder how many of us, or our descendants, would be able to do so well under such trying circumstances.

"The Country School Teacher"
Mary Jeanette Roberts

Stronghurst, IL
Interviewed May 20, 1998

URING HIS HIGH SCHOOL YEARS my son had a lawn mowing business. Occasionally he would "hire" me to assist him. One afternoon while I was talking to one of his customers, a nurse named Terri, I mentioned that I was looking to interview folks who had lived during the Depression. She told me that her mother, Mary Jeanette Roberts, might be a good candidate because "she has some good stories about teaching then." Several years later, as Terri was walking past my home, she told me that her mother was now visiting her and asked if I was still interested in doing the interview. We set up an appointment for the next day at Terri's home. Her mother was now in her 90's but was sprightly and quick-witted. She laughed a lot during our talk and had wonderful recall of details and specific anecdotes:

I was born in a state that I did not like - Missouri. I'll tell you why later. My father.... his name was Edwin Allison....was suffering from spinal meningitis. Our family had moved from Monmouth, Illinois to Kirksville, Missouri where he could be treated at an osteopathic hospital run by a nationally famous doctor named Still. Dad and his father, who was a banker in Monmouth, bought a 20-acre farm near Kirksville. They didn't actually do any farming; our family just rented the farmhouse there so that my father could get fresh air. My mother was pregnant with me, and one Sunday on September 30, 1906 while Dad and my older brother, Donald, were at church, I was born in that farmhouse. My aunt, Mom's sister, helped with the delivery. Mom told me that when Dad came home from church and saw a little girl, he was "disgusted" because he wanted a boy. Apparently, he was so angry that he said to my mom, "I wanted another boy. You can call her Mary Jeanette, but I'm going to call that child Bill." So that's how Mary Jeanette Allison came into this world. I guess that he eventually got over me being a girl, because the only name I recall him using was my real name.

The hospital in which Mary Jeanette's father was treated still exists as an osteopathic teaching hospital. In fact, it was the first such hospital in the United States. Andrew Taylor Still, the doctor mentioned by Mary Jeanette, was actually the first American to practice "osteopathic medicine." His father had been one of the early doctors in Virginia and his son followed in his footsteps. After serving as a doctor for the Union Army in the Civil War, he moved to Kansas where he was treating settlers and Native Americans, often during several types of epidemics (cholera, smallpox, tuberculosis). Based on his experiences he decided that there had to be a better way to care for patients. After three of his own children died of spinal meningitis, he began to develop a philosophy of medicine that believed in the body's inherent ability to heal itself. He experimented with treatments that minimized the use of drugs and soon moved to Kirksville, Missouri to set up practice using his new techniques which focused on prevention and a healthy lifestyle. Based on his results, Dr. Still became nationally famous, and soon patients were traveling from all over the U.S. to receive his care.

Due to the increasing demand for similar physicians, he started the first American School of Osteopathy there in Kirksville in 1892. His medical school was one of the first to encourage women to attend, and his first graduating class had five women among the 18 students. Today over 50% of osteopathic medical students are female and nearly 25% of American physicians are D.O.'s (Doctor of Osteopathy). It is not surprising, therefore, that Mary Jeanette's family came to Kirksville, which was only 150 miles from their home in Monmouth, seeking treatment from Dr. Still for her father's disease.

There are two types of meningitis: viral and bacterial. Of course, Mary Jeanette did not know which type afflicted her father, but both types were problematic during her early years. The disease is an inflammation of the membranes (called meninges) surrounding the brain and the spinal cord. Both types produce symptoms which include fever, headache, and a stiff neck. The viral form is more common, but less deadly, and often disappears without treatment. Most children now receive vaccines to prevent the disease. The bacterial version can be deadly, and without the antibiotics available today, was a serious threat on the frontier. It could be, and often was, fatal within 24 hours. This may have been the type which killed Dr. Still's three children.

Mary Jeanette resumed telling me about her childhood:

After about one year in Kirksville, my father's health improved, and we moved back to Illinois to a small town called Stronghurst...it is in the west-central part of the state near the Mississippi River. Burlington, Iowa is across the river from where we were, and northern Missouri is also close. My grandfather had started a state bank in Stronghurst, and my dad was part owner. I still have a ten-dollar bill from that bank signed by both of them.

My father not wanting me at birth was not the worst thing that happened to me as I was growing up. In the summer just before I was four, I caught fire - me and my dress. I was severely burned and almost died. I don't remember any of this, but my mother told me about it over and over as I was growing up. It was a summer day, and I was wearing an organdy dress...that's real thin material....and a gust of wind blew an ember up from a fire where we were burning trash. It hit my dress which immediately caught fire. I panicked, of course, and started to run, which made the fire worse. By the time my mother got my dress off me, I was severely burned all over my body. Everyone assumed that I was going to die. There was an older lady from Sweden who lived near us and she would put sheets in the oven to sterilize them. She would tear the sheets into strips and put some special salve, which she made, on my arms and body before wrapping the strips around the burns. She and my mother also poured molasses and butter on the wounds. I would scream whenever they did this. In fact, I apparently did a lot of screaming throughout this ordeal. One day, when removing the bandages, the flesh dropped off my right arm down to the muscle. Our local doctor wanted to remove my arm because he thought that gangrene had set in. My mother wouldn't allow him to do it, and....it was a miracle....the burns started to slowly heal. My parents hired a nurse to stay with me for nearly two months. I ended up with terrible scars on both arms and my mid-section for the rest of my life. I have always worn long sleeve dresses and shirts since then.

I had not heard of organdy material when Mary Jeanette mentioned her dress. I later learned that it is "the sheerest and crispest cotton cloth made." Apparently, it was extremely popular in the early 1900's for use in dresses for young girls; several websites show photos of girls in these dresses which flare out because of the stiffness of the material. It is understandable that this thin cotton would be highly flammable. Fabric flowers are often made using organdy.

Gangrene was a nightmare for most physicians in the early 1900's. It is caused by a lack of blood flow to skin cells; if bacteria enter the infected area, it rapidly grows and enters the circulatory system causing sepsis (blood poisoning) and ultimately death. Over 80% of patients will die without treatment which, in Mary Jeanette's time, consisted of amputating the infected limb. It was certainly a risk for her mother to override the doctor's recommendation.

After my burns healed, things were relatively normal for me until we moved less than 20 miles north to Monmouth, Illinois where the Presbyterian college, Monmouth, was located. It was a music college, and my mom was on the Board of Directors of the women's dormitory. We were living with my dad's parents in a large house. They were Scotch and my grandfather was also a banker. I went to grade school there for three years and was very happy. But then my dad and his brother, when I was about ten years old, had this scheme to get rich farming back over in Missouri. They bought a large wheat farm nine miles outside of Butler, Missouri. It was all the way on the other side of the state, practically in Kansas. All of a sudden, I was going to a one-room country school. I had to walk about a mile and a half each way. We had one teacher for all eight grades. Fortunately, she was very good....I remember her name because we had her every year....she had long, beautiful red hair and was named Blanche Duzan. Because of my scars, I continued to wear long sleeves all the time and roasted in those hot summers! Our farm did well the first few years, then the crops all failed due to big floods. Dad started having financial problems....and this was long before the Depression.

I went to high school in Butler but hated it because I was now a country girl, and most of my classmates were city girls. My dad would drive me the nine miles up there to Butler on a Monday morning, and I would then live with a family in town until Friday when he came to pick me up. Dad paid them for my staying there, but I always felt like an outsider. It definitely interfered with my grades. Like I said earlier, I hated Missouri.

I had decided that I really wanted to be a teacher like Miss Duzan. At that time in high school if you wanted to be a teacher you did not take science classes, but more agriculture-oriented lessons. I graduated from Butler High School with a certificate to teach, and at age 19, I went to work as a teacher in a country school. It was one of the best in that county and I was paid $75 a month. Like in most of the other country schools, I taught all grades in a one-room building. That first year I had only seven students - all boys. The mothers would bring in hot lunches for all of us. Each student had to have their parents buy them a book for their grade level, and that's what I used to teach them. I would just follow along with what was in the book. That year I had one student in

1st grade, one in 2nd, and the rest in the 7th and 8th grades. I just loved teaching that year!

We had a Ford car and a Ford tractor on the farm and that's how I learned to drive. You had to turn the crank to start them. I sometimes got a sore arm from cranking but never got seriously hurt like some people. I used to drive with "three feet" - meaning that I always kept my right foot on the gas, my left foot on the brake and then switched the left one to the clutch when I needed to shift. Later in life during a driver's license test the policeman told me that I shouldn't be doing this. I told him that I had been driving that way since I was 13 and hadn't had a wreck yet. He still failed me on the test.

I wanted to become a fully-licensed teacher, so I applied to Emporia Teachers College, which was up in Kansas north of Wichita, but only 20 miles west of us. It was known to be one of the best teacher colleges in the U.S. I had some money that I had saved from teaching and my parents gave me $200 more to pay for classes. To get by I worked in the girls' dorm basically for my meals. I was staying with a close-by farm family but went home on weekends. Every morning when I walked to classes I had to cross a field where there was an old gander which would come running at me and try to snap me!

I had not dated in high school, so it was here that I met my first "beau." He had a great horse and buggy, and he would take me for rides. His horse was so well-trained that he could let go of the reins and play his blues harp - that's what we called a harmonica - all the way home. It was not that romantic a deal....neither one of us were too disappointed when I had to leave school at the end of my first year and come home when my dad went broke. His two partners declared bankruptcy and there was no money to pay for my college tuition.

Our family moved back to Stronghurst, Illinois, so I went back there to live with them. I got a job that fall teaching again....this time it was Maple Grove Country School. The bad news was that I had to take a pay cut and was only making $70 a month. One of my aunts lived near this school and I stayed with her. This time I had 25 students, including *five Mexican youngsters from the same family....their father worked on the railroad. The daughter was in the 8th grade and was real smart, but the younger brothers were something else. The first grader did not know English well and kept throwing spit balls at the blackboard when he thought I wasn't looking. When the time for recess came, I pulled him aside and managed to convey to him that he had to stay inside and make spitballs for me the whole recess. As I turned to go outside to supervise the rest of the class, his older brother, who was in 6th grade, grabbed me and said, "My brother's not going to stay in here and make spitballs all recess." Before I knew what happened, he put a knife blade against my neck. I was petrified, but just stood there and looked sternly at him. Fortunately, the older sister, the 8th grader, intervened and took the knife from him. He got into big trouble for this but was just warned by the School Board that he would be expelled if he did anything again. He never bothered me after that.*

All my 8th graders had to take a test at the end of the school year over at the county seat. Teachers worried about this because if any of your students failed, they had to repeat 8th grade, and it was deemed to be your fault. But none of mine ever failed. The teachers in those schools were responsible for everything, including the upkeep of the building. In winter we had to get there early and start the fire in the big ole stove that had an iron jacket around it. We were allowed to date but couldn't get married.

I taught at Maple Grove for two years, then got a better position which paid more, $85 a month, at North School. I lived with a family near the school but had to pay them $20 a month room and board. It was here that I had a blind date and met my future husband. His name was Merle J. Roberts. He had just started teaching agriculture at Stronghurst High School. When one of his friends told him that he ought to be dating, he replied that he couldn't afford it because he hadn't received his first paycheck yet. His friend said, "Don't worry. I'll pay for the evening for all of us." So, the girlfriend of this friend of his said, "I know two country schoolteachers. One is named Dorothy and the other is Mary Jeanette. Which one do you want?"

North School Pupils

Jeanette Roberts (on right) and her students.

Well Merle chose me based just on my name. I'm glad that I wasn't a Bill! [lots of laughter by both of us on this one]. For our date, the first thing we did was to go up in an airplane over the Mississippi. I was petrified! When Merle and I came down all four of us went to dinner, then took a boat down through the locks of the dam. When the evening was over, I said to myself, "Well, that'll be the end of him." But my cousin saw him a few weeks later and told him that I was having problems with some of the chickens we were raising. Next thing I know he is coming over to show me what I was doing wrong. He taught ag and knew all that stuff. From that point on, my mother invited him over for chicken dinner every Sunday night. Later, after we were married, he used to kid me saying that it wasn't Mary Jeanette that hooked him, it was her Mom's chicken dinners!

We started to date, but my father had a stroke, and I kept working to help with the money. By now I was making $100 a month, but things were tight. Merle wanted to get married, but I told him that I was not getting married to anyone until I got my college degree. Although my grandfather still had money, he wouldn't help me pay for school. But I was determined, so in 1930 I went back up to Emporia and resumed my education. I worked like a dog, again in the women's dorm. Each day I would also walk a mile into town and wash dishes at The Women's Tea Room. They paid me a little and allowed me to eat there and take home food for my breakfast. I ate plenty! I also did a lot of babysitting for professor's families to make money for school. One thing I did for fun was to be a member of The Gibson Players. We toured and put on plays. Because I was older, I usually got "old lady parts." But I loved it!

Throughout my days at Emporia, I corresponded with Merle. My cousin kept telling me that I was crazy to leave Merle back in Stronghurst "with all those young women who adore him." I guess we both dated a little; I had a few dates up there, and he had some. We told each other about the dates and often laughed. Merle did come up to see me twice, but it was a long drive. I returned home during the summers and worked on our 40-acre farm to help keep it going.

I graduated in 1933 with a B.S. in English and Speech. Merle drove my Mom up for the graduation and took us home afterwards. I was 28 years old, and now that I had a degree, I wanted to get a job teaching high school. I soon found out that with the Depression in full swing all those jobs were precious and had been long taken. I had to do something, so I went back teaching at a country school. I always was bitter because the men doing all that road work for the W.P.A. [Works Progress Administration, one of President Roosevelt's New Deal programs to put the unemployed back to work] were making more than me.

This was a different country school than the ones I taught at before. It was called Rankin School and the $65 a month I was being paid was quite a pay cut from the $100 a month I had been making before I went back to school at Emporia. Things were very difficult all over, and I was just happy to have a job. I needed to work because we were in danger of losing the farm. My salary was a big help. I was living at home with my parents and had to ride a horse six miles each way to the school. Of course, teachers were not allowed to wear trousers in the classroom, so I wore coveralls to and from school while riding that horse and put on a dress before the students got there. My class had only 13 students, but *they were a nice group - all kids from good farming families. As usual, I had to get there early to start the pot belly stove on winter mornings, then bank it before leaving in the afternoon. Occasionally in winter Merle would show up in his car to give me a ride home after school on the really cold days. I really loved this because his car had a heater! On these occasions I just tied up the reins and that horse could always find the way home by itself.*

In early 1934 Dad knew some folks who ran a small high school near that North School where I had taught when I met Merle. He talked to them, and they had heard good things about my teaching at the country school. They hired me to begin teaching English and Latin that fall if I would take a mythology course for the Latin. I took a correspondence course on that during the summer, and come September, I was teaching high school at Terre Haute High School. It's not pronounced like the Terre Haute in Indiana….we always said, "Tare Hut." I had learned Latin in high school, but never liked it, so I spent most of the year teaching my students Latin grammar. I made them diagram every sentence. At the end of the year, they knew a lot about sentence structure and conjugating verbs, but not much vocabulary.

Most of the boy students at Terre Haute were athletes and got there each morning by carpooling with one of them driving. The girls rode with them, but that meant that they always had to wait after school for the sports practices to end. We had a lot of Singer sewing machines there, so I told the girls that I would teach them how to sew. We used old flower sacks and made dish towels. One girl told me, "I'm not sewing ole dish towels." I explained to her that her parents probably couldn't afford to buy material for her to make clothes because she had no patterns and would just keep ruining the material. She was sort of bull-headed but ended up learning to make pajamas. It turned out well because she ended up in Canada and wrote to thank me because "I wouldn't have made it through college if you had not taught me sewing because I paid for most of my tuition by making hats for all the other girls." That is the real pay of teaching.

I taught there from 1934 to 1938 - right in the middle of the Depression *while making $150 a month. I lived at home and drove our family car the ten miles back and forth while my family used their truck on the farm. In addition to teaching I also was responsible for putting on all the plays and taking students to Declamation Contests. We had about 120 students in the school, and my class sizes were generally about a dozen. I found that, although the pay was higher, I did not like teaching high school as much as being in those country schools teaching the youngsters. It was more of a challenge when you had to do everything.*

Mary Jeannette mentioned taking students to Declamation Contests. These events were very popular in high schools during the first half of the 20th century. At first only boys were allowed to compete, but by the 1930's some contests allowed girls. Declamation consists of memorizing a famous speech (or parts of it) and delivering the content, not as the original orator might have said it, but in a dramatic style which emphasizes the content. Many universities awarded significant prizes for winners, sometimes even scholarships.

Merle and I wanted to get married, but female teachers were not allowed to marry, and I needed the money to support our family. Merle was now teaching "ag" up at a high school in Genoa near Rockford.... that one is pronounced "ja-NO-a." His principal told him, "You can only go see your girlfriend on weekends once a month. Teachers in this school have weekend responsibilities." What this meant was that Merle had to attend student plays and sporting events to make sure that no problems developed. So, when school ended for both of us in May 1938 we decided to get married.

The ceremony took place on July 5, 1938 in my parent's home. We didn't have money for a big wedding, but we did go on a honeymoon in Merle's car. He had rigged it up so that the seats folded down and had a roll-up mattress that we could sleep on. We drove up to Colorado and Yellowstone and then went up to Canada. We never stayed in a hotel and slept in the car. It was a great adventure!

Now that I was married, I was not allowed to teach. Neither of us were young, so we immediately started a family. We lived in a rented house in Genoa and had a big garden. I canned vegetables and meat so that we could make it through the winters. Terri, our first daughter, came the next May. Looking back, we were poor, but no one told us.

Merle continued teaching there in Genoa. For social reasons, I had to join the Women's Club in town. After I had our second child, Jerry, in 1943, I also joined the PEO and went to their National Convention in Philadelphia in 1950. My dad died in 1944 due to complications from his earlier stroke. Merle and I were together until he passed away earlier this year. I still live in Genoa....and it's still pronounced the same.

When Mary Jeanette used the term "PEO" I did not quiz her on this, but later learned that the full name is "PEO Sisterhood" which stands for Philanthropic Educational Organization. It still exists and claims to have over 200,000 members. The focus is to provide "educational opportunities for female students worldwide." It started with a group of seven women educators in 1869 and has grown to nearly 6000 local chapters.

Mary Jeanette and I ended our conversation on the sad note of Merle's passing. As I reflected on her own life, it was not difficult to grasp the significance of her role in American education. These young, single women who manned (intentional use of this verb) the one-room schoolhouses of our nation during its progression from frontier to "modernity" were absolute heroes. Often only in their late teens or early 20's they not only taught small groups of youngsters (some from immigrant families who knew no English) reading, writing, arithmetic, history, and geography, but in doing so they also helped to fulfill our Founding Fathers' dream of an educated citizenry by creating knowledgeable homogeneity. Each day began at 9 A.M. with the Pledge of Allegiance (which was first written in 1892) and ended at 4 P.M. There was a 15-minute recess and an hour for lunch. Pictures of Washington and Lincoln were typically on the walls. These young ladies had to be the "jills" of all trades: fire stoker, janitor, nurse, sports supervisor, peacekeeper....and teacher of all subjects and all grades. There are countless sources of online information, photographs, and videos about these "country schools." A good starting place is the website for the Country School Association of America (CSAA). The next time I hear one of my former teaching colleagues complaining about online teaching during COVID, I plan to ask if they would prefer to ride a horse six miles each way to teach.

During our long talk Mary Jeanette and I often stopped to share teaching stories. Hers were usually far better than mine (I never experienced a knife at my neck). Even though our classroom days were separated by 50 years, we still shared a common love of our daily interaction with students. Teachers can be more than instructors and role models; often lasting friendships develop. She mentioned to me several times how later in life she frequently heard from her students with children of their own remembering fondly their days together in those small schoolhouses and high school classrooms. There was one area of our conversation when I could go one-up on Mary Jeanette: diagramming sentences. In my Catholic high school in Kentucky we learned during each of our four years of high school how to diagram sentences in English, Latin, AND Greek. She laughed heartily at this.

Mary Jeanette's ironclad determination to emulate her first "country school" teacher, Blanche Duzan, was remarkable. Throughout all the challenges she faced, she never lost sight of her goal. Countless American children have been the beneficiaries. Her comment, "We were poor, but no one told us," serves as an excellent summary of the lives of so many Americans during the trials of the Great Depression.

"On His Own"
Arden Babcock

Wenatchee, WA
Interviewed June 21, 1996

D UE TO HEAVIER THAN ANTICIPATED mid-day traffic, I arrived 20 minutes late for my interview with Arden. He was gracious about my tardiness when I arrived at his trailer in Deer Park, Washington. He showed me around his home and garden and invited me to join him for a cup of coffee. I was immediately struck by Arden's neatly trimmed white beard and large glasses giving him an appearance of a grizzled "old-timer." I was almost certain that Arden was a life-long smoker because of his hollow cheeks and a slight cigarette scent about him. He was wearing a short-sleeved white shirt open at the collar with dark trousers. I found myself frequently staring at the shirt because it had an unusual light vertical striping sewn into the fabric. As we began to talk, he removed a ball cap lettered with "North Central Credit Union" and relaxed into a heavily padded rocking chair. His voice was strong as he recounted his early years:

I'm Arden Babcock. My middle name is Eugene, but I never used it. I was born on January 6, 1919 in Spokane, Washington. I'm not sure, but I think I was born in a hospital. What exactly happened then has never been totally clear to me because my mother - her name was Grace Mullins - died from the flu during that large epidemic shortly after I was born. She was Scotch- Irish right out of the hills of Kentucky - up in the Cumberland Gap area. Her father, my granddad, was one of the toughest, meanest old birds you ever met. We didn't get along. One of my sisters traced our history back to a widow named Mullins who came over on the Mayflower. She had two sons and we all are descended from one of them. My father, Fay Babcock, was a Canadian and apparently just left. He dumped me. I think that I saw him twice in my lifetime - not good memories.

There was indeed a woman named Alice Mullins on the Mayflower manifest for the sailing to Plymouth Colony in Massachusetts in 1620. She came with her husband, William, an 18-year old daughter, Priscilla, and a 14-year old son, Joseph, who (according to Arden's sister's research) became the forefather of the Mullins family in America. I am not sure why the parents were not the ones she considered first in their American lineage. This was the only time Arden mentioned any brothers or sisters; I did not attempt to verify the validity of his sister's research. In view of the actions of Fay Babcock, the family history apparently did not convey much sense of duty. Arden grimaced when discussing his father and then continued:

As a youngster I was shuttled around between several of my aunts on my mother's side. For a while I lived with one of them named Aunt May in the Spokane area. I know that I went to part of grade school there. But she died in 1930 and I was sent across the state to Everett to live with another aunt. That's where Boeing has some of its biggest aircraft plants now. I kept going to grade school over there, but I don't remember the name of the school. I was being "shoveled from pillar to post." One more mouth to feed during the Depression was apparently one too many; I guess that's why I kept getting moved. After being with this aunt and that aunt, I was 14 when I wound up with my granddad back in Spokane, but we couldn't get along. It's a long story. I never could figure out why he was so mean to me. He was born during the Civil War and came out here to work with the railroads when they were coming through down in the Palouse country. I guess he was just a "hard man." It got so bad between me and Granddad that I just took off for Wenatchee. I later learned that he died at 96 while mowing his lawn.

The Palouse is a region of the Northwest encompassing parts of Idaho, Washington, and Oregon. The origin of the word, Palouse, is unclear - some say it is based on the name of the indigenous inhabitants, while others claim that it is derived from the French word, pelouse, referring to "land with thick, short grass." This name was later given to the local Indians (known as *The Palouse Tribe*) who were famous for breeding spotted horses which came to be known as "Appaloosa." Currently "The Palouse" is used to refer to the entire wheat-growing region of these northwestern states. The success of wheat farmers, coupled with the new railroads here, led to a land rush in the late 1800's. Although several cities rapidly developed in the area, Spokane became the major hub and partially led to it being known as "The Capital of the Inland Empire."

Here's why I headed to Wenatchee. My Aunt May, the one I had stayed with first, had a son who was a lot older than me....maybe 20 years older. In fact, when I was living with her, he was supposed to take care of me, but he really didn't. Well, I knew he was out in Wenatchee, and I had a few bucks, so I got myself a train ticket to go live with him. His name was Vasco Morgan; he was a pimp. He got me a job sweeping hallways and cleaning up in a local whorehouse. It was in the Chelan Hotel. I was getting paid a dollar a day and had a small room in the basement. There were maybe 15 to 20 girls working there. They never really bothered me except to sometimes complain about the floors; I never got close to any of them, if you know what I mean. It was just business for those women. I was happy because thirty bucks a month for a 15-year-old was good money in the early 30's.

Somehow the local School Board heard about my situation and wanted to institutionalize me - you know, put me in jail or an insane asylum or something. I got scared. One of the girls working there talked to me and gave me some advice. She told me to put an ad in the paper asking for a place where I could work for room and board. So I did. That's how my parents got me - through a newspaper ad! I say "parents" because they became my true parents since I never felt that I really had any. They took me in and raised me just like I had been their own child. I called them Mom and Dad. Their names were Roy and Esther Beaton. They never officially adopted me, so I never took their last name.

I was not able to determine if the Chelan "hotel" where Arden worked was in Wenatchee or actually in the smaller city of Chelan, some thirty miles to the north.

My "new" parents were living on a dairy farm. They had been rather well-off before the Depression. They owned the Hupmobile dealership in Wenatchee and were part owners of a grocery store. But they lost everything except the farm when the economy crashed around 1930 and had to try to make a living on this ranch. We had a herd of 25 cows - all Jersey-Guernseys - and Mom had a one-acre vegetable garden. We also had pigs, chickens, and rabbits which we raised. My mom and me had a deal on the garden. We both worked it, and she would take enough for us to eat and for her to can, and I got the rest to sell in town. I would sell all types of vegetables, but often it was not for money, but for coffee, sugar, and other things to take home. There was a lot of barter in those days. With all the animals and what we grew, no one went hungry at our place! Mom was Swiss-German and knew how to cook and to stretch out a penny.

Arden and I stopped here to talk vegetable gardening. As a teen I also worked on our family farm in Kentucky. It was called a "truck farm" because after we harvested vegetables in the summer, they were loaded onto our pickup truck and taken to town to sell to grocery stores. Like Arden, as a teen, I also raised rabbits to eat and sell - at one time I had 300 rabbits. Contrary to conventional wisdom, domestic rabbits do not "automatically" multiply but require carefully planned breeding and nurturing.

I forgot to tell you....I had a one-year-old brother. His name was Kenneth and I helped raise him. I even took him on dates with me in Dad's 1929 Hupmobile. It was a 4-door sedan with a "straight-8" engine. I think that a lot of the girls liked Kenneth more than me! I didn't need a lot of money to go on dates because gas was only 10-15 cents a gallon then and the girls never expected you to spend much. Mostly during high school there....it was Wenatchee High....I hung out with four buddies. We did everything together and chased the same girls. A fellow named Hank was my really good buddy. I was tall and played a little basketball, but really didn't have time for it because I had to work on the ranch. Every morning I had to be up for the 4:15 milking. We milked daily at 4:15 in the morning and 4:15 in the afternoon.

The Hupmobile was a car built from 1909 to 1938. The company, the Hupp Motor Car Company, was founded in Detroit by Bobby Hupp and a fellow who had worked for Oldsmobile. They began manufacturing with an initial investment of only $25,000 and produced 500 automobiles in their first year. By 1910 they were making 5000 cars a year. For a short period, their cars were unique for American vehicles because they were the only ones with an all-steel body. Hupp left the company in 1913, but the name remained the same. One of the earlier Hupmobiles was modified to become the first Greyhound bus! Sales continued to grow during the 1920's, but a new strategy in 1925 to shift from 4-cylinder cars to the 8-cylinder model (the one driven by Arden) led to declining sales due to the increased cost. In the early 1930's Hupp merged with Graham-Paige Motor Company to produce highly-styled, more expensive vehicles. This proved to be a disastrous decision leading to the company's closure in 1939. I might add that as a Physics teacher, I always questioned the use of "Motor" for the name of an automobile company. Gasoline cars are propelled by engines, not motors, which are electric. Although there are a few motors in modern gas and diesel vehicles, they are not the motive force. I have been unable to find any reason for this mis-naming. Arden now began a lengthy tutorial concerning dairy farming:

When we did that milking of those cows, it was all by hand. The automatic milking machines which some of the larger dairies had were still unreliable and you had to watch them closely. If you kept the vacuum on too long on the teat, it could draw blood, so we did our cows all by hand. I was really good at it - I could milk two cows to my dad's one. As soon as we got through milking, we would pour the milk through a strainer into a vat in our cool room. We had electricity in our farmhouse but none in the barn, so we had to use ice in the summer to keep it cool. We would then bottle it up and put it in our delivery truck to take to customers on my Dad's milk route. He sold it for 5 cents a quart. It was, of course, raw milk then; no one around us that I know of pasteurized milk then. The raw milk that we sold had the cream in it and would rise to the top of the bottles. That way our customers could shake the bottle to mix it up, or skim off the cream to use however they wanted. All the milk that we didn't use to sell on the route was handled differently. We would pour it into a separator which we spun by hand. The skim milk is heavier and gets slung to the outside - you know, centrifugal force. The fat globules stay in the center because they are lighter. It works best when the milk is still warm. We could separate about 15 quarts in five minutes or so. That cream was our real cash crop because we sold it by the pound to plants that made butter. The skim milk left over we fed to our pigs....you couldn't sell it to no one at that time.

It is well known that the process of "pasteurization" received its name from the French biologist and chemist, Louis Pasteur. Some of his first work (1861) concentrated not on milk, but on the souring of certain wines during fermentation. His experiments led him to conclude that the growth of micro-organisms was responsible. This discovery led him to invent a process which heated the wine between 140- and 210-degrees Fahrenheit. In 1865 he patented the process "to fight the diseases of wine." Within a few years his "pasteurization process" was applied to beer and milk. Pasteur is also responsible for the word "vaccination." He invented vaccines for rabies, anthrax, and some forms of cholera.

Raw milk can be deadly, especially if it is not used quickly. Several life-threatening diseases, such as tuberculosis (TB), can be carried by contaminants in non-pasteurized milk. One of the women I interviewed for this book contracted TB in Los Angeles at the age of nine. None of her siblings or parents was infected; her disease may well have been the result of drinking raw milk. The first U.S. law mandating pasteurization of milk was passed in Chicago in 1908, but there were no national regulations until the late 1940's. Today the sale of raw milk remains legal in 28 states. Arden continued telling me more about dairy farming; I chose not to get into a Physics discussion with him concerning "centrifugal" versus what I believe should be "centripetal."

All breeds of dairy cows do not produce the same milk. The Jerseys give you a lot of butterfat, maybe 35-40%. We never liked Holsteins because they give you a lot of milk, but very little cream, and cream was how we made our money. That's why we had Jersey-Guernsey's - they gave us the best of both worlds. You know, we bred those cows every year, not to get calves, but to have the cow bring in fresh milk. Six weeks before the calf was born, we would stop milking the cow and let it go dry. Then, the day after the calf arrived, we would take the calf away and now have a cow with lots of fresh milk. The calves were pretty much worthless. You could buy them anywhere for 75 cents each. Some of the larger farms would give them away if you hauled them off. I know of several of the big outfits which had lime pits. They just killed the calves and threw them into those pits where the bodies would rapidly decay.

We lost the ranch sometime in the mid-1930's when we couldn't make enough money to pay our bills for irrigation and feed. The bank just took it. I wasn't out of high school yet and we moved into town. Dad was desperate, but he was able to get a job with the WPA putting in a sewer system for the town. [Works Progress Administration, one of the New Deal programs started by President Roosevelt to put people back to work]. He also did some odd jobs around town. Mom and Dad had a little money saved and were able to buy a dilapidated house in Wenatchee for $1000 with nothing down and payments of $14 a month. Dad always said that "we went right down next to the dole." He also always told me when he was working for the WPA that you had better keep working, because "there are always ten other guys waiting to take that job." Mom finally got a job as a bookkeeper for a local loan shark. She kept that job until she retired many years later.

During this tough time for us, I worked in the orchards all around the area for ten cents an hour, ten hours a day. I did a lot of cherry *and apple picking and spraying the trees to kill apple worms and the coddling moth. Both would ruin the crop. We sprayed with arsenic, lead, and sulfur. Most of those fields will never grow anything much again except apples and corn due to those chemicals. I think that I must have developed some form of tolerance for the arsenic because I never got sick. One summer my buddy Hank and I made some real good money because of those worms and moths. During the previous year farmers around Wenatchee who couldn't afford to have their orchards sprayed had to let government guys come in with bulldozers to knock 'em down in order to try to limit the spread of the bugs. So, Hank and I came up with the idea of buying a buzz saw for $10 and hooking it up with a belt to the wheels of an old Model A truck which we would jack up. That sucker had a 30-inch blade. We would go into those pushed-over trees and cut up a lot of cords of wood. We would sell it for $1 a cord if they picked it up at the orchard, or for $2 if we delivered it to them. We sold over 150 cords of wood that summer. At that time, I was working half a day at a lumber yard and half a day at high school. That's why it took me until I was 20 to graduate. At the lumber yard they would pay me in building materials, and I would take these home for me and Dad to remodel that old $1000 house.*

In high school in those days my favorite part of the day was the Smith-Hughes Carpentry class. Every year, as part of this class, we would build a house from scratch. There was some government money for the materials and by the time the school year was over, we had built a nice house. The art class would do the decorating and local furniture companies provided some furniture that they could use for advertising when the open house took place before the house was sold. I'm not sure where that money went, but we sure learned a lot. I loved doing this!

Arden's favorite class was the result of the Smith-Hughes Act of 1917 that provided federal aid to states to promote vocational education in agriculture, industrial trades, and home economics. It was named after Senators Hoke Smith and D.M. Hughes, both from Georgia. Participation reached its zenith prior to WW II. Although many modern historians are critical of the legislation for separating students by gender and placing them in "tracks that reinforce treatment of students on class and race," others, including myself (speaking as a retired classroom teacher), bemoan the loss of such vocational training in our current high schools. Now, instead of providing training for actual good-paying jobs, such as carpentry, plumbing, etc., we are turning out many high school graduates whose best chance for economic success lies in being an "educated" burger flipper.

When I finally got out of high school in 1940, I enlisted in the National Guard in Wenatchee in September. My reasoning was that the national draft had just started and, by enlisting for a year, I would then get a high number for the draft and probably not be selected. Well, that didn't work. Not too long after I was in the Guard, the Feds took it over from the states, and extended my enlistment. Our outfit was an anti-aircraft battery. We went to Fort Lewis on the west side of the state to train, and in February 1941 we got sent up to the Aleutian Islands. Then Pearl Harbor came, and I was stuck in Alaska for the duration of the war. That was the longest "year" of my life: five years, ten months, and one day! [Here both Arden and I shared a long laugh at his joke]. We were 2400 miles out into the Pacific. Due to the ocean all around, it wasn't as cold as you might imagine, but it was miserable due to the damp fog all the time. The joke was, "Get assigned to the Aleutians. You got it made! It has an ocean view and a squaw under every tree west of Dutch Harbor." I quickly found out that there were NO trees anywhere up there! I ended up spending 44 months in the Aleutians. After the Japs invaded Attu, we were sent to Shemya, a real small island about 40 miles northeast of there. It's about two miles wide and four miles long. The U.S. built a runway on it which took up most of the island. Our mission was "perimeter anti-aircraft." If the weather cooperated, we would get a supply ship once a month....often it didn't show up. The worst part was the total isolation. In 1943 I was involved in the invasion of Attu. When we got ashore, we set up an anti-aircraft unit on the beach, but never saw a Jap airplane.

The American-Japanese war in the Aleutians involved the Japanese not only invading, but occupying, American territory. In July 1942 Japan captured the two remote islands of Attu and Kiska in the Aleutian Islands chain. Their motives were unclear - possibly a diversionary tactic for the invasion of Midway Island, or a guard against the U.S. being able to launch an invasion of Japan from the islands. Regardless, Americans were shocked that Japanese troops were now firmly entrenched on U.S. soil. In early 1943, American forces were able to establish a blockade of the islands and ultimately regain control of both islands several months later. The fighting on Attu was bloody and intense, including a suicidal "banzai" attack by the remaining Japanese soldiers. Arden did not discuss how he was involved in the American invasion of Attu but did tell me that he was "shot at many times."

After the war ended, I stayed in the Army for a year or so. I was at Victorville in California and then at Fort Bragg in North Carolina and then back to Fort Bliss where I was discharged. When I got out of the Army, I came home. I went to work for an apple warehouse and then a cabinet shop. It was low pay, but then I got a chance to go to work for the state highway department. I stayed there for 32 years. I started out on bridge crews and was a bridge carpenter. I ended up being a Maintenance Supervisor. After I retired. I started my own little contracting business doing home repair and did several building projects.

I was married in 1949 to Ruby Snider. We were married over in Coeur d' Alene, Idaho....sort of snuck away, although we were both older. It's a long story. See, I was married before when I was in the Army. It had been a high school love affair and when I came home from being away for nearly two years, I found that I was a "Proud Papa." It just ended.... in a divorce. I met Ruby when she was married to the guy I worked with in the cabinet shop. We were all friends, and when her husband died, we decided to get married. We have eight kids: seven boys and a girl. Two of the boys are from her first marriage. They've all done real well - a couple are electronics engineers. Ruby and I lived in Alaska for several years in a fifth wheel [a large RV travel trailer requiring a unique hitch, usually in the bed of the towing pickup truck] and three of our kids are still up there. One is a musher; he has 38 dogs!

At this point in our conversation Arden and I traded Alaska stories - his from living there and mine from having traveled there with my wife on several occasions. As we were agreeing that we both liked Anchorage better than Fairbanks, Ruby walked in from work. She was a close friend and working colleague in the medical field with Coco, the wife of my best friend. When I returned to Coco's home, I thanked her for arranging the interview with Arden, who had such an interesting Depression-era story. As a young man who basically raised himself from his earliest years, Arden found a new family, served his country honorably in the wilds of Alaska, and returned to raise his own large family. It is yet another uniquely American success story from that era.

"The Anabaptists"
Daniel and Elizabeth Bonträger and Daniel Beachy

Elkhart County, Indiana
Interviewed May 1995

The Bonträgers

T HE RELIGIOUS COMMUNITY IN NORTHERN Indiana has long interested me. Whenever I visited relatives in the region, there was no shortage of traditional horse and buggy vehicles on the roads. I initially believed that they were associated with Amish farmers. I made this assumption based on my familiarity with the Amish communities in Pennsylvania I had seen and read about over the years. It turns out that my assumption totally oversimplified the past 450 years of historical and social events associated with this religion.

Most of the farmers I had seen here in Indiana were not Amish, but various sects of religious groups which had their beginnings in the Reformation in Central Europe in the early 1500's. Martin Luther's rebellion in 1517 against the sale of indulgences by the Catholic Church led to an avalanche of like-minded thinkers and theologians not only in other parts of Germany, but also in other regions of Europe. Luther's writings influenced one of the first leaders of the Reformation in Switzerland, a priest named Huldrych Zwingli, who was pastor of a large church in Zurich in 1523. Zwingli's literal interpretation of the Bible led to removing icons and organs from churches, no longer requiring celibacy for priests, replacing mass by a simpler service emphasizing Bible readings and communion, and declaring that church laws are binding only if they agree with Scripture.

At about the same time, a young Dutch priest named Menno Simons learned of a man who had been executed because he had been re-baptized. After reading the Bible for the first time (by his own admission, this was not unusual for Catholic priests at the time to have not read the Bible), he joined others in what is now the Netherlands in rejecting the baptism of infants as contrary to what is written in the Bible. This group of like-minded thinkers became known as "Anabaptists" (from the Greek, *anabaptezein*, which means to baptize again....it was originally a highly derogative term in the Middle Ages) because of their belief that a Christian can be legitimately baptized only when old enough to make an informed confession of faith. These new views were not taken lightly by the religious or government authorities (often the same) who launched all-out war on a group of Anabaptists who had brutally taken over a medieval town. In the ensuring battle in 1535, Simons' brother, Pieter, was killed along with 300 other Anabaptists, including 37 who were beheaded. Few of those in power loved the Anabaptists; they managed to offend not only the Pope, but also Martin Luther. Simons went into hiding because the Pope had a standing offer of 100 gold guilders for Menno's arrest. A Dutch man was executed merely for housing Simons.

When Simons emerged from hiding, he had become a pacifist who rejected the violence of the early Anabaptists and developed a strong opposition to any military service. He traveled to Zurich, where he embraced much of Zwingli's teachings which denied the doctrine of transubstantiation - that the bread and wine used in Catholic communions is transformed into the body and blood of Jesus Christ. However, he soon broke with Zwingli over infant baptism and military service. He argued that the Christian's duty is to suffer, not fight. Over the next 25 years, due to his writings and teaching, Simons became one of the most influential Anabaptists in Europe. His followers were initially called Mennonists, but later became known as Mennonites. Today there are nearly two million Mennonites world-wide in over 75 countries.

Over 100 years later, in 1693, Jakob Amman, a young Swiss man, joined the Anabaptist movement and became a prominent leader among what were mostly Mennonites. Soon quarrels developed among these Swiss Mennonites over social shunning of those who had been excommunicated and other issues, such as foot washing! Those who followed Amman became known simply as Amish; his opponents remained Mennonites, often labeled Amish Mennonites. To avoid continuing persecution in Europe, the Amish group first came to America in 1717. They initially settled in Philadelphia, but a group of more conservative members, now called Old Order Amish, moved west to near Reading, Pennsylvania, which remains a strongly Amish region today. When Amish Mennonites arrived in the U.S., they moved further west of the Amish region, first into Ohio and Indiana, then further west. In general, the Old Order Amish are far more insular and do not attempt outreach or embrace higher education, while the Amish Mennonites have established universities and sent missionaries all over the world.

Having familiarized myself with some of this basic understanding of the Mennonite history and culture, I was able to arrange a meeting with a local Mennonite couple, Daniel and Elizabeth Bonträger. They were living in a large white farmhouse outside Goshen, Indiana. Because of what I had heard about some of the local Mennonites, I was surprised to notice while entering their driveway that their home had electricity. Both Daniel and Elizabeth were waiting outside to greet me. Daniel had a trimmed white beard, with no mustache, and Elizabeth was wearing the traditional Mennonite bonnet with a plain, dark, full-length dress. They were holding hands, and both wore glasses. Elizabeth seemed to have a continuous smile, while Daniel was more reserved, but friendly. They quickly invited me inside to chat. As I was sitting down, Elizabeth brought me a glass of cold water. When asked about their birth places, 80-year old Daniel spoke first. Elizabeth often finished his sentences.

I was born on December 12, 1914 here in Elkhart County. Our last name, Bonträger, was originally Bornträger, but got changed. Our family had 6 boys and 4 girls....all of us were born at home. One of my brothers still uses Bornträger. It's German and my grandfather always spoke German to me. Bornträger means carrier of water.

My parents were farmers. Their ancestors were Amish and came here to Indiana in 1840 from western Pennsylvania. There have been several schisms in the church since then. The first one occurred here in the 1850's when a new group moved in from a different county in Pennsylvania. The two groups couldn't agree on various matters and ended up splitting into separate churches. Ours was called Amish Mennonites, and the other, more conservative group, was Old Order Mennonites. In 1927 there was another schism over whether to have missions. Those wanting to have missionaries became what were called Beachy Mennonites, named after a leader named Moses Beachy who started this branch back in Pennsylvania. So, we are now Beachy Mennonites and gather for services in a meeting house about a mile and a half east of here. We have 16-18 families, nearly 300 people who get together there, mostly Yoders and Bornträgers and Beachys. There are Old Order Mennonites here in the county, but we generally do not mix. They do not have meeting houses but get together in each other's homes.

I originally went to school in a 2-room schoolhouse not too far from my home, which I walked to. In January 1925 a new school got built and opened and I went there until I was 15. Around here we only had two years of high school then, so that's all I had.

Elizabeth, still smiling, now joined the conversation:

We first met when we were both at that new schoolhouse. Daniel is almost exactly two years older than me. I was also born in December, but in 1916. Both of us ended up having to work during the Depression and didn't get married until 1938 when we were in our early 20's. By that time, it was a little better than in the early 30's. My family were Old Order Mennonites, which is more conservative than what we're now, Beachy Mennonites. I'm not originally from around here. I was born in Haven, Kansas and our family came here on a train when I was four years old. Believe it or not, I remember that. I was a Yoder....there are lots of those around here. You may have met some in town. My family had 11 children, but only 6 lived past childhood. Daniel and I have 8 children....they are all married and doing well.

My family were farmers. In 1930 my father had over a thousand dollars in a bank in Topeka, Indiana, and when he went to get it, the bank was closed. He lost it all. The people we owed money to were real good when they heard about us losing the money. They just told my father to pay whatever he could each month. During this time, we didn't buy anything. I had a pair of shoes and a couple of dresses. The farm where we were renting, they decided they had to sell it, so we had to move. From there, we moved every year until I got married because every farm we moved to, they ended up having to sell it. I started working when I was 16 and got two and a half dollars a week working for families where a baby had been born. I worked in 19, maybe 20, places after they had a new baby. I had to get the milk from the cows, wash the clothes, get and carry the water to the house....that came out to about 33 cents a day. We turned all this money over to my father. It helped our family get along.

As Elizabeth was obviously becoming upset by these memories, Daniel interjected:

We had it better because my parents owned a 120-acre farm. I made my money by raising rabbits. When they were grown, I could sell them live for a nickel a pound...the local butcher would pay me 25 cents for a 5-pound rabbit. My father had a federal Land Bank loan for five thousand dollars before the Depression came along, but Dad was able to make those payments at 4% interest all during the 30's. We did not have any extra money to spend, of course. We rotated crops...corn, oats, wheat, and hay on an annual basis. We cultivated all of it except 15 acres of marsh. We also raised cows, hogs, sheep, and chickens and had some horses for work. Us boys in the family would often hire ourselves out to other farmers for 20 to 35 dollars a month, which you had to bring home until you were 21.

When I turned 21, I got a job in a carpenter crew over in Elkhart. Another fellow would give us a ride over and back. I was making 50 cents an hour to start; my uncle was experienced, and he was getting 60 cents an hour. That was good money for me, over $20/week. I could keep all that money and still get food and lodging at home. I next worked at Penn Electric in Goshen and learned carpentry and plumbing. I was making 60 cents an hour, and a local fellow gave me a ride into town. When the union came in, we got a raise. I didn't join the union, but still had to pay the dues. That winter was real cold. A neighbor boy and I each cut a hundred cord of wood for 80 cents a cord. We did that all with hand saws. We each made $40 doing that wood.

That next summer, me and three other boys went together and bought a '28 Ford for $100 and drove out to Kansas. We worked there for the harvest for $3 a day, which was good compared to farm work back home. We then went up to Colorado Springs, and after that, drove up to see a rodeo in Cheyenne, Wyoming. We never rented a cabin; we always would spread a blanket alongside the road and sleep there. When we got to Yellowstone, three of us slept outside as always, but one fellow was afraid of bears and slept inside the Ford. He was right because the next morning we saw a huge grizzly....we were lucky. Usually we only stopped for one meal a day...the rest of our meals were snacks because we had no money except for gas which was 20 cents a gallon. When we reached Eugene, Oregon we got on picking pears for $5 a day....which was great money. On the way back the starter motor broke on the Ford, and we had to use the crank to start it. When it was my turn, it kicked and broke my right arm. I had it set and couldn't work for 4 weeks. We had a lot of adventure on that trip!

Elizabeth now picked up the conversation while Daniel was still laughing about his summer trip.

My brother worked on some road projects for the WPA. All their work was done with a shovel and a wheelbarrow. Some of the poor people in Goshen would come out to work in the fields for 50 cents a day weeding the mint fields...some of the farmers here got rich on mint.

Although we had met in that school many years earlier, I did not know that Daniel even liked me. When he got back from that trip out west, he asked me to marry, but we agreed not to do it until Daniel had saved $1000. We had a nice wedding. My parents fed a lot of our friends afterwards. None of our children drink or smoke, and all have jobs. At Christmas each year we still get most of our family together, except for one of our daughters who is on a mission in Belize.

I had heard that many Amish do not want to have their picture taken, but Elizabeth and Daniel readily agreed. Apparently, the Mennonites have no such problems. They held hands during each photo taken, both inside and outside their home. As I was departing, Elizabeth's final words to me were, "You know, we've been married 57 years now and are still best friends," She was wearing that same smile.

The next day I was able to arrange a meeting with another Mennonite recommended by my relative. His first name was also Daniel, and believe it or not, his last name was Beachy the same as the Moses Beachy who had begun the new branch of Mennonites which the Bonträgers had told me about. Daniel was a very personable man, younger in appearance than either of the Bonträgers. He was working in his office as a manager of "The Depot," a huge combination thrift and furniture store run by local Mennonites in Goshen. Like Daniel Bonträger, he had a trimmed white beard, but no mustache - two characteristics which I later learned were a sign of an older married Mennonite. Throughout our conversation he sat at his desk while taking occasional phone calls and answering questions from employees, but not in a distracting manner. He began by telling me about his early years:

I was born at home on a farm about 20 miles from here in LaGrange County. It was a Sunday, February 19, 1922. I had an older brother and two younger sisters. My mother was a Bonträger. We raised cows, horses and chickens and cultivated 80 acres. The farm had been owned originally by Grandfather Beachy. One of my earliest memories was walking around the farm with my father and his dog.

Daniel Beachy in his office.

I walked to my first school which had one classroom for 42 children of all grades. I really liked it because I could listen to what the grade ahead was being taught so I already knew it when I got there. I remember all my teachers from that school [he proceeded to list each by name]. After 4th grade I was transferred to a new, centralized school. We got there in a hack - that was what we called a horse-drawn wagon that had benches up and down each side. In the middle there was a steel "V" running the length of the hack where the driver burned charcoal to keep us warm during winter. It didn't work that well. Later we got busses, but we still called them hacks.

My father died from pneumonia in 1928 when I was six. He had gotten the flu in the 1918 epidemic and it damaged his lungs badly and since then he always had trouble breathing. Dad had been the farmer, so now we had to move. My mother sold the farm and rented a house from a member of the church. She sold everything except two cows, 50 chickens and one horse. We got milk from the cows, and eggs and meat from the chickens. She began a "truck patch" on a piece of land that came with the house - that term means raising vegetables to eat and to sell. We dug it up by hand. The church was good to mother. Someone would go around to each of the member's farms and ask for "grains for Emma." These farmers would donate corn, wheat, oats, and hay. It was a very difficult time. Mother would do some sewing for money and sold some eggs, but we didn't have much. Each of us had only one pair of shoes, and we ate a lot of dry cereal like corn flakes because it was cheaper than hot cereal.

In 1930 one of Mother's uncles had an opportunity to buy a 160-acre farm with a good size barn and a big house. One of our relatives mentioned to him that Mother had some money saved from selling our farm and that she might be willing to lend it to him with interest, of course. This was a difficult decision for her to make, but after considerable prayer and discussion with other relatives, she decided to do it. When she went up to the bank in Topeka where her $700 was in savings, the banker tried to talk her out of withdrawing the money for a loan to a relative. Mother thought about it for several minutes, but decided that, because she had given her word to her uncle, she was going to do it. She got the $700 und.....the next day the bank closed! In later years we often wondered if that banker knew that the bank was going under the next day and that was why he was trying so hard to get mother not to withdraw her money. It turned out to be a good loan for mother because her uncle paid her interest and some of the principal each six months. Within three years it was fully paid.

After two years we moved to another house on a small farm owned by a member of the church. It was a mint farm. The land was what we called "muck" - very dark soil from previous marshland containing a lot of decaying vegetable matter. The farmer would mow that mint just like hay, and then distill it in an 8 by 8 ft steel drum using steam. The mint oil would come out the bottom and was sold in barrels. It got good money, $1 a pound. At one point it went up to $30 a pound, before dropping back to $2. Still that was good. These mint farmers sold it to dealers *who then re-sold it....not sure where, but probably a lot went to the chewing gum manufacturers in Chicago.*

I went eight years to school but had to work part time from age 8 as a "chore boy" for my uncle on his farm. In 4th and 5th grades I was the janitor at our school. I had to get there early to start the fire for heat and to sweep the floors - they were coated with linseed oil. I got 10 cents a day, and 15 cents during the winter when I had to do the fire. I used this money to buy school clothes. When I got to fifteen years old in 1937, I quit school to work, but I had to get a permit from the truant officer.

As a child I played a lot of games with other boys around us. We went to a local swimming hole during the summer and fished using bent pins for hooks. Most of our entertainment was associated with the church, but activities stopped at night because we had no electricity. We used kerosene lanterns, but that was not free. In November of 1937 we moved to a farm with one of my uncles, while I worked on another farm for $35 a month, but I was also getting room and board there. One of my younger brothers was also "farmed out" like this. When one of the local widowers....his name was Martin Yoder....asked my mother to marry him, she moved to his farm, but he didn't need us boys to work for him so we kept doing work on other farms.

I did this farm work until 1943 when I was 21. That's when I married Viola. She was six months younger than me and we had known each other since we were 13. She had worked on her parent's farm doing "boy's work" - she did not have any brothers. After our marriage we rented an 80-acre farm on a 50-50 basis from the owner. It was all done on a handshake basis He bought the cows and chickens and a horse for us and he got half of everything we grew and raised, including the milk and eggs. With the war now going on, I got a "farm deferment" which was based on points depending on how many acres you were farming and how many cattle you were raising. So, I stayed farming all during the war. Viola and I formed a good team. I did most of the field work and she took care of everything else.

We were Old Order Amish and did not use meeting houses like the

Mennonites. We met in houses then and did not have missionaries. Of course, we had no electricity and lived within certain boundaries with other Amish. In the late 40's our congregation voted to allow electricity and telephones, and after a few more years, cars.

For the next 45 minutes Daniel Beachy gave me his version of church history beginning with the Anabaptists in Switzerland. He spent considerable time discussing Zwingli and the various schisms which had taken place since the 1500's. He said that Peter Beachy had come to Baltimore in 1776, "a very famous year for America," and that Moses Beachy was a "very distant relative." When he told me that the original spelling of his name in German was Bitschi, he laughed heartily saying that he was "always grateful that they changed it because you can figure out how they pronounced it."

In our final minutes Daniel told me of his later life as a builder. He was involved in the construction of most of Goshen College and many other projects in the county. His final thoughts returned to his mother during those hard times of the Depression, "She did not know when a dollar might come." As I was leaving, Daniel stopped me and said, "I have a lot of appreciation for our church. People that had a church were the advantaged ones."

Neither of the Mennonites I interviewed who had dealings with that Topeka bank which failed in 1930 mentioned its name. Because Topeka has always been a small farming community in LaGrange County (currently just over 1000 residents), it is probably the same bank. As stock market traders always say, timing is everything. Emma Beachy was lucky (by a day), while the Bonträger family was not.

There were approximately 25,000 banks in the U.S. when the Depression began in 1929. As the economy began to crumble, more and more bank customers began to draw out their savings; some simply needed the money to get by, while others feared that their bank would fail. With less money available to loan, bank profits began to evaporate. At the same time, farmers had less money to spend in town, creating lesser deposits by businesses, many of which were failing. In essence, the economy was rapidly sinking, and the banks were going down with it. On at least four separate occasions between the end of 1930 and early 1933, there were "bank panics" where depositors lost faith and attempted to withdraw their savings only to find that there was no money in their bank to return to them. During this period, 11,000 banks disappeared and most of their customers lost all their savings. In December 1931, one bank in New York, the Bank of the United States, collapsed with over $200 million in deposits mostly gone.

By 1933 Americans had lost $140 billion due to bank failures - an enormous sum considering the value of a dollar in those days. One of President Roosevelt's initial acts upon taking office in March 1933 was to try to salvage the banking system. His first step was to declare a national 3-day "bank holiday" during which all banks were closed until they were found to be solvent. This step was credited with saving at least 1000 more banks that were in danger of going under. It was during his "fireside chat" radio speech announcing the bank holiday that Roosevelt gave one of his most memorable quotes, "The only thing we have to fear is fear itself." As part of Roosevelt's "New Deal," Congress passed the Bank Act of 1933 which established the Federal Deposit Insurance Corporation (FDIC) to protect bank customers by insuring deposits up to $2500 (the limit has since steadily increased). There still have been occasional bank failures since the early 1930's, but, due to the FDIC, no small investors like the two Mennonite families have lost one cent.

When Daniel Beachy mentioned that he had received a "farm deferment" during WW II, I was caught by surprise. I had never heard of such an exception during the Korean or Vietnam wars. I later did some research and learned that when America's first-ever peacetime draft was initiated in September 1940 prior to the entry of the United States into the war, all men from 18 to 35 were required to register (following Pearl Harbor, the upper age was extended to 64). Married men with dependents were initially excluded from being drafted and were given the classification III-A. By early 1943 the Selective Service (which ran the draft) was falling behind on the required number of inductions to fight the war. Black Americans, who had been required to register, but were not initially subject to the draft, were now conscripted. Shortages remained, so the III-A classification was eliminated, and fathers of children were now being drafted. There were exceptions, but Daniel would undoubtedly have been eligible for the draft. However, at the same time, there was also a desperate need for men with expertise to work on farms to provide food for the nation and the army. Accordingly, farm deferments were offered based, as Daniel Beachy correctly recalled, on the number of "animal units" on that person's farm. The initial guidelines for exemption were based on cows (at least eight dairy cows), but the criteria quickly became flexible. For example, three beef cows were deemed equal to one milk cow; 250 chickens or 9 hogs also equaled one cow. I do not know if Daniel, based on his Mennonite faith, would have claimed conscientious objector status to avoid service (as many other Amish and Mennonites did), but that was not necessary due to his farm deferment.

Over the next several days after leaving Indiana I kept thinking of Daniel's parting words about the importance of the church to their communities. The various sects of Amish and Mennonites whom I met were indeed survivors. Their historical roots fighting persecution in Europe centuries ago seemed to be reflected in finding ways to pull together during the depths of the Depression. Their success was indeed a testament to their hard work, frugality and....faith. An entire nation of modern-day pacifist Anabaptists would probably not survive long in our currently dangerous world brimming with nuclear weapons and enemies eager to take advantage of any vulnerabilities. The Mennonites require a peaceful world to prosper and survive, along with others willing to defend the nation. For the moment they have both.

"The Caddy and the Dancer"
Pat and Martha Callahan

Seattle, WA
Interviewed June 19,1996

S OME OF THE FOLKS WHOM I interviewed were still pre-teens when
the Depression began in late 1929. However, their memories of that
era remained clear and vivid, especially when recalling family trauma
due to loss of jobs, savings, homes, and businesses. Such was the case with
a husband and wife I met while walking around downtown Seattle. We had
been in a local coffee shop when I began our conversation, and they quickly
invited me to their apartment a few blocks away. It was in a high-rise with
a view of many of the skyscrapers in the center of the city.

Pat was tall and casually dressed; his wife, Martha (she insisted that I
call her Marty) was wearing a smart outfit with a crisp, white blouse. I
was struck by the beauty of her white hair. Both were thin and gave the
appearance of highly active seniors. Pat spoke with a smooth voice, almost

like a professional television or radio personality. I would describe Marty as "perky" - her voice was youthful and full of life.

After Marty ensured that I had some iced tea, Pat began our conversation:

I was born on February 7, 1919 here in Seattle, but I did not know my actual parents - never learned who they were because I was adopted shortly after my birth. My new parents named me, Patrick Joseph Callahan....obviously a VERY Catholic name. My father - his name was Claude - was a shoe salesman. He was considerably older than my mother because it was his second marriage....his first wife died. My mother, Katherine, did occasional work as a substitute teacher. They sent me, of course, to a Catholic grade school, Immaculate Conception. My father had a stroke in 1929, and he lived for three more years, but he could not work for the last three years until he died in 1932. I was 13 at the time and I remember how difficult it had become to make payments on our house. I actually had begun to work when I was 8, selling newspapers and magazines to make some extra money for the family. We had always rented some rooms in our home, and my parents and I all slept in one little bedroom. All the kids I knew then had some type of job.

After father died, it was just mother and me, and I became pretty wild and was mostly on my own. Mother continued to be a substitute teacher, but the jobs were few and far between. With my father gone, she rented out seven rooms in our house to be able to make the payments. She put a hot plate in each bedroom, and the men and women who rented shared two bathrooms. Most of them were single....I remember a nurse and a violin teacher....there was only one married couple that I recall. One of my most vivid memories of that time was when Mother and I would be in our pantry at 6:45 in the morning every weekday where we would pray that the phone would ring so that she could get a substitute teaching job that day. When there were no phone calls, we would both cry.

In 1939 Mother lost the house, but through our prayers she was able to find another house for rent. It was a rent-with-lease option and the people who owned the house were real good about it because they had another house. Most of the furnishings in both of those houses came from auctions which took place every Tuesday down at Bushnell's on Second Avenue.

Because I was getting into trouble so much, Mother decided to send me to St. Martin's High School. It was a boarding school for just boys and was run by the Benedictine Brothers and priests. All my buddies who I had been hanging around with and getting into trouble with were making bets that I wouldn't last there three weeks. I should have taken some of those bets because I stayed all four years! It was truly fortunate that Mom sent me there, because I learned discipline, and with all the fellows I went to school with, I now had the big family that I never had. I went there from 1934-38. It was not thought of as a "college prep" school, but now that I think about it, about 2/3 of those in my class did go on to college. I didn't because we could not afford it and I wasn't interested. I remember that we had three years of Latin; there were 18 of us in the graduating class. The school was close enough that I could walk home if I needed to, maybe about a mile. The Benedictines were strict, but they allowed us to smoke....everyone did then. Cigarettes cost 10 cents a pack. I don't know how Mother paid for that school because it had tuition. They may have not charged her much because while I was at the school, I worked in the dorms making beds and "flunked" in the refectory. That's what we called it when we were working in the dining room. She once told me that she had talked to the Brothers about not being able to pay and they "were pretty good about it."

As a teen I made money as a caddie every summer. I started out at 15 as a "second class" caddie at Broadmoor Country Club...it was only two miles from downtown, so I could get there easy. I was getting 75 cents for carrying bags 18 holes. Once you got to be a first-class caddie, you got paid 90 cents a loop - that's what we always called doing 18 holes because you always ended up back at the club house where you started. Normally it takes at least 6 months, and sometime a year to get to be a first-class caddie, but I got a break one day. I was in the caddie shack when I got assigned to carry the bags for a fellow named Harry Barnes. He was an insurance man from up in Bellingham and was doing a practice round for the Washington State Seniors Championship. I later learned he had won it the previous two years. He must have liked what I did because after that round he asked me, "How would you like to caddy for me in the tournament?" I immediately said yes. Apparently, he went back to the caddie shack and talked to the Caddie Master because I got promoted to first class caddie the next day. Mr. Barnes then won his third straight title the next day with me carrying his bags. From then on, if he ever came down to the course, I was his caddy.

At that time caddies did not give the golfers much advice, only when they were asked sometime - usually non-members who did not know the course...they would ask us stuff like, "What's over that hill?" Most of the caddies were married...it was hard times, and they needed the money. The Caddie Master would generally give the first jobs each day to the married guys because he knew that they needed the money more than us high school kids. In addition to what we were paid, we would often get tips of a buck a loop. Sundays were big, because we usually would go out with a man for 18 holes in the morning, then his wife would join him for 18 holes in the afternoon. We had Doctors' Day on Thursdays and Ladies Day on Tuesday. I wasn't a fan of Ladies Day because they always played so slow and were lousy tippers. None of the caddies were Black or from Mexico then....a few of us were still in grade school.

After I graduated, I kept on caddying because it was a good opportunity to get a job due to the connections you could make with the golfers. For example, in 1935, a big telephone company executive - his last name was Breen - offered jobs to three of the older married caddies. Unfortunately for me, Mr. Breen died before I got out of high school, so I lost that connection. Everyone wanted a job with the phone company then because no one got fired. If you got on, it was pretty much for lifetime.

When I graduated from high school in 1938, regular jobs were scarce. I couldn't get a steady job other than caddying, so I did a lot of different things and lived at home. I was a doorman at a downtown theater and also worked in several stock rooms. By 1939 I was finally able to save up $75 and bought a 1930 Model A Roadster. It was old, but it worked.

I also had a few bucks from the National Guard. I had gone into it when

I was still in high school because you got a dollar for the meetings which they held once each week. During the summers we spent three weeks on duty at Camp Murray, which was near Fort Lewis down near Tacoma. Everyone my age joined the Guard then because when we were at camp, the big attraction was drinking beer at the "Slop Shoot" - that was what the beer hall was called. You could get beer there no matter your age so long as you were in the Guard, and we got paid a dollar a day for that three weeks. I stayed in the Guard three years but did not re-enlist; it got federalized after I got out.

It was at this point that Marty interrupted Pat's National Guard memories. She had been sitting quietly during our talk, but at several points obviously wanted to add some comments.

Pat had no business being at the dance where he met me. It was sometime during the fall of 1938. The PTA in our high school would regularly put on dances in the Field House. It was supposed to be just for those of us at Franklin High School, and he showed up. You know, he crashed it. He was 19 and had not even gone to our school. I went to all of these dances with my best friends, Maxine, Ramona, and Bertha.... Maxine is still my best friend....I call her my sister. The four of us went everywhere together. Dancing was our big thing. We all smoked Philip Morris cigarettes because we wanted the boys to know that we were women of the world - you know, so that none of them would try to take advantage of us. All during high school I liked to date as much as I could because they paid for everything and it was fun.

As I said, Pat had no business being at that dance, but when I saw that he was a good dancer, I told my girlfriends that I wanted to meet him. At the time I wouldn't consider going out with a guy unless he was a good dancer. I was terrible then....if a guy asked me to dance, and I had seen that he wasn't a good dancer, I would say something like, "Oh, excuse me, I have to go to the ladies room." Isn't that stupid?

But Pat was a particularly good dancer, and we ended up going with each other for three years. Oh, we fought a lot, but I guess everyone did. Part of those three years is when we were engaged, six months before our marriage in August 1941. We drove up to Victoria [British Columbia, not far north of Seattle] for our honeymoon in that Model A Pat had. While we were dating and Pat was working at the theater, he would let me and my girlfriends in free. I couldn't get any jobs while I was in high school, not even babysitting, so I never had much money. Even though it only cost 10 cents to get into the movies, I couldn't afford it.

My dad had a good business when I was little. It was a moving and storage company....we were not rich, but we were a lot better off than most. His name was John Henry Schulte....I was full-blooded German. He had an office downtown, and I was not even aware of the Depression then. But things got bad when he lost his office and had to begin working out of our home. We lived in Rainer Valley then, which everyone else called "Garlic Gulch." But Dad died when I was 14, and Mom had to sell the business. My older brother, Hank - he was two years older than me - became the "man of the house." I resented that he could now boss me around and tell me what I could and could not do. He was a really good student and studied all the time. Like Pat, he joined the National Guard. He always said that his goal was to get as far as possible in the Guard. He got promoted a lot and when the Guard got federalized, he was the youngest Master Sergeant in the entire U.S. Army. Hank got sent to OCS [Officer Candidate School] and learned to fly. He ended up in Europe as an aviation spotter for the 146th Field Artillery but got shot down over Germany and was a POW until the end of the war. We got along better when he came home.

In high school I had studied typing, shorthand, office machines, and Business English, so after we got married, I was able to get a job as a secretary to the Personnel Director at Webster Brinkley and make $50 a month.

When Marty paused here, Pat interrupted with a big laugh:

Yeah, she was making fifty, but spending thirty on cigarettes! Neither of us smoke now....we both quit long ago. Near the end of the 30's I worked on the railroad, but I didn't like it. I had been putting in applications for the phone company every year, and the month after we were married, I *got lucky and started for them at $26 a week. A few months after Pearl Harbor happened, I decided to enlist in the Marines even though it was less than a year after we were married. I spent most of the war on ships in the South Pacific as part of Marine detachments. The only landing I made was in Japan in July 1945 as part of getting a location ready for MacArthur signing the Armistice. I was on Iowa, one of the battleships, when we learned that there was a Jap sub in the area and I went up to our forward gun mount hoping to be able to see any torpedoes so I could shoot them out of the water before they hit us. When I came back from the war, I went back to the phone company, but was now making $54 a week. I stayed with them until I retired in '81.*

You know, you asked me about our lives during the "Great Depression." None of us called it that then. It was just hard times.

Following that comment, Pat and Marty told me about their three children and spent the next half hour showing me family photos. They both bragged about their oldest son, Patrick, who was a priest for 15 years before leaving the clergy. When I asked to take photos of them, they insisted that we do so on their balcony overlooking Seattle. Marty also wanted me to know how successful Pat had been working all those years for the phone company. "He spent the first 20 years with them in the plant, but in 1961 he was promoted to sales and did real well there."

We also talked golf for some time. When Pat caddied in the 1930's, he did not initially have any clubs of his own, but was able, as he put it, "to pick up a club here and there, so I pretty soon had a set." He indicated that he was not a "decent golfer" when he was caddying because "when I played golf, I wasn't making any money. So I didn't play much then!" Marty wanted me to know that Pat was now a "very good golfer." When I asked how good, Pat told me that he used to have a handicap of 12, but that it was now 17 (meaning that his average score for 18 holes was about 89 - not bad for someone in his late 70's).

On the elevator to the ground floor, I was struck by what a warm, happy couple Marty and Pat were. Although I had just met them, they were eager to share their life stories with a total stranger in their apartment. Both had lost their fathers at an early age during the initial years of the Depression, resulting in significant financial setbacks for their families. But they both persevered, each in their own way to survive the new challenges.

I also found it interesting that most young men seemed to find some way during the 30's to get a car. This was obviously an especially important goal....sort of a way of declaring both your freedom and your manhood. You may not have much else, but you had a car. And everyone that I interviewed remembered the price of gas at the time. In Pat's case, it was 16 cents a gallon. You always remember the important stuff.

"Turpentine Man"
J.C. Evans

Key West, Florida
Interviewed March 18, 1996

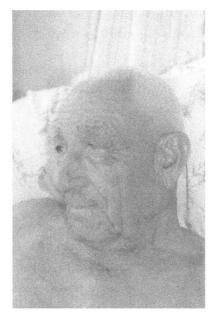

O N A FISHING TRIP TO the Florida Keys with my brother-in-law, Lynn, I found myself in Key Largo, in search of "the elusive bonefish." After hiring a local guide, we finally enjoyed some success in the local shallows where we hooked a couple of those silvery, incredibly fast fish, took the obligatory photos, and released them. After paying the guide $300, we drove to the end of U.S. Route 1 in Key West to engage in some Jimmy Buffet style celebration.

The next morning, I was near the end of a long line in the Key West post office. Because my intention was only to buy a few post card stamps, I almost gave up and was planning to come back later....until I noticed that the fellow in front of me was an older Black man with one leg. On a whim, I said to him, "Excuse me, sir, how old are you?"

A grizzled, older face topped by closely cropped white hair quickly turned around and slowly looked me up and down. He then muttered directly into my face, "What the hell's it to you?"

I calmly replied, "I'm interested in talking to people who lived during the Great Depression and thought that you might have been around then, and..." Before I could finish, he interrupted me in a voice the rest of the queue could easily hear, "You're damn right I did! It was the best time of my life." His craggy face then broke into a broad grin.

Thus, I met J.C. Evans. He quickly warmed up and we began a pleasant conversation as the queue moved at a glacial pace. By the time he reached the clerk, J.C. had invited me to come to his home that afternoon at 2:00 so we could talk.

His home was in an area just to the west of Duval Street, the town's main thoroughfare. Throughout the day, but particularly in the morning, on the southern end of Duval, not too far from the Ernest Hemingway House, pedestrians can hear roosters crowing from somewhere just a block or two away. I soon learned that many of those chickens were roaming J.C.'s neighborhood. When I told Lynn about my upcoming rendezvous, he insisted on accompanying me "just to be safe."

It turned out that J.C.'s home was in what appeared to be a converted garage. After winding our way around several chickens and one rather aggressive rooster in the front yard, we were greeted at the door by a tall black woman in a sleeveless V-neck blouse. Apparently, J.C. had told her of our visit, but she covered her mouth with her right hand in surprise when we asked to see him. Judging by her reaction, I suspected that it may have been a while since two White guys dropped by for a chit-chat. Based on a quick glance, I guessed that she was somewhere between 30 and 60 and had led an "interesting" life. Neither J.C. nor his female companion discussed their relationship, but she obviously lived with him and was some type of caretaker. As soon as she saw my tape recorder and notebook, she warmed to us and introduced herself as Bettijo, which she immediately spelled for us. Lynn intervened by asking if she would like to go over to Duval Street for a drink while I talked to J.C. She readily agreed.

J.C. did not get up, remaining comfortably seated in a large, overstuffed chair covered with a flowery throw. Although the one-story structure had no visible air conditioning, the room was comfortable with tropical spring breezes coming through a window with a series of open slats. J.C. was shirtless, sitting with his back to the window. His black and white, vertically striped underwear was clearly visible above a black belt holding up his white trousers. The button at his waist was not fastened giving me the impression that he was in full comfort mode. While we talked, J.C. leaned both elbows on the sides of the chair, except when raising both his arms to describe tools and events. For a man of 85 years, he looked extremely healthy with an impressive upper body physique. He was not wearing shoes or socks, and it was obvious that he did not have a prosthetic device on his missing right leg. He was clean-shaven, and his overall demeanor gave the impression of a seasoned man who was very much at ease with strangers.

J.C. spoke with a strong, animated southern accent. On only a few occasions during our two-hour chat did I have to ask him to repeat previous words. He did patiently correct me whenever I misunderstood his descriptions of the technical aspects of his work, and occasionally sipped a glass of iced tea while we talked. As per most of my interviews, I began by asking the date and location of his birth.

I grew up on a farm outside Sylvester, Georgia. I was born there on that farm on August 3rd, 1910. I was the second oldest of five boys and four girls. My given name was James Zane Evans, but I always went by J.C. 'cause I liked that better. My father was a sharecropper; we didn't own the land….just rented it to farm cotton, peanuts, and corn. I only went to the second grade, so I can't spell real good. Momma died early and Daddy did not make us go to school. We also raised hogs, cows, and chickens. Us boys had a good time. We lived 10 miles out from town and would take a wagon or a buggy when we went there. We had one horse and some mules. We didn't play many games. When we weren't working in the fields, we just walked around and talked. Our house had three bedrooms. After my momma died, daddy remarried and had two more boys and one girl. The little girls slept in the bed with my parents and us boys had two beds in our own room. As a teen I could go anywhere, but always had to be back home by sundown. That was a rule. We didn't have electricity; all our lights were lamp lights with kerosene. We did all our cooking on a wood stove. During the winter we ate pretty much what we had grew....a lot of sweet potatoes.

When I was in my teens, I went to school a little, but not much....never really liked it much. I left home in 1929 when I was 19 to go to work in the turpentine woods outside Doyle, Georgia, which was about 15 miles north of us. I had learned how because when I was at home I would go into the local woods with my older brother, K.C., and became friends with one of the workers who showed us what you had to do. In the woods I had 7300 trees that were mine....that means I was responsible for all those trees. I got paid $1.25 a week for each thousand trees, so I was making about $9-10 a week. We got paid at the end of each month after our expenses for meals from the commissary were deducted. A fellow named Nelson Moree owned the turpentine forest. All us workers lived in the Turpentine Quarters, that's what it was called. There were about 40-50 of us in there, all colored men. We would get up early when the sun came up and ride on a wagon to our part of the woods. We always carried our lunch out there.

Getting the gum out of the trees would begin in March and end in October. During the winter we raked around each of our trees so that when they burned the grass each year, your trees would not burn. We got paid 50 cents for each 100 trees we raked. I didn't like raking and only did 150-175 trees a day. Some of the other fellows would do 200. At the end of the month, they would look into a book and see what I earned and what I had spent in the commissary and I would generally get about $25-30, which was good money during those times.

Like I said, everyone working in the woods was colored, except for the wood riders. They were White and would come through the woods on a horse to make sure you were working. If you were taking good care of the trees, they never bothered you. Mostly we were out there by ourselves, except for the cows that they put out there to eat the grass around the trees. When the Depression hit in the 30's we did not get paid as much. Sometimes we would get only 50 cents a day. So, in late 1932 I went back to the farm to work for Daddy. But I liked working in the turpentine woods a lot better, so in 1934 I went back to the woods. The owner, Moree, died and his wife sold out to another White fellow named Len Tallas. He was good to work for. When the war broke out, I went into the Army.

But let me tell you, I liked working in the woods. We ate good....meat, eggs, and canned goods. The meat was mostly ham and chicken, but we also had some fish. You could get any kind you wanted in town, especially mullets. They were good and you could buy 5 or 6 big ones for a dollar. A lot of us had gramophones to listen to records in the Turpentine Quarters on weekends. There was no electricity, and those gramophones worked by winding 'em up. We had to pay 75 cents in town for a record - they weren't cheap, but we had a few of them among us. There was no work in the woods on Saturdays or Sundays, and sometimes I could get done with my trees by noon on Friday, so I had time off to go into town to chase some women. I never got married...came close, but the war broke out and I didn't want to leave a wife behind when I went off in the Army. On Sunday everybody went to church. I was a Methodist, and the service went from 11 to 3 in the afternoon. It was about 5-6 miles from the Turpentine Quarters and we generally rode over there in a car.

I was generally saving about $30 a month, and come 1932, I had enough money to get my own car, a used 1930 Ford that cost me $350. It ran pretty good and was a black 2-door coupe. Everyone thinks that all those cars were always black, but that 28 Ford came in a dark blue. I didn't have the whole 350 to pay for it, but you could put something down, like 50 or 60 dollars, and pay the rest as you go. Gas was 20 cents a gallon, so I always had a way to get into town and do stuff there. I kept that car for two years but tore it up. It just wore out, so I junked it.

It was a year-round job in the woods. We even stayed there in the Turpentine Quarters during the holidays. I fell off a wagon in'35 and busted my shoulder. My older brother, K.C., he was two years older, also worked in the forest, and he took care of me. If you got sick, someone else had to cover your boxes and you didn't get paid, because he was getting your money. Like I said, I went home to Daddy's farm to work a couple of times, but I always came back to the woods because I liked it better and could make some money.

At this point in our conversation, J.C. leaned forward in his chair and became considerably more animated. As he began to explain exactly how he harvested the "gum" from the pine trees, he gestured with his arms and called me over to correct my sketches of the process. I had assumed that the gum was the sap, but I later learned that it is a resin (actually, an oleoresin) that the tree exudes onto the cut surface of the wood. This gradual process acts as a natural protectant to seal the cut. By doing this the tree effectively blocks microorganisms and insects which could kill it.

You asked me what I did all day out there in the woods. Well, it was hard work. Like I told you, we always left the Turpentine Quarters early in the morning to avoid the heat and to have as much daylight as possible. We brought our tools with us....we didn't have to buy 'em, but we were the ones who had to keep 'em sharp....used a grinding stone to keep the pullers sharp. You always start real low on a new tree. First you gotta hack away the bark on one side. Then you use your puller....it had to have real sharp blades to make these streaks in the wood....they were V-shaped but you cut the streaks so they won't touch at the bottom of the V.....that way the gum could have someplace to run down the middle so that you can catch it. You would make maybe 20 or so of these streaks close together with your puller. Like I said, that puller needed to be sharp to cut the wood, and even then, it was real hard to pull it through that pine. At the bottom of the streak on each side I would nail a piece of metal same angle as the streak to make all the gum go into a cup which I nailed below....always used three-penny nails. That gum was white and sticky and moved real slow, so it took days to fill up the cup.

Harvesting gum from a pine tree.

I would go around the woods checking each cup and, when it was full, empty it into a bucket, then when that was full, pour all that gum into a 60-gallon wooden barrel. Two dipper boys would come around with a mule and wagon every three weeks and roll the barrels up onto it using skid poles. Then they would take those barrels back to the distillery where the gum would get steam distilled in a copper still to get the turpentine off. The stuff that was left, they sold that too....not sure what it got used for, but they didn't throw away nothin'. Most streaks would give you two of those cups each week....usually you could get a quart every three weeks out of a tree. Once that streak stopped producing gum, you just move up higher on the tree and pull new streaks and move the cup up. Those streaks don't grow back, so a tree would usually last six years as you moved up, then they cut 'em down and sent 'em off to the sawmill. Some people who would see our cuts on the trees called them cat faces cuz they looked like cat whiskers. I never heard any of our boys call them that.

The "stuff" which J.C. described as being left in the distilling process was the result of a rather clever operation. The initial product, the gum, as J.C. called it, is the "oleoresin" (sometimes shortened to "resin"). After being hauled from the forests to the distillery it was dumped into a wood-fired copper distilling unit which was heated to temperatures between 212 and 320 F, the point at which the turpentine vaporizes into a gas. This vapor rises to the top of the still where it enters tubing which is run through cooling water to condense the vapor into liquid turpentine (chemical formula C-10, H-16) which is then collected into shipping containers. The hot fluid remaining in the bottom of the still is then drained through cotton wadding to remove any solids. As it cools it becomes a substance known as "rosin." Depending primarily on the age of the pine tree from which the gum was taken, the rosin can vary from a nearly totally black, to a very pale, glassy substance. It is used to make soap and various waxes, and a host of other commercial products. Little did I know that those "rosin bags" used (legally) by generations of baseball players to improve their grip on the ball and bat actually contains white rosin powder which may have been derived from some of those pine trees worked by J.C. and his successors.

We had three of those wood riders, older White men, that I told you about. Each was responsible for five crops....that's we called a stand of trees like mine. They would ride through most days and see how you and the trees were doing. They would look at your streaks and let you know if it don't look good. Most of these fellows had been working a long time and knew how to put in a proper streak. I never had any trouble with the riders....they would call you by your name and treated you pretty good. The wood riders also made sure that no one else was coming around while we were working in the woods. I remember one rider yelling to some man that came around looking to get us to work for him, "Get out of here! Don't mess with my hands!"

Like I told you...I went back to Daddy's farm a few times, but I always come back to the woods. Sometimes people in town would ask me how I knew which trees were mine. I always told 'em, "I know my trees."

J.C. now wanted to see my notebook to make sure that I had the streaks drawn correctly. He took my pencil and made a few corrections before proceeding to tell me about his life after the woods. During WW II he spent all his time in the Army building bases and runways at several locations throughout the South. He first came to Key West in 1944 to do some military work and later shuttled around south Florida doing mostly construction jobs. When J.C. was working on the Navy barracks here in 1955, he was sent to Cuba on a cable boat. His memory was that "it was before Castro and everything was good." For the next 35 years J.C. continued construction work in Florida, often in Key West. When I asked him about his right leg, he matter-of-factly replied, "Got my leg cut off in 1990 while running a ditching machine."

"You were working at 80?" I asked.

"Hell, I'd be working now if it weren't for this damn leg. Sometimes I still walk pretty good."

I later learned that J.C.'s off-hand comment about men coming into the Georgia forests looking to lure away workers was common practice. As the Georgia pines began to become less productive in the mid-1930's and the spent trees were sent off to sawmills, the empty fields were not replanted. The turpentine industry simply shifted south into the forests of northern Florida with recruiters being sent into Georgia to hire skilled hands to work the virgin pine forests.

Lynn and Bettijo returned as J.C. and I were talking about Roosevelt's public work programs, the WPA (Works Progress Administration) and the CCC (Civilian Conservation Corps). Beginning in the mid-1930's these programs provided jobs for out-of-work Americans and were in full force in southern Georgia. J.C. said that neither he nor any member of his family "ever worked out there, but I knew some who did." He also added that one of his younger brothers (this one named "J.T.") went with him to Florida in the last part of 1938 to pick beans and peas for 15 cents a hamper. "We could make $3-4 a day doing it." In 1939 he moved to working in a sugar cane farm in southern Florida where he cut cane with "a cut crew" for 30 cents/hr. J.C. had something of a wry smile when he added, "On that job I had to work all day Monday through Saturday, so I left after a year to go into the Army, which looked real good after cutting that cane."

Because I felt that we had begun to overstay our time with J.C. and Bettijo,

I chose not to ask about his ancestors and their history during slavery. I assumed that his father became a sharecropper in the steps of earlier relatives who had received land during Reconstruction following the end of the Civil War, but then, as happened to many Black families, had it swindled away by Whites who then rented the same property back to them. Such was tragically the case throughout much of that part of Georgia. During our discussion J.C. mentioned that he had never voted until he went into the Army because, as he put it, "You got no property, you got no vote." Sharecroppers, black or white, were not allowed to vote because they did not own the land they worked. Once again, this was the accepted way of life in the South, no matter what federal law stated.

We also did not have time to discuss what his sisters did, other than to work on the family farm. He did not mention their names, whether they married, had children, or remained in touch with him. Near the end of our conversation, J.C. mentioned that the government took over all the turpentine woods during WW II, but I have found no mention of this in history sources. I do know that "crude turpentine" is still being produced by tapping pine trees, although the methods are now more sophisticated and less labor-intensive than during J.C.'s time in the woods. Other forms of turpentine production now include steam distilling of shredded pine wood and processing by-products obtained by cooking wood pulp to make certain types of paper.

As we departed, chickens were still roaming the yard. Bettijo pulled me aside and told me not to worry about J.C. because "he gets a disability check." I smiled and thanked her for taking such good care of him and for keeping Lynn happily occupied during the interview, but also saying to myself, "No worries, Bettijo, this man *knows* how to survive."

That number, 7300, stuck in my mind for several days - the number of "his" trees which J.C. worked each week. Just doing some simple arithmetic, that means that on any given day, he tended to an average of roughly 1500 trees, or 125 every hour, working from sunup to sundown. To do this he had to inspect, and then do the necessary work on each tree in about 30 seconds! J.C. did not mention how many steps he walked each day carrying those heavy tools, nor where he obtained water during those hot, muggy

Georgia summers - all for $10 a week. Rather than bemoaning his fate, J.C. embraced it and found happiness in his solitary days in the woods. Despite the seemingly endless hard work, he was obviously proud of mastering a skill which many others could, or would, not do. He described his life in the turpentine woods in obviously proud, matter-of-fact tones, as if saying, "This is what I had to do to survive, and I did it."

Thinking of J.C., I find myself recalling Albert Camus' famous 1942 essay, *The Myth of Sisyphus*, in which he argued that he imagined Sisyphus to be quite happy eternally pushing a large boulder up a hill each day only to have it roll back down again for another uphill struggle. J.C. certainly seemed to be the 1930's parallel - a man doing hard labor daily while regarding it as a joyful journey. Can you imagine many current Americans willing to endure this type of work and lifestyle?

And standing in line at a Post Office nearly 25 years later continues to bring a smile to my face. What a wonderfully serendipitous chance encounter years ago that brought J.C. Evans into my life!

"The Country Girl"
Thelma Steiner Holveck

Scottsdale, Arizona
Interviewed July 20, 1997

"IHAVE A LOT OF THINGS I can show you about the early days here." Thelma Holveck was speaking to me in an excited voice. I had just met this youthful-looking octogenarian while walking in downtown Scottsdale. She was wearing a bright red, long-sleeve shirt with white buttons and a blue denim, full-length skirt cinched at the waist by a wide brown belt featuring a large silver buckle. Her weathered face added to the impression that I had just met a cowgirl. Thelma had responded with a big smile when I said "Hello" as I was walking by. She was sitting in the shade in the driveway leading to her home on Osborne Road. When I asked if she had lived here in the 1930's, she readily agreed to talk to me about earlier days in Scottsdale. Little did I know at that moment that I had accidentally hit the mother-lode of local history. Thelma was not only a native of the city but was one of the founders of the Scottsdale Historical Society.

After retrieving a notepad and tape recorder from my rental car (I was in the Phoenix area visiting relatives), I returned to Thelma's home to begin the interview.

Neither of my parents were from here originally. My father, Jacob Steiner, was born on a farm in Iowa. He had been in San Francisco during the 1906 earthquake but went to Oregon afterwards to work. Up there he met my mom, Lorene Bingaman, who had just finished training to be a nurse. You only needed a grade school education at the time to get into nursing training. After they got married up in Washington - not sure why there - they moved to Santa Barbara, California where Dad got work as a carpenter and cement finisher. My grandmother, Mom's mother, came along and lived with them.

They probably would have stayed in California, but in 1911 the Theodore Roosevelt Dam [in central Arizona] had just been completed right below where the Salt River and Tonto Creek come together. That dam allowed water to be brought by canal into the valley below for irrigation. There had always been a lot of really bad floods on that Salt River, so the dam served several purposes. Mostly it created a lot of new potential farmland. When word about this reached Santa Barbara from men who had worked on the dam and canal, my dad and many other people in California became interested in getting some of this land because it was being sold by the Federal Land Bank for $10 an acre. Dad took a train east to Tempe [city east of Phoenix] and found his way over to here in Scottsdale, where he bought 10 acres to start a farm. That was in 1912, the year that Arizona became a state. Later that year my mother and grandmother came over in a train with all our belongings on a flatcar on that same train.

I was born not far from here on a farm just north of what is now McDowell Street on October 5, 1915. My birth took place at home, but my younger sister, Labeula, was delivered at a nursing home over in Tempe. Mother was a nurse; she delivered a lot of other folk's babies with the doctor who delivered me. His name was B.B. Mouer....he later went into politics and became our Governor for four years during the Depression. I used to joke with my girlfriends then that I had come into this world courtesy of our Governor! He also had some major role in the administration of what was then the Teacher's College over in Tempe - that's what it was called before it became Arizona State University....it's so huge now!

Our father built us a house on his new land. When we needed things, we took a wagon over to Tempe and got them. Mom was kept busy as a nurse due to the 1918-19 flu epidemic and all the childhood diseases that were around. You probably can't imagine this now, but then many children would get sick drinking coal oil and other poison stuff. Mom told me that many times children who did this were saved by having them drink sweet cream.

My sister was born in January 1919. We used to fight a lot as we grew up, but now we're best friends. Growing up on the farm was really great. We had plenty of food and the farm was doing well. Dad got irrigation water from the canals, and we grew our own vegetables and had farm animals of all sorts - milk cows, goats, chickens, ducks, pigs, and sheep, but mostly cows. We also had some guinea hens which, believe it or not, would alert us when skunks or weasels or coyotes were around. We had grapefruit and orange trees in our yard. There were all sorts of fruit and nut trees: almonds, olives, citrus, grapes, pomegranates. We made jams and canned everything. We even made our own lard, but had to buy coffee, flour, cornmeal, and sugar in town. You couldn't drink the irrigation water, so we had to drive off each day to get three large cans of water from a safe source in Tempe. That's why I learned to drive when I was twelve...I had to go get the water. I never got a driver's license until sometime in the '30s

Labuela (8) and Thelma (11)

One of my first chores was to help milk the cows. I learned to milk by hand, but sometime in the late 20's we got a milking machine that was run by a gasoline motor. We didn't have electricity yet. We sold the milk and cream to some of the resorts which had sprung up in the area due to the climate. One of them was Graves Guest Ranch - it probably sounds strange now, but then they catered not only to vacationers, but also to tuberculosis patients! During the summers when my sister and I were not in school, we would get to go along on the deliveries. That resort had a Black fellow who was the cook. His name was Jim, and I always remember him because he would occasionally slip us a biscuit he had baked. As far as I know, he was the only Black person in Scottsdale at the time.

It's hot here in the summer, and we would usually sleep outside with nets over us. After electricity finally became available sometime in the 30's, we got one of the first evaporated coolers - it was sort of an air conditioner. You would put wet excelsior in the back and use an electric fan to blow air over it - it would give you a cool breeze, but it was very noisy.

"Excelsior" refers to thin wood shavings which absorb water and stay moist for a considerable time while air is blown over the shavings. The resulting evaporation of the moisture removed heat from the air as it passed through the shavings resulting in noticeably cooler air entering the room.

As our farm prospered, Dad bought more and more acreage, all on credit. Soon after we arrived, he bought 20 more acres, then 80 - soon we had 110 acres. In the late 20's he also bought our first tractor; it was a Fordson....a lot of neighboring farms were also buying them. They were popular and were cheap, like the Model T cars. But Dad had diabetes, and it started to get real bad. We were weighing his food for him to try to control his diabetes, but he loved ice cream and that didn't help. He got extremely sick and died in 1928 - he was only 55. Just before he died, Dad had bought 40 more acres over near where McDowell Street is now, but, like everything we had, it was just on paper because he had done everything on credit. He had always said that he didn't want to be buried in the desert, so we had him put in the ground over in Tempe.

We were by then no longer making payments on the land or equipment, and the banks kept threatening to take it all away. I remember my mom frequently saying, "No one owns anything." When the Depression first started, I didn't really notice anything different, because I was a teen. My grandmother had been receiving $30 a month pension [Thelma did not explain this, but apparently her grandfather, who had long ago passed away, was a veteran], and when she died in 1931, things really got rough. Our local bank, Farmer's State Bank, closed early in 1932, and soon after that, the Federal Land Bank of Berkeley foreclosed on our 110 acres. So, we had to move to the remaining 40 acres where we put up a shack to live in. We had a bunkhouse, sort of, where a man who worked the cows for us lived. He was supposed to be paid, but we couldn't, so he just worked for room and board. We weren't making payments on that land either, so some bank in Phoenix, I think, took that land. We lost everything....the tractor, machinery, trailers....everything "went." Before the Depression, I had it pretty good....good clothes, music *lessons, no worries. I always had chores, but we always had plenty of food. When I graduated from high school in 1932, it suddenly hit me that I now had to be a grown up.*

I had begun to work at Byers Grocery Store here in Scottsdale filling orders. People would come in with a list and I would go around the store filling it. Everyone would buy on credit and pay at the end of the month. We had a lot of Indian trade because they always had some money and were very good about paying at the end of the month. The Mexicans too, because they got paid weekly for their work on the farms. Soon the butcher who worked there, Earl Shipp, bought out Mr. Byers and renamed it Earl's. A lot of the people who couldn't pay would sign their land over to Earl. He ended up with a lot of land...he's still alive and is past 85 now. While I was in school, I worked every Saturday for a dollar a day. But I learned a lot and ended up working in three different grocery stores. After high school I had gone into South Phoenix to work for a family, but I got so homesick I came home and did more grocery store work.

Mother died on January 20, 1935....the same day in January that Labeula had been born on. She had gall bladder problems, but we had no money to have it treated. Her colic got so bad that she got took to St. Joseph Hospital in Phoenix where they operated on her, but she never came out of it. I was there, and when they told me that my mother had died during the operation, I keeled over on the floor, and they just let me lay there....no idea how long. We had no relatives anywhere near, so there

were just the two of us girls; I was 19 and my sister was 16. But our neighbors were wonderful. I don't know how we would have survived. A close family friend, Mrs. Caldwell, helped us out and was appointed our legal guardian. Because our remaining land was taken away from us by a bank in Phoenix, we had to move into a little house here in town, which we rented for $8 a month. It was right next to Fant's Grocery where I was working. My sister got a job where she went to live with the Willmouth family to take care of their children. There was no pay, of course, but she got room and board.

I did not ask Thelma more about her mother's "colic" nor how it was diagnosed. She mentioned gall bladder problems, so I assume that this had been a long-standing problem that had at some point required seeing a physician. The pain, according to the online sources I viewed, can be intense and comes in episodes lasting from a few minutes to several hours. Patients now can benefit from various imaging tests (x-rays, ultrasound and/or CT scans) to determine the cause of gall bladder issues. Many current surgeries are often performed using minimally invasive techniques, typically with favorable outcomes. Unfortunately for Thelma's mother, such tests and procedures were many decades away

Mom was supposed to have started a WPA [Works Progress Administration] job at a TB sanitarium in Tempe just before she died, so Mrs. Caldwell talked to the WPA people and was able to get me on with the WPA in Scottsdale. I did whatever they wanted me to do...all sorts of things, like handing out meat and cheese to folks who needed food. I was paid $68 a month. Next year they sent me over to Tempe, and again I did whatever they told me to do. I figured that I was doing more than most of the other workers, so I complained and got more pay. I worked in an office but never had any training. A woman named Mrs. Bouse was my boss.

Here Thelma paused and offered to fill up my iced tea. When she came back, she began telling me about her education.

I didn't get to go to school until I was seven because our farm was too far from the school to walk, and my parents were too busy to take

me there. But then the teacher, Mrs. Florence Roth, heard about my situation and would come by to pick me up and take me to "The Little Red School House." That's what it was called. It had two rooms and lots of windows to keep us cool. Shortly afterwards we got a school bus to take us there. In 1927 Scottsdale Grammar School was built, and I got to start 7th grade there. The next year they moved all of us 7th and 8th graders over to the high school building, which I thought was great because the girls could now take home economics and the boys took shop. When I graduated from Scottsdale High School in 1932, I wanted to go to college and become a nurse like Mom, but we had no money, so that never happened. I did date some in high school, but never high school boys....they had no money and no cars! So, I generally went out with older fellows in town who did have cars. We would sometimes go over to Phoenix to watch the picture shows. I remember seeing "The Covered Wagon" - I think it was a silent.

Thelma was correct. *The Covered Wagon* was indeed a silent movie, a "western" which had first come out in 1924. The plot, according to IMDb, concerns two wagon caravans which travel together from Kansas City to Oregon. Along the way, the pioneers are faced with heat, snow, hunger, and attacks by Indians. And, of course, a love triangle develops involving members of the two wagons. As Thelma recalled the movie, I could tell that it was one of her fonder memories of those years. After a pause accentuated by a large smile, Thelma returned to thoughts of her WPA work.

Shortly after I had got that raise from the WPA, an opening took place at the Scottsdale Grammar School. They needed a librarian and someone to do ditto work for the teachers, so I got the job and was still being paid by the WPA. As the librarian, I would often drive over to Phoenix in my 1929 Chevy to pick up books from the Maricopa County Library when the teachers wanted some books we didn't have. I also did a lot of typing. After a year or so, the Principal told me they needed a secretary at the high school, so I took that job. Now I was being paid by the school district and was getting $108 a month. There was a fellow I was dating who wanted to get married, but I was making more than him and if I did get married, I would lose my job. You may not know this, but teachers and all the female staff at schools then were not allowed to marry. If you did, they fired you. This all changed, at least in Arizona, when the war started in '41 because they suddenly had a shortage of men teachers, and I guess married women started to look good to them! Basically, they had to let us be married because otherwise they wouldn't have had enough teachers.

Speaking of marriage, after our mother's death, my sister, Labeula, found a job up in Prescott in 1936 taking care of two small children for a man whose wife had died. Turns out that they fell in love and got married. That was a pretty good one....they've now been married over 60 years. I met my husband, George Holworth, when he came here to Scottsdale to visit a friend he had met while working for the CCC [Civilian Conservation Corps] in Colorado. He was a truck driver up there and began doing that work in 1933. They were making roads all over Colorado. He even met the architect, Frank Lloyd Wright, there during his time in the CCC. His parents got $20 a month and he got $5. He was very proud of that CCC work he did and even took me back up there to show me some of the projects which they had done. When he finished his time with the CCC, he couldn't find a job near his parents' home in Chickasha, Oklahoma, so he came down to Arizona. He was able to get on as an electrician and helped build the Camelback Inn near here. I met him while he was doing some work at the school; we started dating in the late 1930's.

I worked for the school system from 1935 until 1942. George and I were married in May of '42 after he joined the Navy. I kept working at the school until that fall. After his initial Navy training, he was assigned to Treasure Island near San Francisco where they repaired ships, I suppose due to his skills as an electrician. I loved my job at the high school, but wanted to be with George, so I rented my house and moved out there in the fall of '42. I found a job as a secretary up at the college, UC Berkeley, but then quickly got a better offer from the Golden State Agency, which was part of State Farm. I initially just typed up insurance policies, but I soon became their bookkeeper. They were some of the sweetest people I ever worked for. George and I were together until the Navy sent him overseas to the Philippines early in 1945. He ended up in Brisbane, Australia, but when the war ended, he couldn't get a place on a ship to *come home. He kept waiting and waiting, but they were filling most of the ships with "war brides." He was really angry about this.*

That house that I was living in before we got married came through a real blessing. My uncle in Iowa, who I had never seen, died in 1936 and left both me and my sister $1000 each. My mother had always wanted me to be able to take care of myself and had taught me to be resourceful. So, I took that money and bought a lot on Main Street for $125. I used the rest of the money to hire a local man to build me a little frame house on that lot. I sold it for $32,000 in 1959. I never had to make a payment on it. I was able to invest that money to buy this house I'm in now. One thing I learned from losing our farm and all our other equipment is that if I don't buy something on credit, no one can ever take it from me. My sister used her money to buy a lot next to mine, but they borrowed $5000 and had a two-bedroom house built on it. They still live there.

I first voted in 1936 and, of course, voted for Roosevelt. I've always been a Democrat because I have no idea what I would have done without the WPA. I was very grateful to that man. Who knows what would have happened to me if he had not been President?

Thelma then began to show me albums of photos of Scottsdale during her childhood years and numerous clippings from the Arizona Republic in which she was profiled as one of the original natives of Scottsdale. In one newspaper photo she is dressed exactly as she was for our interview. Although Thelma did not tell me, she continued to work for the city of Scottsdale until she retired as the assistant city clerk in 1980 at age 75. She also neglected to tell me that the year before I met her, she had been inducted into the "Scottsdale Hall of Fame."

Thelma's husband, George, died of lung cancer in 1985. Their only son, also named George, stopped by during our discussion. We traded high school teaching stories drawn from his current position teaching World History and my previous days as a Physics teacher. He told me that Thelma still drives a 1981 Chevy El Camino and keeps his dad's 1977 Chevy Camaro to use for "special occasions." Apparently the Holvek's are a very loyal Chevrolet family.

Evidently her father had room in his heart for Ford vehicles - at least tractors. That Fordson tractor which he had bought on time in the 1920's was, as the name suggests, built by Ford. "Fordson" was the brand name for a line of both tractors and trucks. Like the Model T Ford car, the tractors were originally mass-produced from 1917-20 by Henry Ford & Son, Inc. From 1920-28 the company operated under the name Ford Motor Company, and then added Ltd to its name in 1929, but the tractors always remained "Fordsons." Henry Ford, himself, had grown up around farmers, and when he began to build cars, soon started using various components to build an experimental tractor which he completed in 1907. He called it "an automobile plow." Other entrepreneurs were also building tractors and in 1915 a competitor hired a fellow, also with the last name of Ford, in order to use his name with the intention of building a "Ford" tractor. Their goal was not to build large quantities of tractors, but to force Henry Ford to buy them out so that he could use the name. Ford outsmarted them by calling his tractor the "Fordson," which he immediately trademarked. Within a year he had sold over 6000 of these, because they were small, general purpose tractors, ideal for small farms, and inexpensive ($750). By the time Thelma's father purchased his tractor, Henry Ford had built over 500,000 Fordsons. One of the design flaws was painfully familiar to me, that is, the tendency to flip over backwards. Like Thelma, I was a farm boy who started to drive at age 12. On at least two occasions I nearly lost my life when our Farmall tractor (a competitive brand built by International Harvester Company....it was about the same size as the Holveck's Fordson) began to flip over. In each case, I was saved by the hydraulically operated disk on the back of the tractor keeping it from flipping over.

Thelma's recounting of how her father purchased his initial 10 acres of land in Scottsdale in 1912 through the Federal Land Bank has been difficult for me to verify. President Woodrow Wilson did not establish the Land Bank until 1916. He took this action to set up 16 regional banks with the purpose of providing low-cost financing to farmers and ranchers. It may have been that Thelma's father purchased that initial land under a different program, then used the Land Bank to add the additional acres at later dates. Nonetheless, it was an extremely popular program - so much so, that by 1922 nearly 75,000 farmers had borrowed nearly 1/4 billion dollars.

Because it could be used to buy not only land, but also equipment and animal feed, many farmers, including Thelma's father, quickly became over-extended. When the economic ravages of the Depression engulfed them, many farmers found themselves unable to make payments. This lesson was indelibly imprinted on Thelma; several times during our conversation she bragged about never having to make payments "on anything."

I did not comment when Thelma told me that she would have been fired as a teacher if she were married. I was embarrassed that, although I had been a classroom teacher for many years, I was unaware of the history of this discriminatory practice. I later learned that during Thelma's time working for the school district, there were no national rules concerning school employment practices. It was up to each school district (in some cases, states) to adapt qualifications and guidelines for hiring personnel. As late as the mid-1930's nearly two thirds of American school districts required female staff to resign if they married. In many rural areas, the rules were strict and typically involved a double standard for men and women. Men could marry; women could not. Some school systems forbade smoking or drinking, or even "loitering in ice cream stores." Many midwestern farmers did not want their children to be taught by a pregnant woman, nor to have to find a replacement teacher if the woman had a child. In their view, the most expedient way to avoid these "problems" was simply to fire any woman who married (or became pregnant outside of marriage). The arrival of American involvement in WW II immediately created a drastic need for more female teachers because many of their male colleagues joined the military services or found higher-paying jobs in war-time industrial plants. The long-standing discriminatory restrictions were quickly lifted and never reinstated.

Another theme that Thelma returned to frequently during our two hours together was her concern that "young people nowadays do not want to work like we did." When discussing the CCC, for example, she opined that what this country needs right now is another CCC to get these youngsters working. It was obvious from all of Thelma's volunteer work following her retirement that she continued to have no aversion to work and had little empathy for others who choose not to work.

Due to a plane reservation, I had to leave Thelma before she could show me as much of the memorabilia of early Scottsdale as she intended. Much to my surprise, I received a package from her less than a month later with copies of newspaper clippings and photographs which she felt might aid my understanding of her life and times. Then two years later another large envelope arrived with a sweet note and yet more material.

Thelma Holveck was an American original worthy of admiration.

"The Embalmer"
Jim Sieving

Buffalo, New York
Interviewed July 14, 1997

WHILE VISITING AUNT JEAN, ONE of my late mother's sisters in Scottsdale, Arizona, she mentioned that one of her neighbors who lived close-by in the same trailer park had "some good stories" from his days during the Great Depression. When I expressed interest, she telephoned him and arranged an interview.

Jim Sieving warmly greeted me as I entered his double-wide trailer. I noticed that quite a few framed photographs and certificates were hung neatly on the walls of each room. During our ensuing conversation, he proudly explained the significance of each one, including a U.S. government discharge certificate for James Corrie, his maternal grandfather, who had served in the Indiana Infantry during the Civil War. Jim's eyebrows were full, white, and exactly matched neatly combed hair. His hairline had slightly receded, but the overall impression was one of an articulate gentleman enjoying his senior years. Jim said he had come to the Phoenix area in 1958, he told me because he and his wife, Holly, believed that the climate would be favorable for one of his daughters who had rheumatic fever. He also quickly added that both he and his wife liked the Phoenix area based on a previous vacation here. When Holly passed away in 1978, Jim had no desire to move elsewhere.

Throughout our talk, Jim spoke with little emotion, other than an occasional chuckle following an amusing anecdote. As we discussed his family background and his memories, I was impressed with this 87-year old's recall of dates and specifics. Whenever I had follow-up questions, he was eager to ensure that I fully understood all the details. He began with his family history:

I was born on November 1, 1909 at home on our farm outside Hanover, Indiana. My mother, Nancy Jane Currie, was Scotch-Irish, but she was always called "Nanny." My father, Edward Henry Sieving, was very German. Both sets of their parents were local farmers who had come to the U.S. via different routes, before ending up In Cincinnati [Ohio...about 50 miles to the east]. I am not sure how or why they came to Indiana, but I suppose it was because of the good farmland. I had a sister, Ina, who was 10 years older than me; she became a life-long schoolteacher there. My father farmed until I was six, then we moved into town where he started making a living as a carpenter. He was good at making things and had steady work. I began first grade while we were on the farm....I remember it well because we had all 8 grades in one schoolroom. My parents told me that the small schoolhouse was the reason they moved into town so that we could go to "a proper school." It turned out that it was an upgrade....we now had a 4-room schoolhouse - two grades in each room!

I went on to high school there and graduated in 1927. Hanover was a college town, and those four rooms were in one of the college buildings called Classic Hall. The town rented the rooms instead of building a separate building for the high school. I don't know what they have now. My father built one of the fountains and a well house on the college campus, and I heard recently that they are still there.

Here I interrupted Jim to tell him that I had been on the Hanover College campus in 1960 when the small Kentucky college I was attending (prior to the Naval Academy) played a basketball game vs. Hanover. Our team (Villa Madonna College) won....but it was a night game during the winter so I could not tell Jim if those fountains were there. We both laughed at the coincidence.

Like I said, I graduated in 1927, but I couldn't do anything there because there weren't any jobs. So, I went down to New Albany [Indiana, across the Ohio River from Louisville, Kentucky]. It was maybe 40 miles from home. I went there to take some courses at a business college, but as soon as I arrived, I heard that the telephone company was hiring. I forgot about the business college and immediately got a job with Indiana Bell. I started out as a cable splicer's helper - an apprentice - and was making $21 a week. I started living in a rooming house run by an older man who lived alone. I don't remember his name, but he had a band and played piano. I know that he was in the Elks. He rented two rooms to four of us, so I had a roommate who also worked for the telephone company. I could save some money because food was cheap. We ate all our meals at local restaurants and a cup of coffee was a nickel everywhere. I could get a bowl of oatmeal also for a nickel. A good noon meal would cost you a quarter - maybe sometimes 35 cents. In the evening I generally just had coffee and a slice of pie - 5 cents each. We would go bowling for entertainment.

I did this telephone work in New Albany until next year, 1928. Most of my work involved climbing poles to do work up on top. I saved up enough money to buy myself a new Ford Roadster that summer. Then my job started to take me from town to town in Indiana. Some guy up in Indianapolis would tell us where to go next. I was traveling to towns all over the state: Anderson, Bedford, Bloomington, and up north to South Bend and Terre Haute. We would generally be in a town from 4 to 8 weeks, then move on. It was all repair work, so we would fix it and go to the next place. I had it pretty easy compared to a lot of guys my age at that time. I had a good job, a car, and there were plenty of phone operators to date. These women were in every town and, my being in the phone company, I knew how to meet them.

Jim paused here for a long chuckle, and probably some good memories. Many small cities still had phone service controlled by an operator sitting at a switchboard. When you "ringed her" by turning a hand crank in your home, she would answer. After you told her to whom you wished to speak, she would physically connect your phone to the other person's phone by plugging a wire from your phone jack into a female jack wired to the phone you were trying to reach to complete the circuit. If you wished to make a call beyond the operator's area (a "long distance" call), she would have to connect your line to a central office where that connection would be made by another operator there. Because the operators, almost exclusively women, could listen to any call, there was no privacy. The operator sat facing the panel of jacks and had columns of switches and toggles on a desk in front of her. If several people wanted to talk at the same time, the operator had to be dexterous and sharp. Not everyone could do this job.

Much of American phone service in rural areas and small cities in the first half of the 20th century involved "party lines" in which multiple homes were on the same line. This type of service meant that only one of the homes could be using the phone at a given time. For example, even by the late 1950's, our home in rural Kentucky had 10 families on one party line. Our ring was "4 shorts." Others were 1, 2, and 3 short rings, and a single long ring. I never understood why, but we could not hear the rings for the other 5 families. Whenever we wanted to make a call, we had to pick up the phone to listen if someone else was using the system. We had dial tones, and could make calls without an operator, but there was no privacy for a call. A popular past time was to pick up the phone and listen to other people talking. Often when on a call, I would hear the unmistakable sound of someone else's phone being picked up to listen in. If you did not want your neighbors to know what you were talking about, you did not use the phone for those conversations. You can imagine the gossip possibilities!

The 1928 Ford Roadster which Jim mentioned was essentially a bare bones convertible with a rumble seat. He told me that "it was the first year with a stick shift" and that he paid $465 for it new. I did some research on the Roadster but could not find any information on the type of transmission. Jim added that he kept it only two years before trading it in for a coupe. He did not mention which brand of car this was but did say that the reason he sold the Roadster was that "I got tired of getting wet and cold all the time." None of these cars had heaters. If you are interested in buying your own 1928 Ford Roadster today, there are several available online starting at roughly $15,000. Most have been rebuilt with new engines, transmissions, and "creature comforts" such as a heater! After discussing roads in Indiana at the time (not good), Jim began telling me about his experiences during the early 1930's.

Things didn't start out too bad for me after the stock market crashed. I hardly knew it because I had my job and no worries. After three years with the phone company, I had finished my apprenticeship and became a certified splicer. When the banks in Indiana closed, I lost some money, but only about $40. Because I worked for Indiana Bell, I had been eligible to buy AT&T stock at a low price even when it still had a par value of $100 per share. Sometimes I would sell it at that price even though the market value had fallen to $40. This really helped me when I got laid off in 1932, because I couldn't find a job doing anything. I went back home to Hanover and stayed with my parents. They had a nice garden and Dad would do carpenter work around town, mostly for food. A lot of bartering was going on because people had no money. We still had a Model T, and we would raise a pig or a calf out on my uncle's farm and bring it home. There wasn't much else for me to do at home, but I kept looking for work. I heard that a fella got hurt working over in Burns County where they were building a highway toward Louisville. I went over there and got that job, but it paid only 20 cents an hour. You can do the math....for 40 hours a week I was getting $8. Compare this to the $40 a week I had been making with the phone company!

When that job ended, I had no work. I came back home again and was getting restless, so in early 1933 I took off with my buddy, Tom Bruther, to hitchhike to Florida. We got over to Kentucky, then caught rides all the way down Routes 27 and 41 to Tampa. I had told my parents to send me some letters in care of General Delivery there in Tampa, so I knew what was going on back home. We didn't stay there in Florida very long because there was no work. We got home by "riding the rails"- you know, hopping freight trains - up to Atlanta, then hopped some others....I think it was the L&N, from there to Cincinnati. There were usually lots of other fellows riding on those trains, and they could generally tell you where to get off to go to someone's house who would give you food. It was an adventure, but tough, and I went hungry some nights.

While Jim excused himself to get us some iced tea, I thought about how I had shared some similar adventures, although many years later. Throughout my 17 years growing up in Kentucky, we always lived either next, or close, to train tracks. I was familiar with some aspects of Jim's train adventures. One of our "sports" was to hop onto the handrails of slow-moving freight trains at one end of town and hop off as the train began to exit town. It was not for the faint of heart. Several years before my adventures, an older boy named Doug, who lived near us in Bellevue, Kentucky, was trying to hop a freight train, but fell off and had his arm severed on the rail by the train wheel. He later owned a dry cleaners behind our home and often talked about it. Remarkably he became a very good golfer using one arm. As late as the 1950's railroads had detectives who monitored trains for "hoppers." We called these detectives "railroad dicks" and often ran away when we saw them starting to watch us. Boys are wired to do stupid things. Ironically, I also did a road trip with a buddy to Tampa, Florida, possibly along the same route that Jim had hitchhiked a generation earlier. In my case, I was driving a '59 Renault Dauphine. As with Jim, our trip did not end well; I burned out the engine and had to spend all our money to have the engine re-built. Hitchhiking was also still prevalent even in the 1960's, and I did a lot of it. Like Jim, I always found it easy to get rides by sticking out my thumb. I once hitchhiked from Florida to Kentucky having only 11 cents in my pocket. Jim did not expand on his hitchhiking experiences, possibly because it was such a common way for young men to travel then.

Jim returned with two glasses of tea and immediately picked up his thoughts following his return to Indiana....

When I got home, I said to myself, "This is enough of this....I'm going to find some way to make a living." I still had some of that AT&T stock, so I went to my sister, Ina, who still had her teaching job, and offered her a deal. I would sign over all my stock to her if she would give me $1000. She agreed. I took the money and went to Cincinnati to stay with one of my other sisters. I had heard about an embalming school there when I was riding the rails, so I spent $750 to enroll in the Cincinnati College of Embalming out on Reading Road. It was a good course, nine months long. I didn't know this at the time, but some funeral director in Buffalo had written to the school asking if they had any students looking for work. Apparently, this fellow knew of a former graduate of the school and liked his work. I was on the train to Buffalo the next day following graduation.

It was raining all night, and I fell asleep in my seat on the train. When I woke up in Buffalo the next morning, there was a foot of snow on the ground and the temperature was minus 5! I had no overcoat and a no snowshoes. Welcome to Buffalo!! I went to the address that I had been given and saw a sign saying, "Thomas V. Ray Funeral Home." When I went inside to meet my new boss, his first words were, " We've got a funeral tomorrow at 8 A.M. Get working."

*This fellow, Mr. Ray, had the Catholic funeral business in Buffalo locked up. He had two sisters who were nuns, and that was probably the connection. There was another funeral home in town that did all the Protestants. I was Protestant, but that didn't matter. What did matter was using "V" in the name of the funeral home whenever I answered the phone. It had to be Thomas **V**. Ray. I got chewed out several times for forgetting the V. Mr. Ray had two sons and a daughter, but none were in the business with him. One of the sons was totally worthless, and the other was a lawyer. I never met his daughter or his wife. He paid me $30 a week, and I lived in a room in the funeral home. Although I now had a skill, I was still making less than I did for the phone company. But I had a job.*

Mr. Ray had one other embalmer working for him. He was from Bradford,

Pennsylvania; his name was Gordon Healey. He was 2 to 3 years older than me, but we got along ok. I never learned what he was getting paid.

I interrupted Jim at this point and asked just what was involved in preparing a deceased body for a funeral. I had been to what seemed like countless funerals as a child. Neither my parents nor any of their friends with children ever hired a babysitter. If it was a wedding or a funeral or a party, I went. Part of the ritual at the funerals was that my parents always insisted, if it was an open-casket viewing, that I had to go up to the casket, kneel on the "kneeler" in front and say a prayer while I viewed the body. If it was a female relative, I was instructed to kiss the body on the cheeks. Gross! But that was how we did it. At any rate, I had always been interested in what happened before the viewing. Jim obliged....in great detail.

This may surprise you, but most of the deaths at that time, at least in Buffalo, occurred in the home. The body always stayed in the home. We would go there with our equipment and do the embalming where they died. When we got finished embalming, we would put the body on a couch until the family made arrangements for a casket - it was usually just a wooden box, although some paid more for metal. If someone died in a hospital, we would bring the body to the funeral home and take care of everything there.

When we arrived at the home, we would put a large rubber sheet under the body, and then lift them into a metal "cooling tray" which had some ice to keep the body cool. Then I would make an incision into one of three arteries to drain the blood....the femoral, the axillary, or the carotid. If I couldn't get into one, I would go to another where I could get in. I would also open an artery so that I could get the blood to drain from the vein. The embalming fluid we used was formaldehyde; they used to use arsenic, but people doing that stuff were getting sick and dying. In the homes we always used a hand pump to put about 3 to 4 pints of formaldehyde into the body. If the body was at the funeral home, we would just use gravity feed. Some funeral businesses, the bad ones, would dilute the embalming fluid with water and use only one pint to save money, but we always did it by the book. Well, not exactly, because I never wore any protective gear or gloves, although I was supposed to. I never had any idea what the person died of, and never wanted to know....they were all the same to me. When I got finished putting in the fluid, I would sew up the incision just like a surgeon so that there was no leakage. I had practiced this over and over in school. We never took the blood with us; it was just flushed down the toilet.

Once the body was embalmed, I would bathe the deceased person and put clean underwear and socks on them. That was a rule. Same thing for women, even the bra. If it was going to be an open casket showing, the family would choose the other clothes that they wanted the person to wear and we would put those on. Part of my job was to apply makeup, both for men and women; I learned how to do that in school in Cincinnati. During my first years, we would also do the hair, mostly just comb it. Finally, we started asking if the relatives wanted us to get a hairdresser, but it was expensive, because most of those women were afraid and wouldn't accept the job unless the family paid big bucks. When I was finished, Mr. Ray would come and do a final inspection to make sure everything had been done properly.

I told you that we did mostly Catholic funerals. Well, when a nun died, things were done different. At that time, nuns always had to go anywhere in pairs, so when a nun was being embalmed, there had to be two nuns present when we did it. The Mother Superior had directed that. Often the nuns would ask questions as I worked. Sometimes the young nuns were so scared that I thought they were going to faint. We were never allowed to remove any underclothing from a nun, so they may have got buried in dirty underwear. We did a lot of priests, several bishops, and even a cardinal, but none of them required special procedures. Although we did mostly Catholics, we also had some Protestant and Jewish customers. The Protestants were essentially the same for us, but the Jewish deaths were always rush jobs because of their religious rules about quick burials. A lot of them were not even embalmed. We never told the relatives.

Most of the showings were in people's homes. For this there were usually two days of "visitation" where friends and relatives would come...often with food. We had two rooms in the funeral home for showing. When these took place, I wore striped trousers and a cut-away coat. Mr. Ray did not own a hearse or a limo, so he rented them from a local livery company. I was on call seven days a week, and never had a vacation. Other than the low pay, I liked my job.

Following this detailed, *very* detailed, explanation of the embalming process, I needed a break and excused myself to use the bathroom in the double-wide. Jim had patiently provided far more information than I had anticipated, including a lengthy discussion of rigor mortis (that I will not share), but I did not want to interrupt him as he was obviously enjoying telling what he did for a living for so many years. When I returned, he started to talk about his family life:

I got married on September 6, 1936 to Elizabeth Cauvet. She always preferred to be called Holly. We met in a strange manner. One night when I was working, a friend who was married had been at a party. He was with his wife and her girlfriend, and when they saw the lights on in the funeral home, they stopped by to say hello. So, my future wife met me in our morgue where I was cleaning up instruments which I had been using. Pretty romantic, huh? Her birthday was on November fifteen, and mine was on November first, so we always joked that we were "payday buddies" because the first and the fifteenth were always the paydays then. Holly had been born in Yonkers (New York), but her parents were now in Buffalo because he was a railroad man. When we met, she was a clerk for Liberty Mutual Life Insurance in Buffalo but had previously worked at Macys in Manhattan. After we started dating, neither of us had much money, so we mostly went to movies for a quarter each or a local dance. During our engagement, Holly lived with her parents, and I still was staying in the funeral home. Holly wanted to get married back in the New York area where her brothers and sisters and all her friends lived, so she chose a Presbyterian church that she liked in Pocantico Hills, New York. The minister who married us was extremely popular; later he was the one who did the burial service at that same church for John D. Rockefeller. We took my car, a '35 Ford 4-door sedan, on our honeymoon to Annapolis and then to Atlantic City. When we got back to Buffalo, we rented an apartment in a husband's and wife's house on Ashland Avenue for $25 a month.

We were both back at our jobs until the funeral home business started to decline. Mr. Ray wanted to bring his nephew into the business, so he let me go in September 1937. I was very bitter because that nephew had no training. I needed a job bad, so I contacted the National Caskets Company in New York City because I knew that they did business with all the funeral homes around the area. They pointed me toward the Quirk Funeral Home in Englewood, New Jersey, just across the George Washington bridge from NYC. It was another Catholic-oriented operation and was owned by Mr. Joseph Quirk. He had his own hearse, but I was his only employee. I had to work my ass off for him, but I needed a job because our first daughter, Bonnie, was born in January 1938. I worked for Quirk all through the war. I had a low draft number and assumed that I would be drafted, but the fellow at the draft board called me not long after I registered and said to forget about the service. I never knew what happened there. What I do know is that Quirk never gave me a raise, even though guys like me working in industry were now making a lot more during the war. As soon as the war ended, I quit Quirk and bought a small trailer to go to California to work in the oil fields.

Jim spent the next 30 minutes talking about the rest of his life until he ended up in Scottsdale. He stayed in California only six months before bringing his family back to the New York City region - this time he worked for a funeral home in Dalton, New York, near Mitchel Field, an Air Force Base, on Long Island. Jim mentioned that this funeral home had a contract with the military so some of his work involved trying to piece together bodies of military men who had been in tragic accidents. He told me of one situation where 13 servicemen had been killed in an explosion and he was literally piecing together parts of bodies by trying to pair arms and legs with correct torsos. By this time, he had three daughters. As I mentioned earlier, they moved to Arizona in 1958 where Jim worked for funeral homes, first in Phoenix, then in Scottsdale.

I could not confirm a detail which Jim mentioned about his wedding, that is, the church in which he was married in Pocantico Hills, New York. He told me that it was Presbyterian, and that John D. Rockefeller's burial service took place there. The Rockefeller family had begun purchasing property in the area in 1893 and built the Union Church of Pocantico Hills in 1921.

By all accounts, it is a beautiful structure with stained glass windows by Matisse and Chagall. I could not confirm if it had any association with Presbyterians or what denomination the minister belonged to who married Jim and Holly, but I suspect that it was the church Jim had mentioned. It sounded to me like a wedding location that a young woman from nearby Yonkers, New York, less than 20 minutes away, would dream about. The only other church I could locate in Pocantico Hills was Catholic.

Most of us probably would not choose to hear the details of embalming or other aspects of funerals. But, listening to Jim's story, I realized how integral his profession is to a civilized society. This fact was possibly the reason why he was not among the ten million American men drafted for WW II. Those involved in the funeral business had critical skills which were deemed essential to the wartime effort.

As a youngster in rural Indiana, Jim had probably never considered becoming an embalmer, nor envisioned a career preparing bodies for burial. But hard economic times change many things, both nationally and on a personal level. To his credit, Jim saw an opportunity to establish a career in the midst of extremely difficult economic conditions and he took it. When I had the privilege to interview him at age 87 in Arizona, Jim was living comfortably and seemed, with good cause, to be proud of his professional accomplishments, a marriage of over 40 years, and three loving daughters.

"The Restauranteur"
Diana Pipinos

Los Angeles, CA
Interviewed July 18, 1997

Diana (with hand on chin) at Red Cross camp
following 1933 earthquake

D IANA WAS LIVING ON GARRISON Street in San Diego directly
across from one of my Navy roommates and his wife whom I was
visiting. When they learned about my interest in interviewing
Depression-era survivors, they introduced me to Diana. She and her
husband, Hercules, moved to San Diego in 1968 when they purchased the
Fisherman's Wharf Grotto restaurant, a few blocks down the hill on the
harbor front. Hercules was killed in 1989 in what Diana described as "a
horrific automobile accident."

Diana was smartly dressed in a dark V-neck blouse with a necklace that looked remarkably like a rosary (but wasn't). She spoke quietly at first but became animated as we proceeded with our discussion. She did not want her photo taken and seemed initially to be unsure of my motives for talking to her, but soon appeared flattered that there might be interest in her life and times. Diana began by telling me about her childhood:

I was born on January 30, 1921, so I was a teenager during most of the Depression. Mother always told me that she was hospitalized for my delivery because I was a breech baby. Each of the other five children in our family was born at home, but I arrived into the world in a hospital - it was General Hospital...like the TV show. Our home was right in the middle of Los Angeles. My father was very Greek; he came to the U.S. through Ellis Island in 1909. I still have his immigration papers. He came with nothing and went to live with family friends who were in Holyoke, Massachusetts. I don't know how, but he ended up in Los Angeles a few years later. That's where he met my mother. She was Dutch, an Updike, and was living in Bristol, Virginia. I don't know much about her family or what they were doing in Bristol. Her older sister, who was then living in L.A., had earlier met a Greek fellow in Bristol when he was working there. She married him and they moved to California. In 1913 she wrote my mom in Virginia and said that they knew a fellow whom they thought might be a "good fit" for her. She suggested that Mom come to California for a visit and to meet him. Mom got permission from her parents to go, and after her sister sent train fare, at just 17 Mom got on the train and came to L.A. My grandparents thought that their daughter was going out there only to see her sister. They must have been surprised when she was married a few months later. I guess it must have been a pretty good fit!

My father opened his first business, a coffee house, when he had been here in the U.S. only four years. Shortly afterwards he went into the wholesale produce business. Most of the Greek immigrants seemed to want to own their own companies. I had a good early childhood. One of my first memories was going to the beach a lot while my dad fished from the Redondo Beach Pier in Los Angeles. All of us kids in our family were two years apart and we did everything together as a family. I had a hard time with my appetite....not sure why, but when I was nine years old, I was diagnosed with tuberculosis. It was first noticed by the school nurse at Raymond Avenue Elementary when she saw lumps on my neck. Most other children were happy and healthy, but I wasn't. My oldest sister developed infantile paralysis, polio, at about the same time. My parents put me into a Catholic sanitarium called Mother Cabrini in Burbank, California.

I was terrified of the nuns there. They slapped us frequently and seemed to try to get away with as much as possible in terms of abuse. We always had to take two doses of cod liver oil every day - one first thing in the morning before we ate, and the other at night before we went to bed. I'll never forget that smell and the terrible taste. Remember, I had trouble with my appetite before I got there....well, the food was terrible. They frequently served soup with pasta in it. Often there were bugs in the soup. Whenever we complained about the bugs, the nuns would say, "Well, take out the bugs." Even though there were only girls there, we were never allowed to take showers in the nude. The nuns made us wear special dresses in the shower so that we would not be naked. There was one nun in particular that I remember....her name was Sister Louisa. If you got too near her, she would yell, "Don't touch me! I'm holy!" Later I always joked that the nuns, who were always dressed in black, reminded me of Edgar Allen Poe's poem, The Raven. There was also a lot of religion. We had to go to Mass twice a day. My parents were allowed to visit, and they would come over on a red streetcar on some Sundays. The treatment for the TB was for us to bake out in the sun and to eat "proper food" which they made me eat. I already told you about the soup, but I guess that the fresh air did help me because in just over a year, I was declared cured and allowed to go home. I think that they used chest x-rays to make this decision, but I'm not sure about that. I still have scars on my neck from the TB.

After Diana told me about her experiences as a 9-year-old at Mother Cabrini's, I shared with her some "growing up Catholic" stories from my childhood. Corporal punishment was standard practice in both my grade school and high school classes. One priest named Father McClanahan had a wooden paddle he had drilled holes in to make it aerodynamically perfect as he swung it onto our bent-over teenage rear ends when we misbehaved. In retrospect, although many of our collective "growing up Catholic" stories make for amusing anecdotes, most of my buddies now agree that it was a positive influence in our lives, and we were fortunate to have had the disciplinary experience. Although Diana's father was Greek Orthodox, she did not attend Catholic services or schools; her mother was not Catholic and made those decisions. In the case of Diana's parents choosing a TB sanitarium, the denomination probably was of no concern. As far as I can determine, there were no other children's sanitariums in the Los Angeles area at that time.

Mother Cabrini was a remarkably interesting person. Her full name was Mother Frances Xavier Cabrini. She told interviewers that as a young nun in northern Italy, she added St. Francis Xavier to her religious name because she admired him so much. Although she had intended to become a missionary in China, the Pope urged her to assist the flood of Italian immigrants coming to America. During her lifetime (she died in 1917) she founded and staffed more than 67 schools, orphanages, and hospitals in the U.S. and around the world. The group of nuns she founded, the Missionary Sisters of the Sacred Heart of Jesus, focused on what the Pope had recommended, that is, assisting fellow Italian immigrants to the U.S. When she landed in New York in 1889, she was not immediately welcomed by the local Archbishop. In a short time, however, she was able to gather donations to not only feed the poor, but also open hospitals in New York and Chicago while also starting orphanages. Mother Cabrini first came to California in the late 1890's. Once there, she added more nuns to her order and immediately built the Villa Cabrini Academy, a school for girls. I could not determine when the sanitarium for girls was opened.

The Catholic Church canonized Mother Cabrini a saint in 1946, and in 1950 she was declared the patron saint of immigrants. Just recently Colorado passed legislation to replace Columbus Day with "Cabrini Day" because of the work she did with immigrant miners and their families in Colorado. There are currently numerous Catholic churches in the U.S. bearing her name.

Because of the climate in Southern California, Los Angeles was long billed as a favorable area for those afflicted with tuberculosis. In the early 1900's there were at least six sanitariums in the Los Angeles region. It was such a draw to cure tuberculosis that at least one developer offered to donate land to build another sanitarium to increase his adjacent property's value. The treatment which Diana received was standard for the time: sun, relaxation, and good food. There were no antibiotics or other effective measures, so, as one brochure of the time advertised, "We offer TLC and a warm environment." I have been unable to locate information on the Mother Cabrini sanitarium, but Diana told me that it has long since closed. There are, however, several buildings in Los Angeles which bear the Cabrini name, including a church and a shrine.

Although one can understand Diana's feelings about her treatment by the nuns, it is important to remember that these women (all volunteered to become nuns) were essentially indentured servants working in a difficult, dangerous environment with no pay. They were probably eating the same soup as the young girls for whom they cared. It was truly a labor of love for their Lord. Diana continued by discussing her life after the sanitarium:

Our family home was a two-story house with a basement. We always had three girls in one bedroom and the three boys were in another. Dad always made wine down there in that basement - lots of wine. It was during Prohibition and, as a young girl, I remember police officers and detectives coming to our home on a regular basis and leaving with Mason jars filled with wine. Everyone then was on the take. Dad also bartered for haircuts and other services with his wine.

One of my memories from my childhood during the 20's and 30's was of Aimee Semple McPherson. She was a Canadian who came to L.A. and was a hugely popular Pentecostal preacher. She would have thousands of followers at her sermons and built a huge building for her church in Echo Park, called the Angelus Temple. My dad was supportive of her charity work, because he felt that she was helping a lot of poor people during the hard times of the Depression. He donated lots of produce to her from his food business. Poverty at that time in L.A. was horrible. I remember food lines stretching around the block. Children had no clothes to go to school. Of course, because of Dad's business, we always had plenty of food in our house. In fact, every Greek I knew had food - maybe not much else, but always food.

Aimee Semple McPherson, also known as Sister Aimee, was indeed one of the best-known women in America during her heyday from 1918 through the Depression. During the early days of her career as a preacher, she traveled the East Coast in her "Gospel Car," a Packard convertible, which was painted with religious slogans. She often delivered sermons while standing in the back seat. After she arrived in California, she started what was one of the first "mega-churches" and sometimes had over 10,000 worshippers at a service. Her Angelus Temple claimed to be the largest Christian congregation in the world at that time. According to church records, 40 million people visited the temple during its first seven years. Stories about her charity work may actually understate how much good her organization did. Not only did she assist those in need locally, she also provided funds for disasters in Japan and Germany. She even persuaded physicians and nurses to provide free clinics for both children and the elderly. During the Depression, her soup kitchens fed nearly two million. Her temple commissary assisted more people, including migrant workers from Mexico, than any other private or public institution.

As a preacher, McPherson was a major national celebrity. To label her flamboyant would be an understatement. She frequently led Sunday parades through Los Angeles with major movie stars and even the mayor. (Diana did not say if she had seen these, but in view of her father's business connections and their home's location in central L.A., it is probable). McPherson used a 50-piece band in her "temple" and had sets built for every service, which always concluded with a dramatic sermon. She often dressed in "interesting outfits," such as a policeman with a helmet in a scenario during which she drove a motorcycle to the pulpit before giving a fire and damnation sermon entitled, "The Green Light is On." McPherson sometimes gave over 20 sermons a week and once held a revival in a boxing ring! In 1922 she was the first woman to preach on radio, and even started her own radio station. Of course, as with many celebrities, her life was not without controversy. McPherson was often accused of marital infidelity and, in a 1926 scandal, was allegedly kidnapped and disappeared for five weeks. Many suspected that it was a publicity event. A grand jury was convened to investigate, but the case was subsequently dismissed.

McPherson was ahead of her time in terms of racial issues. She welcomed members of the Black community into her Foursquare Gospel Church when few other church leaders would do so. When she died due to an accidental overdose of sleeping pills in 1944 preceding a revival in Oakland, California, over 50,000 people filed past her casket. The denomination she formed still exists and claims over eight million followers in 90,000 churches in 146 countries. Diana was certainly impressed with this woman and talked about her for nearly ten minutes before returning to her high school years.

I attended Manual Arts High School on Vermont Avenue in L.A. for two years before we moved to a safer area. Then I finished my senior year at Whittier High School. My dad wouldn't allow me to date in high school. By this time, he had several big produce trucks and many drivers, although he generally didn't trust them much, particularly when he found one of them trying to steal his wine. After that he would not let them in our house. I remember him hearing noises one night and running out in his long johns with a shotgun chasing the guy.

We didn't lose any money in the banks when they closed because neither Dad nor any of his Greek friends kept money in banks. I remember vividly watching people standing in lines trying to get their money out when the banks around us all closed. It was horrible.

The 1932 Summer Olympics were held in Los Angeles. We lived near the L.A. Coliseum and USC [University of Southern California] where many of the events were held. During the Olympics we would go to the Coliseum every day and they would let us kids in free when most of the events were over. I was very excited as an 11-year-old to see the athletes and all the flags from all over the world. I really liked watching the discus and the pole vault. I saw several swimming events at the new Swimming Center which was built near the Coliseum. You won't believe this, but they let us kids swim in the Olympic pool after the competition was over.

As a teen I got to see all the big movie stars at the USC football games.

I was disappointed when I saw Myrna Loy because she was rather short and had bowlegs! George Raft was shorter than I imagined and always wore lifts on his shoes. When I saw Clark Gable, I immediately thought that all the men in our own family were better looking. But it was great fun because of all the furs, perfume, and glamor. The stars were always kind to me, whether we saw them at the football games, outside the gates of the studios when they were going in, or at the racetracks. They would always give me their autographs. I remember talking to Sally Eilers - she was a big star then and had been in movies with Spencer Tracy and George Raft. I bumped into Edward G. Robinson at Laguna Beach one day, and we had a long talk. He was shorter and darker in person than I imagined. My girlfriends and I would often hang out near the movie studios, like the Hal Roach Studio and MGM, and would see the stars coming and going out the gate. Dad at this time had a night club/coffee house named Christo's. It was actually, of course, a speakeasy where he served his homemade wine. Charlie Chaplin and Gloria Swanson would come in. I saw Clark Gable with Carole Lombard, and one night I was there when Jean Harlow came in with William Powell. Both gave me their autographs. I think I still have them. I saw a lot of movies when I was growing up. It only cost 10 cents to get in and you could stay all day if you wanted....watching the same movie over and over, of course. I really liked Fred Astaire and Ginger Rogers. Maybe it was because one time a friend told me that I looked like her. So, I dreamed of growing up to be a dancer in the movies like Ginger. Those were two of the movie stars that I never met.

We also saw other events at the Coliseum. During the election campaign of 1932 Roosevelt came and I got to see him ride around the track in an open car while waving. Everyone was cheering loudly. Dad was a big Democrat. I myself did not vote until at least 1975; I just wasn't interested.

The biggest event - the one I remember the most - was the earthquake on March 10, 1933. I had been reading about the 1904-5 Russo-Japanese War. When I heard all these crashing sounds, I thought that we were being bombed! I was in the house....there was a movie theater next door. Dad screamed for us to get out of the house and get into the streets. It was about five in the afternoon. I ran out into the middle of the street and looked back to see my sisters sliding down the steps. I remember Dad going back inside to turn off the gas and water. Our neighbor, Ina, who lived across the street, was killed when a bunch of bricks from a chimney came down and hit her right in front of us. A lot of people died. We slept in our backyard for a week while there were aftershocks going on. We didn't go back to school that year because the school had been severely damaged. There were a lot of fires. It really hit Long Beach the hardest.

The "Long Beach Earthquake" did take place on the date that Diana remembered so clearly. It began at 5:54 P.M. and caused nearly $50 million in damage (in 1933 dollars). The estimated magnitude was 6.4 and caused at least 120 fatalities in Southern California. Diana's neighbor's death was similar to most of the other fatalities, that is, people running from their homes and being hit by falling debris. Buildings collapsed, structures were knocked off their foundations, and chimneys fell. School buildings were among the worst hit, leading to major changes in construction techniques all over California due to legislation introduced in the aftermath. One can only imagine the death toll if the quake had hit a few hours earlier with children inside all the schools which collapsed. Diana showed me a series of photos which she had kept and later mailed me at least 20 copies showing the widespread damage. Her mood became lighter when she started talking about ham radio:

When I was 17, I had a lot of hobbies....my favorite was amateur radio. I took a course and studied Morse Code and got interested in ham radio. I studied real hard and when I took the government test, I was the only girl. I scored higher than all the boys. I got my license - my call was W6SOK. Short wave radio then was all Morse Code, and I did a lot of ham radio. My receiver was a Holocrafter SX 28. Eventually I got a chrome "bug" on my sender. Of course, because it was just code, no one knew I was a girl. You would generally begin by talking about the weather - you might be "talking" to someone anywhere in the world with short wave, depending on the weather conditions, of course. Part of the normal procedure was that after you "talked" to someone, you would then mail each other cards with your contact info on it. When they would find out that I was a girl, they always wanted to know more. Sometimes we would exchange photos via mail.

About this time, in 1938, after I had graduated from high school, I was out walking our dog one day and saw a fellow landing an airplane on a nearby field. He saw me and came over. After we talked for a few minutes, he surprised me by asking, "Do you want to go for a ride?" I think I surprised him even more by saying, "Sure...let me tie up this dog." He flew me over to Long Beach and back. It was a Piper Cub two-seater. It wasn't his plane; he had rented it. I married him a few months later. I was 17, and he was 19. He had a job working for a baker supply company as a temporary job until he got into law enforcement.

After we were married, I kept doing ham radio. On December 7, 1941 I was doing Morse Code when I was suddenly interrupted with a signal saying, "Get off the air. We are being bombed." That was the end of my short-wave days.

Shortly after the war began, my husband enlisted in the Marines. Our marriage was not going well, and we were divorced in 1943. I was shocked to learn that he was shot on the first day of the Mariana landings in June 1944 on Saipan.

Diana chose not to elaborate on this marriage. In her obituary (she died in 2011) there is a son other than her four Pipinos children listed. There were several times during our conversation that Diana was obviously uncomfortable discussing events in her life. She did not tell me what happened to her marriage and just mentioned in passing near the end of our conversation that she had one son in the marriage. She did not say whether her ex-husband was killed in battle or returned to the U.S. after his war injuries. She also did not elaborate on whether her son lived with her, or what happened to him, other than to say that "he became a scientist." I chose not to press her for details on any of these sensitive issues. She resumed talking about how she met her next husband (whose first name she never mentioned, but I later learned):

I met my husband in 1945 right after he got out of the service at the end of the war. He was Greek and had been drafted during the war as soon as he came to the U.S. He was in the Army, but always had problems going A.W.O.L. Eventually they made him the personal cook to a general. I knew him only two weeks before we got married. Our marriage took place at the same Greek Orthodox church in Whittier where I had been first married. My husband had been ready to join the Merchant Marine, but when he met me, he changed his mind and went to work cooking for a large hotel. Not too long later we opened our first restaurant in Los Angeles. We had several restaurants and night clubs there over the years. My husband loved to start a new restaurant; then he would get bored and want to begin a new one. They were always Greek-themed. In 1960 we opened a nightclub in Hollywood where we served food; it was called The Grecian Terrace. Marlon Brando was a regular; he was just like you or me. He had a Polynesian girlfriend at the time and would always join in the Greek dancing we had. A lot of movie stars of that time would show up. Charlton Heston often came in with his wife and was genuinely nice. Ann Margaret always brought her parents and her boyfriend at the time who was Greek. She had such beautiful long red hair; she would also join the dancing. John Huston was a good friend; he always hugged me and had me sit in his lap. Everyone drank ouzo then; it was our big seller. Unfortunately, we had to close that place because it was the time of the hippies and they were sleeping on the street and causing a nuisance. Customers were afraid to drive down Hollywood Boulevard. Also, drugs were becoming a problem there, so we started a new steak house in Downey [California] because it was a better place for business. Not too long afterwards we had an opportunity to buy Fisherman's Grotto here in San Diego, so we moved here.

At this point Diana interrupted her train of thought and told me that she had one son with her first husband and four children with Hercules, two boys and two girls, born in 1946, 52, 53, and 58. She then shifted back to restaurant stories. They kept the Fisherman's Wharf place until the lease ran out in 1977, and then built two other restaurants, one using two railroad cars. They called it "The Napoli Express." Diana was actively involved in running each of their businesses. "I always took care of the books and did everything except cook. We pretty much retired in 1981 when Hercules had a heart attack."

Diana's experiences during the Depression were certainly quite different from so many others I interviewed who had faced economic ravages and displacements during the 1930's. Because of her father's steady income, she never had to be concerned about having meals or doing hard labor to simply survive. She had clothes, hobbies, and, in general, enjoyed "the good life." She did have adversity at an early age in the form of tuberculosis and the "year of hell" (as she described it) in the sanitarium but was fortunate to be healed and live through the 1933 earthquake. Because she had vivid memories of many Los Angelinos around her who were in bread lines and who lost all their savings during the bank failures during those years, she appreciated her good fortune and worked with her husband in their restaurants most of the rest of her life while raising their children. Her memories of Hollywood stars of several eras were obviously cherished memories....I certainly enjoyed hearing them.

"The Coon Hunter"
Willie Eden

Topsail Island, NC
Interviewed May 14, 1995

Annie and Willie Eden

I spotted Willie at Mollies, a seafood restaurant in Surf City, North Carolina where my family and I were dining. The specialty of the restaurant was a large, low-priced, fried seafood platter which attracted both locals and tourists, such as us. There were no reservations, strictly first come-first served. On weekends you had better be prepared to wait in line outside at least 30 minutes to obtain a table.

Surf City is now a popular beach town on Topsail Island, one of the barrier islands along North Carolina's coastline. At the time of my interview, it was connected to the mainland by a "swing bridge" which had the same purpose as a drawbridge, except that the roadway was rotated rather than raised to allow boat passage. Because of its white sand beaches, the island has become an extremely popular summer destination for not only North Carolinians, but also tourists as far away as Canada. The old swing bridge was recently replaced by a high-rise bridge, giving even easier access to both the thousands of year-round residents who now live on Topsail and hordes of tourists. The narrow saltwater passage between Topsail Island and the Carolina mainland is now part of the Inland Waterway allowing small boats to transit up and down the East Coast safely while avoiding the many perils of the Atlantic Ocean.

Willie was just finishing his lunch. From his appearance I suspected that he was well over 75 years old. As I approached his table, I explained that I was gathering information on folks who had lived during the Great Depression. When I asked if he would be interested in talking to me, he nodded his head in agreement, but said nothing. A younger woman with him, in what appeared to be a large family group, eagerly pushed a chair aside for me to join them at their table.

Willie was a thin, short man whose face spoke clearly of many years of outdoor activities in the sun, and probably far too many cigarettes. His ball cap seemed to be a bit large for his head and featured a logo of a sailing ship under the words, "St. Augustine, FL." I introduced myself and pointed to my family at a nearby table; then Willie warmed noticeably and began to patiently answer my questions. His voice was low and often monotone except when he discussed hunting and fishing with great animation. His family, especially the youngsters at the table, seemed interested in listening to his memories. After telling me his full name, he began:

I was born on April 3, 1910 here in Pender County across that water behind you. I had a sister and five brothers. All of us were born at home. The school we had was real small and was about three miles from our farm. We walked, but I didn't go to school much. Not sure how many years I went to that school ....like I said, not much. My daddy was a farmer...his name was Toby Eden. My mama had a long name. I can spell it for you, Amaradaway. She was from Onslow County; it's right next door. We grew ground peas [one of the women at the table interjected, "peanuts"] and corn and we had a spot where we grew vegetables. I got a single barrel shot gun when I was young and did a lot of coon hunting at night with my dad and brothers.

My wife, Annie, that's her sitting over there...we ran away and got married in 1930 down in South Carolina. She was born in 1915, so I was 20 and she was 15 at the wedding. I was the meanest man on the top of the ladder, that's why she liked me. We've got four children, two boys and two girls....that one down on the end is Billy and that is my grandson William next to him. We've got a bunch of grandchildren.... hard to keep track of. How many? Around eight of 'em.

Each member of Willie's family at the table smiled and waved when introduced to me. Annie definitely looked younger than Willie and did not have the sunken facial features of a life-long smoker. She was wearing a long-sleeved dress which caught my eye because of the obvious shoulder pads. One of his grandson's stopped eating and came over to shake my hand. It was a friendly group that gave the impression that I would have been just as welcome in their home for a Sunday supper.

The 30's were not a good time. We lived over in what we called Low End Topsail and had a farm. I was raising tobacco, sweet potatoes, and ground peas. I had my own barn where we cured some of the tobacco and sold it at auctions up in Greenville and Lumberton. It got between a nickel and 25 cents a pound. When it was a nickel, it was a bad year for us. But we always had plenty to eat because of the farm. I'd raise hogs out here on the island [Topsail Island]. I put 'em in my boat and bring 'em over here to this island and let 'em root around til they put on weight, then bring 'em back and sell or butcher them. There was nothing on this here island then, just two or three fish camps. The boat I had, it wasn't big, only about 12-14 foot...we either rowed it or pushed it where the water was shallow. No one down here had motors on their boats. They didn't put a bridge over here until 1940. It was a pontoon bridge when the government was getting ready in case we went to war. They started building some military stuff in case the Germans came. It got carried away by Hazel [a devastating Category 4 hurricane which hit North Carolina in October 1954].

I did a lot of fishin' then....mostly popeye mullet [that is the actual name of this type of fish]. We would take our boats offshore in the ocean and use a seine. There were four of us and we used a 200-yard seine to get the fish. No one used rods and reels for that type of fishin'. September was the best time for the mullet. Some of those popeyes at that time were up to ten pounds. You're not going to find them that large now. We also went after the spots [a type of fish] here in the water between the mainland and where we are now. The best time for them is in the fall. We also got some red snapper and pogies - all of it was good eatin'.... no one here did any shrimping then. Whenever we had a good catch, we would take the fish down to Wilmington and sell 'em. We were always lucky on storms....never got caught out there on the water in a bad one. Our place didn't get hit too bad by Hazel in the 50's, but it killed some people because it came ashore south of here near the border [with South Carolina] and didn't give no warning.

During the winter we always did a lot of coon hunting. We would have to walk about four to five miles to find them. I had some good coon hounds....at night they would find the coons and tree 'em and I would shoot 'em and bring 'em home. We would skin 'em, eat 'em, and sell the fur. My coon dogs were good, but they lasted only a few years because they would get the heartworms. During that time, I tried to make a dollar wherever I could....farming, fishing, and hunting.

I got my first car when I was 17, before I even got married. That's how we got down to South Carolina to get hitched. It was a new Model T and cost me a few hundred dollars. I had saved up some money to get it from doing farm work in the area. That was before the Depression hit. The nearest gas pump was over in Holly Ridge...gas cost 18-20 cents a gallon.

After we got married, we were in the middle of the Depression, but I bought 90 acres on time for a thousand dollars. No bank....just between us two men. I cleared 35 acres of it....we cut all those trees with a big two-man saw. I hauled the lumber in a pickup truck up to Jacksonville [North Carolina, about 30 miles north]. When I sold all the timber from where I cleared those trees, that helped me pay off the loan to the fellow who sold it to me. I paid it off total in ten years. I paid a buddy of mine to build a house there. Annie and I lived in that place 30 years...it's sitting empty now. The electricity didn't come in until sometime during the 30's.

Unless you have used a two-man saw, you may not have an appreciation for the work involved in clearing 35 acres. I grew up on a 14-acre farm, half of which was forest. I cannot imagine the work to do those 7 acres with a gas-powered chain saw, much less cutting down trees by hand. Once the trees are cut, there was still the issue of sawing the trunks into lengths which could be transported in a pickup truck. Willie's tone when telling me about this work was very matter-of-fact as if anyone could have done it.

I also did a lot of other work during the Depression. I sawed logs for 10 cents an hour and cropped and wormed tobacco for 5 cents an hour. I never kept any money in a bank...didn't trust them....kept our money hid at home. We had a cow for milk and had the hogs and chickens for meat. We bought bread and a few other things at a store up in Holly Springs - not much else.

Hoover was bad. We always said afterwards that with him we had caught the devil. When Roosevelt came in, things picked up. We never voted much, but we all voted for him. I got on with the WPA (Works Progress Administration, one of President Roosevelt's New Deal programs) for a year and made some money - not much, about a dollar a day. My job was to load up trucks using a shovel while they were doing some road building. We didn't wear uniforms on that WPA job, just regular coveralls and brogans - those stiff leather work shoes that came up to your ankle. I didn't like that WPA work, but it was money I needed during that time. I never saw any CCC projects around here and no one I knew was in one.

My wife and I and our kids never went anywhere back then. Our main entertainment was picnics. Now we eat out a lot, like today. I still love fish.

With that declaration, Willie started to slowly get up from the table signaling that our conversation was over. A few young children at the table were getting restless and it was obviously time for the family to leave the restaurant. I walked outside with Willie and Annie and took some photos of them in front of Willie's red and white pickup truck and also a few other photos of the two of them with the Inland Waterway in the background. Annie smiled in each photo, but Willie stood solemnly with his arms at his side. He looked tired.

It is doubtful that many 21st century Americans can understand or appreciate a man such as Willie. He not only hunted, but enjoyed eating, raccoon! It may be tempting to dismiss Willie as a stereotypical, uneducated, white, male southerner, but this would be to misunderstand the economically dire conditions under which he was born. Nearly all children in these rural areas at the time were born at home, and many died during childbirth. Few attended school on a regular basis because their work was required on the family farm. There was abundant fish and wildlife in coastal Carolina, but you did not buy it at the supermarket; it had to be caught or shot. There was no mechanized farming. To grow crops and raise farm animals required knowledge, hard manual labor, and quite a bit of luck with respect to the weather. There was no electricity, no telephone, no 'a lot of things' which we now take for granted. If you wanted to eat, you had to find a way to produce the food. Willie told me that there never was much information from "the outside" as he was growing up. And if you wanted entertainment, you had to make it yourself. This was the situation into which Willie and his Pender County peers were born in the early 1900's.

Willie reminded me of many "country men" I grew up with in Kentucky... hard working individuals without pretense. With little formal education they learned not only to survive, but to raise a family using whatever nature and their wits provided. My own father, for example, had to quit school after the third grade to go to work on a horse-drawn milk wagon to help support his family.

Clearing 30 acres of land without power equipment is a daunting task under any conditions. For Willie to do so in the heat (plus insects) of coastal Carolina shows remarkable tenacity and drive. I also cannot imagine rowing a small wooden boat filled with hogs in these same waters where I later found kayaking to be a challenge. Make no mistake; although Willie had a hard life, he could be described as an American success story.

Willie's discussion of coon hunting brought back memories of another aspect of my early teenage years in Kentucky. Most of the men near our farm did not hunt raccoons, but we occasionally went out with a dog at night trying to tree a "possum" (opossum). The procedure is similar: the dog smells a possum in the dark, the possum climbs a tree to avoid the dog, the dog begins to bark like crazy, the hunter arrives at the tree, locates the possum with a flashlight, and shoots the possum. In my case, I would not shoot the animal, but climb the tree while keeping the flashlight on the possum and then jump up and down on the tree branch supporting the possum until it lost its grip and fell to the ground. The dog would immediately grab the possum and shake it vigorously until it "played possum" (go limp while pretending it was dead). I would then carry the "dead" possum by its tail back to my home. In the morning, my father would take the possum into the foundry where he worked to eat it for lunch with his fellow workers. I never asked him how they killed the possums.

Coon hunting differs only in that the dogs must be highly trained - usually by running a young hound with an experienced older dog for a few hunts. Also, the raccoons are shot rather than captured because they are dangerous when cornered and can seriously injure the dog or the hunter with its teeth or very sharp claws. They are excellent climbers - I have seen one actually climb up a gutter downspout. At the time when Willie was doing most of his coon hunting, raccoon fur was prized and could bring a good price. Adult raccoons are large animals, typically 25-35 pounds. Their diet is opportunistic. Although they will eat birds and small mammals, they prefer nuts, berries, eggs, and insects. If they are near water, they will eat fish and reptiles. The raccoons which now live in suburbia have found food left in trashcans to be a favorite; they are very adept at using their "hands" to open trashcan lids. I have never tasted raccoon meat, but for a family in rural North Carolina during the Depression it was probably quite a treat. One raccoon could be translated into several meals. Several recent online sources show numerous recipes for raccoon. One aficionado described his eating experience as "tastes just like chicken!"

It is doubtful that many 21st century Americans are aware of the term "coon hunting," much less the fact that there are still active coon hunting clubs in America. Raccoons are in no danger of extinction in the U.S. In fact, their numbers are increasing dramatically because they have few, if any, natural enemies. They have been frequent visitors at night to our home in suburban Virginia and our camp in the deep woods of northern Maine. Female raccoons have from 2 to 7 babies (kits) in a litter, so it is easy to understand why Willie found so many on his nocturnal hunts. I suspect that if Willie and his hounds were around today, they could be kept busy trying to reduce the nuisance raccoon problem!

"Mormon Missionaries"
Richard and Velma Allen

Fairmont, WV
Interviewed July 15, 1997

WHILE I WAS TRAVELING IN Arizona, I was able to interview several residents at the Arizona Pioneers' Home in Prescott (pronounced biscuit, except with "pres" in front - I was corrected on my pronunciation several times while in the area). Before doing my first interview, the receptionist at the front desk told me that she would attempt to arrange another for me. After completing the interview, I found a well-dressed couple waiting to see me. They both smiled broadly as the man introduced himself and his wife, "Good afternoon! I assume that you are the fellow looking to talk to some of us about our experiences during the Depression. I'm Richard Michael Allen, Senior, and this is my wife, Velma Louise."

After the receptionist brought glasses of ice water for each of us, we moved to the nearby library to chat. Richard was tall - well over six feet - and was wearing a long sleeve white shirt with a thin black bow tie. His creased black trousers were held up with matching suspenders. His black hair contrasted with Velma's pure white hair piled, interestingly, high on her head. She was well over a foot shorter and had an elegant sleeved dress with a long necklace of white beads. Her voice was considerably weaker than Richard's, and I found that he answered most of my questions, including some I asked of Velma. Richard began by telling me about his early days here in Arizona:

I was born on June 8, 1911 in Mesa in Maricopa County. I'm older than our state....it was still a territory then.... we didn't get statehood until February 14, 1912. My parents were living on a farm and I was born at home, the last of six boys and two girls. My father was Warner Hopes Allen, and my mother was Fannie Busby Peterson. We are LDS - you know - The Church of Jesus Christ of Latter-day Saints. That's the full name, but I'm sure you're aware that most people call us Mormons. My great grandfather was one of the original Mormons in western New York State. In 1832 he moved west with our founder, Joseph Smith, and other followers to Kirkland, Ohio. My grandfather had been born in 1830 in New York, the year our church was restored to this Earth. Having suffered persecution in Ohio, most of the group moved to Missouri, but were run out by the locals, so they moved over to Illinois where Smith built an entire new city called Nauvoo - I think that's the correct spelling. Well, that didn't last too long, because Smith was murdered by a mob in 1844 in Carthage, Illinois while he in jail for treason. Hostile groups were causing even more trouble for the Mormons in Illinois and two years later, Brigham Young - I'm sure you've heard of him - became their leader. He then took nearly 10,000 followers on an exodus west. After 17 months of horrendously difficult travel in wagons, they reached the Salt Lake Valley, which was pretty much barren. When Brigham Young saw the land below from the mountains, he declared, "This is the place." During the 1850's over 15,000 Mormons migrated to Utah from the east. Young was the first governor of the Utah territory and was named President of the LDS Church.

My grandmother was born in 1847 in a wagon coming across the plains during that exodus. In 1882, when my father was 16 years old, the family moved south from Salt Lake to Mesa, Arizona to live in a warmer climate. When I was born, my father had a 20-acre homestead right in the middle of Mesa. He raised mostly alfalfa, but also some grains.... wheat, oats, and barley. Alfalfa was the big cash crop because we sold it to all the dairy farmers in the area. After 1911 the farming was excellent there because there was now a reliable source of irrigation water coming from the Roosevelt Dam which had been built up on the Salt River.

Richard's recounting of the history of his family and the LDS church was accurate with respect to the dates associated with the early Mormon church. I chose not to ask him about the phrase, "the year our church was restored to this Earth." I later learned from a Mormon friend that LDS members consider April 6, 1830, when the church was organized by Joseph Smith and five others in Fayette Township, New York, to be the "restoration of the church on Earth." Richard's spelling of Nauvoo was correct. The word "Mormons" was initially a derogatory term applied by those who opposed LDS members, because one of the sacred texts of the LDS religion is *The Book of Mormon*. ("Mormons" was later embraced with pride by LDS members). The LDS church teaches that Mormon was a member of an indigenous American tribe known as Nephites, who descended from Jewish people who had come to America to avoid persecution in their homeland. How they arrived here is not explained in detail. Mormon was a prophet who claimed to have been visited at age 15 by Jesus Christ. At age 16 he was appointed by his tribe to be their military leader. As a prophet himself, Mormon condensed the writings of earlier prophets based on ancient Hebrew texts. Following his death in battle at approximately age 74, his son, Moroni, continued his father's work. After Moroni died, he appeared as an angel near Palmyra, New York to tutor 17-year-old Joseph Smith and reveal sacred records inscribed on golden plates. Based on his memory of Moroni's words, Smith dictated a translation into English to his wife (and others) which was published in 1830 as *The Book of Mormon*.

Richard did not say whether his grandfather had multiple wives, as many of the early Mormons did. His grandfather may have also been involved in the "Utah Mormon War" during 1857-58, but he made no mention of this. Several times during our conversation Richard quoted passages from the Bible, but none from the Book of Mormon or the Doctrine and Covenants (an important LDS book containing revelations from God to Joseph Smith). At no time did Richard attempt to proselytize, and, in fact, we had several interesting and very pleasant exchanges about religion. Although he was obviously a fervent life-long LDS member, he seemed to enjoy very much discussing other religions and the commonalities between them.

Several Arizonans that I interviewed mentioned the significant role which the Theodore Roosevelt Dam played in the development of the entire Phoenix region, not only in terms of irrigation for the expanding number of farms, but also for flood control (there had previously been a series of devastating floods), hydroelectric power for the region, and commercial development of the area. The lake behind the dam (now called Roosevelt Lake) was for many years the largest artificial water reservoir in the world. Several private companies had previously attempted to build an irrigation system for central Arizona, but all failed. The dam, which for many years was simply named "Salt River Dam #1," was the result of The Reclamation Act passed by the U.S. Congress in 1902. It took six years to construct, at a cost of $10 million, and became a symbol of the successful role of federal government in large-scale projects. The paperwork to change the name to Theodore Roosevelt Dam probably cost more than this.

Richard continued telling me about his own childhood:

My earliest memory in Mesa was not a good one. We had a turkey gobbler that thought that I was his personal punching bag. Whenever he would see me in the yard, he would run toward me and jump all over me trying to give me some good pecks. I now laugh about it because that gobbler was only guarding his flock....doing what comes natural. And my oldest brother got bit by a rattlesnake - they were all over the place. He was saved by my uncle who cut him with a knife at the wound and sucked out the venom. I did, of course, have a lot of good memories about growing up there. We always had Easter egg hunts in the grain fields, and my oldest sister gave me a pocketknife when I was just five years old.

Our farm prospered during this time, but when I was seven, during the height of the flu epidemic in 1918, my father sold the farm for a big profit. We then moved up here to the Chino Valley 15 miles north of Prescott to a 60-acre farm with a big house. My parents had gotten tired of the summer heat in Mesa and thought that this location would be better for all of us. Well, that was a bad decision, because the water supply up there from Lake Watson was unreliable. You couldn't depend on it; several years it didn't rain much, and the lake went dry. Another problem was the Banking Panic of 1923. One day Dad told us that we lost everything and were "flat broke." He sold all our farming machinery and said that we were going to go to L.A. to get rich during the building boom out there. My oldest brother had been in the Navy and settled there afterwards. The plan was for us to stay with him. I was 12 years old then and I remember riding in the back seat of our Model T Ford going across the desert. In some places the road was only two tracks for the tires. One night we hit some bumps so hard that my head hit the cross bars scaring me to death. But we stayed in Los Angeles only three months. It wasn't as good for my dad as he had been told, so we hopped back into the Model T and came back to Prescott.

The lake mentioned by Richard today is called "Watson Lake" and is now mostly a recreational area for the Prescott region. The banking panics which took place at regular intervals during the 1920's were mostly local issues caused by crop failures or other economic disruptions. In each case, depositors suddenly attempted to withdraw more money than the bank had on hand, causing the bank to be unable to meet its obligations. There was no national system of deposit insurance protecting bank customers; many lost all their savings. However, I can find no mention of a national Banking Panic of 1923. For a family to lose everything, it would be a devastating blow, no matter the name.

When we returned to Prescott, my second oldest brother, Merle, had earlier returned from his church mission and had borrowed some money to buy a business called The West End Milk Depot. He would buy milk from farmers and sell it out of the store and on milk routes. He was quite a businessman, and after four years he bought out the store next to the depot. He started hiring members of our family to run the business. When my father came back from L.A. Merle hired him. Pretty soon Merle bought a 17-acre dairy farm south of town with a herd of 60 cows and put Dad in charge. I was 14 and a sophomore in high school and my brother put me to work at the Milk Depot. My job was to get up at 4 A.M., fire up the boiler, wash all the empty bottles with steam, bottle the milk, eat breakfast, and then go to school. On school days I slept during all the study halls in high school! In summer I worked all day on the farm.

During my senior year my father wanted me to work only on the farm. We had two vacuum milking machines run by electricity from the Arizona Power Company. The problem was that they would sometimes freeze up in the winter, and we had to milk all those cows by hand. We sold raw milk, but it was always tested by the Health Department. We also had a refrigeration unit to keep the milk cool. I remember standing on the running board of our delivery trucks which one of my brothers was driving and jumping off at each house to drop off milk and bring back the empty bottles. My brother never stopped the truck, so I had to run fast!

Richard's memories of delivering milk strongly resonated with me because my father had the same job in the early 1900's except that he worked on a horse-drawn milk wagon in Newport, Kentucky. He attended school only through the third grade before having to deliver milk full time to help support his family.

I graduated from Prescott High School in 1928. I was tall but very thin and didn't play any sports because I had to work every day. I weighed only 125 pounds then. I didn't have any fancy clothes - just Levi's and bib overalls. I probably looked like someone out of the Grapes of Wrath. I dated some girls within our church, but nothing serious. Right after I graduated, Merle put me in charge of a feed store which he had purchased. He had the Purina franchise in our area. Handling all those large bales of hay and bags of chicken feed really built up my muscles. I delivered all the feed and hay on the back of a Chevy sedan which I had modified by installing a bed on the back. I always took along my .22 with me in case I ran into any rattlesnakes.

I have a funny story about my first date with Velma and that Chevy. Velma was from a family down south near Tucson. Her father was a butcher, and they had enough money to send her to BYU for college. She had completed one year and had stopped in Prescott to visit a girl friend who lived here and was a member of our church. This is how I got to meet Velma. I invited her to go with me while I was delivering feed to some farmers. Well, she agreed - not sure why - and off we went. We were at one farmer's place when I spotted a large rattler next to the Chevy on Velma's side. I grabbed the .22 and shot it dead.

Velma had been sitting quietly alongside Richard during our conversation wearing an almost continuous smile. When the first date story was told, she interjected:

What a first date! I was planning on being a teacher and was enjoying my studies at BYU. I really liked Richard right away - not because he shot that snake! He just seemed like a nice guy. I was born in Tucson in January of 1910, so I was a year and a half older than him. That didn't bother me because he seemed mature and had a good job. Marriage was not an issue because he had not yet been on his mission. I knew that he wouldn't marry until he had completed that, and I wanted to go on a mission myself. Not too many young women did that in those days.

Because Velma spoke in an exceptionally soft voice, I had difficulty hearing her due to background noise from an adjoining room. She appeared to be in declining health, and Richard often completed her sentences.

The first American Mormon female missionaries were not called until 1898 when the (Mormon) President declared the need for "wise and prudent women" to aid in proselytizing. The ladies chosen were in their early 20's and were sent to Liverpool, England. More soon followed to other English cities. They traveled in "tall silk hats and good black clothes." I could not determine why the women were sent abroad rather than to "callings" in the U.S. Velma did not mention how she dressed on her mission.

Missionary work has long been an emphasis for the LDS church. At the beginning of 2020 (pre-COVID) there were over 65,000 full-time missionaries world-wide, in addition to 31,000 others doing charitable work. Many were recalled to their homes during the pandemic. Most of the missionaries are single young men and women in their late teens or early 20's. Men serve for two years and women for 18 months. Older couples whose children are no longer at home can also be called. One of my close friends and his wife were assigned to charitable work in Chile for two years when they were in their early 70's. All missionaries are volunteers, but young Mormon men are "strongly encouraged" to serve. The LDS church has one of the largest programs in the world to teach foreign languages so that the missionaries are fluent when they arrive in a foreign country. The term "to receive a call to serve " or "to be called" refers to the process of designating missionary assignments. Missionaries have no say in the location or nature of their assignment. It is made by church authorities in Salt Lake City based on the needs of the church. Often these calls are big social events where the letter (now email) announcing the destination for the missionary is read aloud to family and friends.

BYU is Brigham Young University and is in Provo, Utah, south of Salt Lake City. When I was teaching it was almost always the first college choice for many of my Mormon high school students. Contrary to popular belief (at least among non-Mormons), the school did not have its origins with Brigham Young. It was founded in 1862 in Provo by Warren Dusenberry and later became a branch of the University of Deseret. When the school experienced financial problems in the mid-1870's, Brigham Young, who was then President of the LDS church, took it over and named it Brigham Young Academy. He wanted to have a school of higher education where "children of the Latter Day Saints can receive a good education unmixed with the pernicious atheistic influences that are found in so many of the higher level schools of the country." For its first years the Academy was owned by the church and was both a high school and a college, but in 1903 BYU became known just as the university. I found it interesting that the university accepted women shortly after its opening, because many state universities did not do so until many years later. Currently well over 95% of the 33,000 BYU students are Mormon. No matter their religion, students are required to exhibit behavior in accordance with LDS teachings, such as abstinence from extramarital relations and homosexuality. There are no statistics on the rate of compliance in this era....Richard now resumed talking and shifted to his days as a missionary:

When I received a call for my mission in 1931, I went up to Salt Lake City to attend missionary training. I was assigned to the East Central States mission in Louisville, Kentucky. After learning how to be a missionary, I took the train out there. When I arrived, I was sent to an additional training conference in Roanoke, Virginia. I got a ride in a Model T to my assignment for the next two years in Fairmont, West Virginia. I don't think that I accomplished a lot during those two years. There was considerable opposition to Mormons, especially by local Christian pastors who believed that we were trying to steal their congregations from them. Talking about our religion there was a tough sell. On one occasion we were in a small town trying to show photos of our missions in South America by doing a slide show on a sheet which we had hung up between two buildings. All of a sudden, dozens of raw eggs came flying over one of the buildings. Several of us were hit....no one was seriously hurt, but I still remember one fellow who was watching the photos. When he got hit, he just stood up and wiped the egg off the front of his overalls and said, "Keep going." But there were also more serious attacks where angry locals came in the middle of the night and threw rocks through the windows of the church. It was just a small chapel that the church owned. Several of us missionaries slept in a tiny apartment in the back. None of us got hurt, but we didn't know if they would try to come in and beat us up or what. Initially there were five of us men there, but by the time I left in 1933, we were down to me and one other fellow.

I was amazed by the situation in West Virginia when I arrived there. It was nothing like Arizona. I mean, we had some poor people in Prescott, but I had never seen anything like this. People were living in abandoned coke ovens! Many children looked thin and underfed. Most of the local population in the coal mining towns were unemployed. The coal companies were letting their miners work half a day one day each month so that they could earn enough to pay their utility bills. We attended a lot of funerals. It was incredibly sad. But we weren't in as bad shape as some of the people we met because we were always receiving financial assistance from the church and from our families. The church gave us a Model T to use to get around the state. It had a rumble seat, but no top. You might have called it dilapidated....one day the windshield fell off when we hit some bumps. When we got to some of the remote areas, we would give help to whoever asked; we did a lot of cleaning of hillsides so that those living there could plant corn and other crops the next year. Most of the people we converted were men who were very dissatisfied with their lives and wanted to do better. These were hardy people. I watched one older man carry a 100-pound sack up a long hill - I doubt that I could have done that.

The coke furnaces that Richard mentioned were commonplace throughout coal mining districts. Coke was a highly valued commodity for making steel. It was produced from certain types of mined coal by heating it in an airless oven at extremely high temperatures (usually 1800 to 2000 degrees Fahrenheit). These high temperatures vaporize organic material and water in the coal leaving a residue that is almost pure carbon. The beehive coke oven was most likely the type which Richard saw. It was typically a brick structure built in the shape of a dome, usually with a diameter of 12-14 ft. and a height of approximately 8 ft. There is a hole in the top through which the coal is dumped to a depth of about 3 ft. Once ignition takes place, the top is closed as the coal burns off the volatile products in the pile of coal. The process takes 2-3 days. The emissions which take place are extremely hazardous, and the people who moved into these abandoned furnaces were undoubtedly exposed to a multitude of dangerous residue. The saying that "Desperate times call for desperate measures" was never truer for these West Virginians. If your family had no shelter, these coke furnaces would at least provide protection from the elements. The plight of so many during his time there in the early 1930's obviously made a lasting impression on Richard....he continued by telling me about his experiences in Pendleton County, West Virginia:

I spent part of my mission in Pendleton County. There were very few roads there. We had some LDS families in that area, and they would often invite us to stay with them. This sounded good, but we quickly learned of two major hazards: bed bugs and scabies. Everywhere we stayed there were bed bugs. You can't get away from them. They find you! They hide in any crevice in a bed: the mattress, the box springs, or any place they can find near a bed. All the mattresses up there were old and had plenty of places for bedbugs to hide. They come out at night to bite you to get your blood. We could sometimes see them when they came out....they're small, red things about the size of an apple seed. The bite itches like crazy. The only good news is that they didn't cause any other diseases. Most of the locals had bed bug powder. I don't know what was in it, but they swore it worked. I would say not so good. On one trip we had two female missionaries with us, and we put them up with the bed bug people. They never forgave us!

The other problem in nearly all these homes was scabies. Everyone simply called it "the itch." These were mites and you couldn't see them. Some of the drug stores up there sold a lotion to prevent them, but it cost a dollar - a huge amount in those days. I tried it once and was immediately sorry because it burned and caused a rash on me worse than the scabies. Eventually some of the local ladies told us to spread lard over your skin, then rub powdered sulfur into it. That worked. It smelled bad, but it worked. The natives knew how to do it.

While we were in Pendleton County, we often worked with the local moonshiners helping them on projects for their stills. It was still Prohibition, but we never felt bad about helping because we just dug ditches and secondary things like that. Everyone paid off the cops, usually with beer. We never drank, of course, but we did convert many of these families who appreciated our help. All in all, when I left West Virginia, it seemed like they were 100 years behind the times. But I liked most of the people I met and felt that I gained a lot from the experience.

When I got back to Arizona in November 1933 Merle put me to work the next day at the feed store. We always joked that returning missionaries get married right away so that you don't get into trouble. So, I got back into touch with Velma and we began to date again. Her father had sold his business in Tucson and had come up to Prescott to work for Merle as a butcher. We were married on February 1, 1935 there in our church in Prescott.

I had to laugh when Richard mentioned "returning missionaries." Several of my female Mormon high school students headed to BYU told me that once they were there, they were going to start looking for a good "RM" to marry. They said that they would not bother dating anyone else. Velma now interrupted Richard. She spoke in her soft voice with Richard interrupting occasionally with additional commentary:

I also went on a mission for a year. Mine was mostly in New York State and some in eastern Pennsylvania - Scranton and Wilkes Barre. I didn't have any of the experiences Richard had in West Virginia. I took the D&RG [Denver and Rio Grande railroad] out of Salt Lake City just like Richard and headed east. Once we got to New York the other lady missionary and I stayed near wherever LDS churches already were, usually in rented rooms using money from back home. I played the piano and several of us women formed a musical group which sang for events. The elders [the name given to male missionaries] always watched over us and made sure we were safe. We were even on the radio several times. There were no dates while you were on mission, and no dancing or swimming. But we would go to meetings with all the male missionaries in our area. It was the most interesting experience of my life.

After a long pause in which it seemed that both Velma and Richard were enjoying fond memories of their missionary days, Richard provided some information about their life after marriage:

Once we were married, we didn't have much money, but we didn't care. I worked in Merle's grocery store for three more years or so, and in 1940 he put me in charge of one of his stores which had been having some problems. I had a good butcher, and one year after I took over, I had that store in the black. I ran that same store until I retired in 1971. One thing I noticed about Prescott was that during the Depression none of us had it too bad, at least compared to what I saw in West Virginia. Most people here had work and we all took care of each other....that was what was important...looking out for one another.

Because I had another interview scheduled to begin shortly, I did not have the opportunity to learn about Richard and Velma's children. He did tell me earlier that they had "six or eight grandchildren who are now on mission." I found it interesting that only one of the Allen family (Merle) had to initially become financially successful for the entire family to enjoy work and stability throughout the challenges of the Depression years. Of course, all his family members were hard workers who used Merle's entrepreneurial success to improve their own lives. I could not decide if Velma was in failing health or if Richard simply had a dominating personality, but he definitely controlled the conversation. What I did know was that this was a marriage which had lasted 62 years and was still full of love.

"The Aviator"
Ken Grant

Seattle, WA
Interviewed June 18, 1996

MY TRAVELS HAD TAKEN ME to the Northwest to visit friends after obtaining a "hop" on a military plane to the Naval Air Station at Whidbey Island, Washington. My first stop was in Seattle at the home of Kay Powers whom I had known for years through a mutual friend. When I mentioned that I was interested in interviewing folks who had lived through the Great Depression, Kay immediately responded, "You have to talk to my dad. He did a lot of flying during the 30's and has some great stories." Two hours later we were in Ken Grant's apartment in downtown Seattle, just to the east of Interstate 5. First Hill Park is just up the street.

Ken was tall with thin, receding white hair. His neatly trimmed beard and mustache were also white, giving the impression of a stately gentleman. He spoke in a clear, deliberate voice with no distinguishable accent, and with excellent grammar. Occasionally his 83-year-old memory would fail him for specific names, which would always bring a mild "hell" or "damn." Ken was obviously well-educated and extremely polite. As usual, I began by asking about his parents and his birth:

I was born on October 1, 1913 in McKenna, Washington - that's about 40 miles south of here. I never heard for certain if I was born in a hospital, but I think so, probably in Tacoma, Washington. My birth name was just Kenneth Grant...I had no middle name. This caused a problem later on in life when I was trying to enter the Marine Corps. They told me I had to have a middle name, or I couldn't become a Marine. So I said, "It's Roscoe" because that was my father's first name, Roscoe. He was from a wealthy family in Morehead, Minnesota, but died when I was just five due to the flu during the epidemic which was raging around the world. 21 million people died world-wide in that epidemic. My paternal grandfather struck it rich in the gold fields in Alaska. He traveled via ship around Cape Horn in South America, then up the California coast to Alaska. He became so wealthy that when he returned to Minnesota, he bought up sawmills, timber, and banks.

It was not clear which years Ken's grandfather was in Alaska. Although there were small numbers of prospectors in Alaska as early as 1870, the major influx occurred from 1897 to 1903 during the Klondike and Nome gold rushes. Because Ken was born in 1913 and had two older brothers, his father had to have been born long before the 1890's, making it very unlikely that his grandfather was in Alaska during either the Klondike or Nome gold rushes. What is probable is that his grandfather may have been one of the first Alaskan prospectors to "strike it rich" sometime after the California gold rush in the 1850's. He then returned to his midwestern roots and used his gold monies to create even more wealth. Ken did not linger on this aspect of his family's past and switched to talking about his mother:

I do not recall how my parents met, but my mother's name was Myrtle Johnson. She was originally from Bozeman, Montana. When my father passed away at my early age, my mother went back to school. She already had a teaching certificate but wanted to have more qualifications. My two older brothers, Gerry and Jim, stayed with my mother who moved to Ellensburg, Washington. I am not sure why I was sent to live with my mother's brother, Paul Johnson, for a year – probably my young age. He was Superintendent of Schools in Clarkson, Washington, which is right in the center of the state....near Walla Walla. When mother finished school, I moved back with her in Ellensburg where she got a job teaching school. It was a small school and she taught both the first and second grades and was the Principal.

I went through grade school and high school there in Ellensburg. We had a three-bedroom home, and from an early age I delivered newspapers: the Portland Oregonian, the Seattle Post Intelligencer, and our local paper, the Ellensburg Record. I also worked on a dairy farm throughout high school, but instead of milking cows, my jobs were to wash bottles and deliver the milk. I played some sports - football one year, and basketball my junior and senior years. My brother, Jim, was really good in basketball, and during my junior year we won the state championship - that's the only time up to now that Ellensburg won the title. The fellows that I hung around with were mostly athletes....we would run home for lunch each day. We ran everywhere. Most summers while I was in high school all of us guys on the basketball team would work at the sawmill in their box factory. That was where they made the wooden boxes for all the apples which were grown in that part of Washington. Of course, we also did all the usual "boy things" like tipping over outhouses on Halloween. One year six of us got caught by the Chief of Police and were put in jail. All the other boys had "high power" parents, like the District Attorney, who came to get them out. After the other five were let go, I was still in there. It was a dirty, stinking jail with rats all over the place. Fortunately, in the morning, when I had not come home, my mother called the sheriff who was a family friend. He came down to the jail and got me out right away. My buddies thought it was hilarious that I had to spend the night in that jail. Mom never yelled at me about it. She was a wonderful mother who knew how to raise boys!

I was not that aware of the Depression in those days. We were not living high style or anything like that, but we always had food and Mom always had her teaching job. We lived near the railroad tracks, and in winter I would pick up coal that had fallen off the trains and bring it home to heat our house. During the summer I would pick up chunks of ice from the refrigerated trains carrying fruit and put that in our ice box. We didn't have a refrigerator and I didn't know anyone who did.

Ellensburg is a small town located in the middle of Washington State just to the northeast of the Yakima River. During Ken's stay there it had a population of approximately 4000 (currently just over 18,000). Because it was the most centrally located city in the state, it was initially considered to be the logical location for the state capital. A fellow named John Shoudy had arrived there in 1871 and established a trading post for miners, trappers, Native Americans, and cattle drivers which he playfully named "Robber's Roost." He chose a more conventional name, Ellensburgh, based on his wife's first name for the surrounding city which he was the first to map. He ultimately had to drop the "h" in 1894 due to a ruling from the U.S. Postal Service and the "Board of Geography Names" (this is an actual government agency established in 1890). Unfortunately for those residents who were lobbying for the city to become the capital, a major fire broke out in 1889 destroying most of the downtown area. Soon thereafter Washington state voters chose Olympia as the capital. It can be argued whether this slight was good or bad for Ellensburg, but what is certain is that the population would have been considerably higher both during Ken's days there and now.

After graduating from high school in 1932, I bought a new Chevy Coupe using the money I had saved up from my work during high school. I don't recall how much it cost, but I remember that I now had no problem getting dates! I didn't go away to college but did one year at Ellensburg Normal School, which was our local college. It is now Central Washington University. In the fall of 1934, my mother loaned me $500 so that I could drive over to Seattle to begin classes at the University of Washington. I had wanted to be an aeronautical engineer but quickly learned that I was not prepared due to not studying much in high school. I switched to several different majors and ended up getting a degree in general studies with a major in air transportation. I don't recall how much tuition was then, but I was totally on my own. I worked my way through school and also repaid my mother that $500. While I was at the university, I lived in a rented house with four other bachelors. The landlady lived in the basement and we fixed all our own meals. We hardly ever ate out in town.

As I said, I worked all the time while in college. One of my first jobs was pumping gas. I was working 10 hours a day seven days a week and still going to classes. That was too much, and my grades weren't good. In 1936 I met a fellow who was an electrical engineer whose hobby was winemaking. He decided to start a winery and asked me to help. I built it with him on 15th Street just below Shepherd's Ambulance. He called it the Conegare Winery. One of the things I remember most is that when I told him that I didn't know anything about wine making, he said, "You don't need to know how. You do what I tell you to do. I'll coach you." So, that's how I learned to make wine. He taught me everything, and during my senior year I actually lived at the winery as a night watchman. Every weekend I was paid 97 cents an hour to make 5000 gallons of wine. In 1936 that was good money!

In late summer, the winery owner would drive his truck to Kent Valley or take a ferry to Vashon Island to buy loganberries. He would bring the berries back and freeze them in 50-gallon drums for use throughout the following months. Every Friday night I would begin by taking one of these drums and dump the berries into a copper cooker to boil them with a small amount of water. This would kill the bacteria to pasteurize the mixture. After the berries were cooked, I would pump the liquid into a 50-gallon barrel, add sugar from 100-pound bags, then dump into it a plastic bucket full of the liquid from a "working keg." This adds some of the yeast which was brewing in that keg. The yeast had originally been brought to Seattle from France by the owner; if you are careful, the yeast will last essentially forever, just like in making sour dough bread. I also added some sulfur "candles" to each 50-gallon barrel to purify the mixture. When I was finished with one drum, I would repeat the process with the next. I would begin winemaking at 2 P.M. on Friday and have 5000 gallons made by Sunday evening. I slept in my clothes every weekend because I had to get up every two hours to do the pumping. The loganberry wine we made was sweet and was ready, if I recall correctly, to bottle in about four weeks. The owner sold it under the Connoisseur *label; apparently the wine sold well, because I kept making those 5000 gallons every weekend.*

There was one batch that I made that may not have been so "connoisseur." Somehow, not sure how it happened, but one night I accidentally dropped my knife into a 5000-gallon vat as it was being made. I panicked at the thought of having to dump that much wine because I knew that the metal from the knife would dissolve in the acid and ruin it. 5000 gallons of wine was worth a lot of money. So, without much thought, I jumped into the vat, found the knife with my toes, went under to get it, and retrieved the knife. Even though my buddy hosed me down, I was purple for several days after that! I never told the owner but always wondered if that batch had a "special flavor."

Ken's loganberry wine stories brought back memories. In early 1969 I was on a submarine, USS GURNARD, in the Seattle area for sound trials and practice torpedo firings following construction at Mare Island, California. Many evenings found bachelors from our crew at one of the "submarine bars" outside the gate of the Bremerton Naval Shipyard. Here I had my first introduction to loganberry wine. None of us ever drank the wine by itself. It was poured into a half-full glass of Olympia beer. This concoction was called "Logy and Oly." On far too many occasions I recall waking up to a lot of purple clothing. I do not recommend that you try it!

In my senior year I joined the Marine Corps (USMC) reserves at Sand Point on Lake Washington in Seattle. I had wanted to get into Marine Corps flight training after graduation, but I knew that the only way most could get in was if you knew a Congressman or had some money connections. However, there was another route which was to have been in the Reserves, so that's why I joined. Our unit met at the Sand Point on Lake Washington in Seattle. At that time this was on the edge of town. I wanted to learn to fly, and fortunately there was a sergeant in the unit who taught flying. He wanted to buy his own plane and was short of money. He took ten of us aside and said, "If each of you give me 50 bucks, I will teach you how to fly as soon as I get the plane." We all thought that was a really good deal, so we gave him the money. The plane was a "Curtiss Pusher." It was built by Curtiss Wright and was called "The CW-1 Junior." The engine was made by Szekely and was small, only 45 horsepower....sort of like a Volkswagen "bug" type. It was mounted behind the cockpit on struts with the single propeller directly behind the engine. Earlier Pushers were biplanes, but this one had wings above the fuselage like a glider. The open cockpit had room for a pilot and one passenger sitting in tandem. I sat directly behind the pilot and he would yell what he was doing, so that is how I learned to fly. I had several close calls in that plane. For starters, the sergeant was way overweight, probably close to 300 pounds, so the plane handled quite differently when he was in it. On my solo flight at Renton Airport, I was up by myself with him down below watching me from the ground. The runway was only 1000-1500 feet long and there was a nursery with tall trees at one end. No matter how many times I tried, I couldn't get the damn thing on the ground because I was going too fast; it was a hot day, and the plane just floated as I tried to come in. Finally, I just stalled the plane and bounced it hard onto the ground. The instructor came running out yelling, "Damn it! I forgot to teach you how to side slip!" He got in and showed me how to side slip in order to land on those short runways. I can tell you that plane always came down easy with his 300 pounds in it no matter the weather. With just me in there, you had to side slip to get the plane down on that short Renton runway.

CW-1 Junior (note propeller behind pilot)

A few years before I interviewed Ken, my wife and I were on a cruise in Alaska. Part of the itinerary involved watching an Alaskan bush pilot demonstrate how to make a landing on a noticeably short grass runway near Anchorage. His prowess at side slipping was incredible. I had always wondered how those Alaskan pilots landed seaplanes on small remote lakes there. Side slipping essentially involves flying the plane sideways with the plane out of balance by using the ailerons to apply bank in one direction while using opposite rudder. This creates more drag so that the glide angle increases without increasing the speed allowing the pilot to descend quickly to land on a short runway. The entire time Ken was discussing side slipping, I had Paul Simon's 1977 song, *Slip Slidin' Away*, stuck in my mind!

Once I got my license, I wanted to take one of my friends from Ellensburg for a flight. So, I took him over on a flight to see my brother on Vashon Island and flew over him at about 200 feet. He told me that he could see the buttons on my shirt. Well, when I took the plane back, one of the other fellows took it up and the engine quit on him at takeoff. If that would have happened an hour earlier, my friend and I would have ended up in the water and probably dead.

When I looked up photos of the Curtiss Pusher aircraft, I found that the version Ken flew was a handsome plane. It was a small, light sport aircraft - just 21 feet in length with a wingspan of 39 feet - designed specifically to be affordable with a cost comparable to many cars of the time. The "Junior" was a totally new design from the previous Pusher biplanes and featured a steel tube fuselage covered with fabric. The open cockpit and the appealing looks were designed, as the ads put it, to allow a customer to "fly the girl friend around a little and sell for under $1500." From design to the first flight took just over two months. The actual retail price came in at $1490 (less than $25,000 today). Just under 300 were sold. It was not clear exactly how the sergeant Ken knew obtained the plane, but he apparently financed it, at least partially, by giving lessons to those ten cadets. The plane did have some design flaws (which Ken did not discuss) because it tended to throw cylinders while in flight. Although there were three cylinders, the problem was that the one which separated would fly directly into the propeller behind, causing the plane to lose power and crash. The other issue was the location of the propeller, which was close to the ground. Several people died walking into it while getting into, or exiting, the aircraft because the only way to start the engine was to manually spin the propeller. Despite these shortcomings, it was a popular aircraft because it had a range of 200 miles and could cruise at 80 mph - both major attractions in the early 1930's.

As soon as I graduated from college in 1937, I got into my Chevy and drove cross country to Marine Corps flight training in Pensacola, Florida. I took my mother with me because she had obtained a teaching job there. While we were driving through Oklahoma, we saw an oil well come in. We had parked our car to watch the activity but had to move it quickly to keep from getting drenched by the oil. I was a cadet while I was in Pensacola. I completed the first 11 months and was in the stunt phase. It turned out that there was bad weather for nearly a month, and I was rusty and got a "down" from my instructor. They gave me another chance, but the instructor was an engineer who was so busy that he said he was going to give every student a down until they stopped assigning him check runs. As to his word, he gave me a down, and with two downs, you're out.

An American Airlines pilot who was there talked to me and told me to go back to Seattle and apply with the Army because they are so desperate for pilots that they are taking all comers. I thought about it but decided that maybe flying for the military was not for me. So, I drove back to Seattle with my mother. No oil well thrills this time! I was probably foolish not to push for another test there in Pensacola; one pilot practically guaranteed that I would pass, but who knows why these things happen? Each one of my flight school classmates was killed in Alaska flying PBY's as bombers against Japanese installations on the Aleutians. There were essentially no navigation aids up there, and every one of them flew into mountains in the bad weather that's always there. So, I guess that my guardian angel was looking after me. One of my high school classmates had flown numerous successful PBY missions up there. One day when he came back, they brought him a sandwich and told him that they were loading him up for another flight. He said, "That was my last flight....you can court martial me, but I'm not going back up there." They didn't know what to do with him; eventually he was sent to Washington, D.C. where he had a highly successful career. He even wrote President Roosevelt's Christmas message one year. I'm certain that if I would have completed flight training, I would've been killed. Many of my classmates who died up there in Alaska were better pilots than me.

The PBY, "Catalina,' was a flying boat, basically a military seaplane. It was first built in 1936 and was last flown by our Armed Forces in the 1980's. Many PBY's were used as patrol bombers after being sent to Alaska in June 1942 following the Japanese raid at Dutch Harbor and the invasion of the Aleutian Islands. All reports indicate that there were indeed heavy losses, not necessarily due to enemy fire, but because of poor visibility and severe wind conditions. There was one squadron of PBY's, VP-41, in Alaska on Pearl Harbor Day, 1941. By the end of 1942, the Navy had five squadrons there. Originally the planes operated from flying boat tenders until bases could be established in the Aleutians. Many of the missions had to take place at night due to the plane's vulnerability against Japanese fighter aircraft. The PBY was the most numerous aircraft of its kind; over 4000 were produced between 1937 and 1945. Although the planes were slow and vulnerable, their missions were many and varied, including not only bombing, but also reconnaissance, search and rescue, and even torpedo attacks (such as at the Battle of Midway in 1942). In view of the extreme dangers associated with flying this plane in wartime conditions, Ken was fortunate not to have succeeded in flight school.

When I came back to Seattle in 1938, I went back over to Ellensburg and worked at the Falderson Peterson service station for a few months but kept trying to get a job with Boeing. On one weekend I went over to Sand Point with the Marines and ran into one of the officers who was the number two test pilot for Boeing. When I told him my story, he immediately said, "Well, show up at Boeing on Monday, and you'll have a job." So, I went to work there where I was "drilling skin."

Here Ken laughed heartily before explaining:

They had these big sheets of aluminum up against a wall so that workers could just drill holes wherever there were marks to put rivets in. We used an electric power drill just like at home. On about the third day, the foreman came by and said, "What the hell are you trying to do?" I told him that I was just trying to keep a job so that I could eat. He was angry and said, "You're drilling about three times as many holes as anyone else. Cool off!" The next day I got a call from one of my college classmates who was in flight test. He was now an Air Force Captain. He said that he heard I was working at Boeing and asked me why I was drilling skin. I told him that I needed a job but really wanted to get into flight test like him. Within two weeks I was working in flight test on B-17's. It was the second series of B-17's being built. One of my jobs was to hang engines and props and then run the engines up for static tests. I loved this job, but the Army insisted that their pilots do all the test flights. We built 12 or 13 of the first B-17's built by Boeing.

My shop foreman, Manny Atkins, was building his own airplane and asked me to help him. We rented a house and built this airplane in his living room. The airplane had been crashed and we were able to get a lot of material and parts from Boeing surplus. Manny and I co-owned the airplane which was a Great Lakes Trainer. It was a stunt aircraft with a 100 HP engine which allowed me to do maneuvers that I couldn't do in the military planes down at Pensacola. The first time I tried to do a snap on top of a loop with the Great Lakes Trainer, I did a double snap. That was one lively airplane! Manny was one hell of a mechanic but did not have much experience as a pilot. A few months after we got the plane together, he took it out for a cross country trip with a buddy and had some engine issues as he was flying up the Columbia. He landed it in a farmer's field and did some damage to the plane. I told him that a smart pilot always flies where there is a road to land on!

Back at Boeing, I found out that we were not going to be actually flying the planes because the Army wanted their own pilots to do all the testing. This was very disappointing. I decided that if I could not fly those planes, I would become an aeronautics professor. So, I went to Los Angeles to take graduate courses at UCLA. A few months later I flew up to Seattle to help Manny get our plane out of the field with a trailer. I am not sure whatever happened to that plane.

While I was down in L.A. taking graduate courses, I got a job with North American where they were building the first B-25's. Then I worked over at Lockheed on the first P-38's. While I was at Lockheed, we also built the early Hudsons for the British. My job was flight engineer testing these planes.

The Hudson was a light bomber and coastal reconnaissance plane which

Lockheed built for the British as early as 1938 before WW II fighting began. The plane was a conversion of one of Lockheed commercial airliners, the Super Electra. The initial order of 200 planes was a huge financial boost to Lockheed, but also set up the company for mass production of other military aircraft when the U.S. entered the war in 1941. Because of America's initial neutrality in the European war in 1939, the Hudsons destined for Britain had to be given clandestine delivery. They were flown to airfields near the U.S.-Canada border, towed by horses or vehicles across the border, flown by Canadian crews to airfields where they were dismantled, loaded into boxes, and shipped by sea to England where they were reassembled. In the summer of 1941 one Hudson actually "captured" a German submarine off Iceland when it ran up a white flag for surrender after being attacked by the aircraft. The damaged sub and its crew were then taken to a British base by Royal Navy ships. The U.S. also used Hudsons for anti-submarine patrols. At least two German submarines were located and destroyed by Hudsons off the U.S. coast in 1942. Ken then switched to tell me about his how he met his wife:

In early 1941 I flew up to Seattle for a weekend where I met my future wife on a blind date set up by a friend and his wife. Margaret was a nurse at a hospital there in Seattle. I hadn't had a date in eight months, and we hit it off very well. We started dating regularly and were married in L.A. two months later. Not dating for eight months is hazardous if you were planning on being single!

Ken had a long laugh at this anecdote and began to show me family photos. We were interrupted by a phone call from a friend who reminded him that they were supposed to have dinner in less than an hour. Ken apologized for having to end our conversation before we had a chance to discuss his life during the war and thereafter. Before I left, he insisted that we go to the roof of the apartment building to take a photo of him in front of his beloved Seattle skyline. We also quickly discussed our mutual heart surgeries; in 1971 he had one of the early open-heart surgeries. I later learned from his granddaughter that Ken and Margaret had four children, two daughters and two sons, and that he had become an air traffic controller, first at Boeing Field in Seattle, then at SEATAC airport which services the entire Seattle region.

Ken is an example of those Americans who were spared the economic ravages of the Great Depression, but still had to scramble for work. Although he lost his father at an early age, he was fortunate because his father's family had financial resources, and his mother always had a good job as a teacher. Still, other than a $500 loan to get to Seattle to begin university studies, as a young man Ken was on his own and worked continuously throughout college to support himself. He also learned to adjust when a window of opportunity suddenly closed. As a friend of mine put it, "When one door closes, you open the next." Instead of going into a tailspin when he failed flight training, he found a way to "reinvent himself" at Boeing and continue his dream of flying.

Ken spoke in modest terms about his experiences in the early days of aviation when Americans were just beginning to realize the potential for both civilian and military aircraft. Who knows why he was "chosen" to fail flight training so that he could live such a full life afterwards, when all his classmates died flying during the war in Alaska? Our early aviators were brave, or foolhardy, based on your opinion - I prefer brave.

"Granddaughter of the Canal"
Virginia Hawkes

Goshen, IN
Interviewed May 5, 1995

NOT EVERYONE SUFFERED MIGHTILY DURING the Great Depression. If the breadwinner in your family held a steady job and had savings which survived the stock market crash of 1929, there was a good chance that you would not have the same struggles as many other Americans. I am not talking about the "super-rich", but rather families for which life remained comfortable relative to the vast majority of their fellow citizens. Of course, there were inconveniences for these families, but, for the most part, there were few life-altering financial events.

Such was the case for Virginia Hawkes. She was born on December 20, 1910 in New Haven, Connecticut. Her father, Donald French Stevens, a Cornell graduate, was an executive for the Baltimore and Ohio (B&O)

railroad. Her mother, Mayme Bagley Stevens, was a homemaker. Due to the nature of her father's work, the family (including her two older brothers) moved frequently during Virginia's childhood. Six weeks after Virginia's birth, her family moved to New York City, then Garrett, IN, followed by Grafton, WV, Newark, OH, Newcastle, PA, Akron, OH, and finally, Cleveland, where she attended high school. Due to these frequent family moves, both of her brothers attended a military school in Minnesota in the 1920's. Upon graduation from high school in 1928 Virginia was sent off to two years at Pine Manor College in Wellesley, MA, which she described as "a finishing school." When I asked what she had studied, Virginia laughed, "I was studying to be a lady…that's what we did at the time." In 1930 she began classes at Goucher College outside Baltimore where her parents then lived.

I learned about Virginia from a cousin who lived in Goshen, IN and was in the "Library Club" with her. When I telephoned Virginia to request that we meet for an interview, her response was, "How soon can you come over?" As I entered her beautiful, older home the next day, her first words to me were, "We paid $4200 for this house when we bought it in 1937." Although it was a warm, spring day, Virginia was wearing a V-neck sweater over a striped long-sleeve shirt with checkered pants. Her pure white hair appeared to be fresh from the hairdresser, giving her the appearance of one of the grand old dames of Goshen. After offering me iced tea, she sat on the sofa, while continually petting her black cat, Kitty, as she spoke. Virginia spoke with a strong voice for a mid-octogenarian and had wonderfully detailed recall of every event from her childhood. Anticipating my visit, she had found several old photos of her family to share. After telling me about her childhood and education, the subject turned to what happened after she became disenchanted with her studies at Goucher.

I went to Goucher for a while, but I really wasn't too crazy about it. My grandfather was taking a trip down to Panama, and he wanted me to go with him, so I did. His name was John Frank Stevens, and he had been hired by Theodore Roosevelt in 1905 to go down to Panama to build the canal there. He was the Chief Engineer, but it was hard for him without his wife who lived in Washington in an apartment with their three sons. Finally, he resigned. Roosevelt was very unhappy with him for doing so and said that he was going to hire someone who could finish it and wouldn't quit. That's when he hired the other guy, I forget his name.

Grandfather and I went down there on a ship which sailed out of New York. There were two ships. We went down on one and back on the other. One ship was named the Ancon and the other was the Cristobal….I don't remember for sure which was which and how Cristobal was spelled, but the accent was on the "o." It was late 1930, and I had a wonderful time because I was still 19, and there weren't many girls down there. It seemed like every man in the whole Army and Navy was there. I had a wonderful time. I could have had a date for breakfast, lunch, dinner, and a dance in the evening. My grandfather was very relaxed….I don't know, I expected him to keep an eye on a girl my age.….I sure would've. But he let me do what I wanted.

We stayed at the Tivoli Hotel. Granddad had built it in 1906 because he was expecting Roosevelt to come down to see how the Canal was going. I don't think it's there anymore. I was there in Panama over a month. Most of the time I went with this one boy named Dorrance Brown. His father was the Governor and the General of the Army. He came up to visit me in Baltimore. When I later mentioned his name to my husband, he said, "Well, that's the family that owns the Campbell Soup Company."

Here Virginia excused herself to answer the phone. While she was gone, I realized that I knew little about her grandfather, John Stevens, and how famous he was. When he returned to Panama with Virginia in 1930, he was essentially a major celebrity regarded with awe by most of Panama. I later read the historian, David McCullough's, meticulously-researched and lengthy 1977 book, *The Path Between the Seas,* in which he detailed the history of the Panama Canal. Two entire chapters discuss John Stevens' role in making the canal a reality. Due to his strong leadership, personal work ethic, and force of will this man essentially single-handedly rescued the canal from disaster during the darkest days of construction in the early 1900's and became one of the most famous Americans in the first decade of the 20th century.

From his work in the American West, John Stevens had already gained fame as an engineer who could build railroads where no one else could. He was totally self-taught and learned all typical engineering disciplines studying on his own at night while building railroads through unimaginably challenging conditions in northern Michigan and the Rockies. His reputation was already well-established when the railroad tycoon, James J. Hill, hired him to find a route to the Pacific for his Great Northern railroad. Stevens' work for Hill made him a legend among railroaders – he even had a pass named after him. Hill, who was one of the wealthiest Americans of his era, was a regular confidant of President Teddy Roosevelt. When Roosevelt told Hill, according to McCullough, that he was looking for someone "who could build the canal," Hill told the President that he knew a man who could do it. Roosevelt immediately summoned Stevens and, over lunch in Oyster Bay offered him the job.

Virginia's grandfather, John Stevens, Chief Engineer, Panama Canal

In late July 1905 Stevens landed in Colón, Panama and immediately took charge of the failing canal-building operation. He formed a close working relationship with Dr. William Gorgas, an Army colonel, who had been appointed by Roosevelt as the Chief Medical Officer in Panama to combat the tropical maladies which were ravaging the workforce (predominantly native Caribbeans), threatening to end the entire project. Together they wiped out the *Stegomyia* mosquito, which was the source of yellow fever, by relentlessly attacking breeding grounds with oil and draining and fumigating nearly every house between Colón on the Caribbean side and Panama City on the Pacific. Stevens, by all accounts, had boundless energy. He used his railroad expertise not only to devise and supervise an ingenious excavation nearly 400 ft. deep in the 9-mile long Culebra Cut through the Continental Divide, but also to build entire communities to house, feed, and support the tens of thousands of workers. He also convinced Roosevelt and Congress that the best route for the canal was not a sea level path involving impossibly greater digging, but one involving a series of dams and locks and a man-made lake using water from the Chagres River.

When Roosevelt sailed to Panama less than two years later in November 1906, he found that engineer Stevens and physician Gorgas had essentially created a miracle. Disease issues had become non-problems and incredibly large machinery was now working non-stop loading excavated dirt and rock into a continuously moving line of railcars for removal to build the Gatún Dam. Roosevelt's visit was the first time a President had left the U.S. while in office, and Stevens wanted to ensure that the trip was a success. The lodging for the President was indeed at the newly constructed Tivoli Hotel where Virginia stayed 25 years later.

Although the circumstances surrounding Stevens' resignation as Chief Engineer of the canal in 1907 remain unclear (at least according to McCullough), most now agree that Stevens was simply exhausted and desperately wanted to return to his family in the U.S. as Virginia suggested in our interview. President Roosevelt was indeed angry with Stevens for resigning and declared that he "would put the canal in charge of men who would stay on the job." Stevens' replacement, an Army Lieutenant Colonel Goethals, did fulfill that desire until the canal was completed in 1915, but most observers still regard Virginia's grandfather, John Stevens, as "the builder of the canal."

When Virginia resumed our conversation, she still had Panama on her mind.

I'm not sure how everyone in the Army ate down there, because I, of course, didn't eat their food. There was a lot of social activities, and people entertained lavishly. After Grandfather Stevens and I sailed back to New York, I returned to our home in Baltimore. Dorrance came up to visit me, and when it was time for him to go back to Panama, he asked me and my mother to come up to New York to see him off, which we did. When we got up to the ship, there was my old friend, Ginger Rogers and her mother, Lela, who was also in show business. They were always awfully close. We had known Ginger and her mom from our time in New York; she was less than a year younger than me but had already been married to one of the men who danced with her. When we saw her there in New York, she was "technically" still married, but not living with the fellow. She ended up getting married at least four times, I think. When we knew her then she had already been in a bunch of movies and was a rising star. She passed away recently....she certainly let herself go, didn't she? I read her autobiography and learned a few things about her that I didn't know. For example, Ginger was a Christian Scientist just like her mother whom she adored.... I guess that's why she never drank, and she never smoked. But she loved ice cream! She was always eating ice cream. That'll put the weight on you!

Dorrance knew Ginger from when both had been in New York before he went down to Panama. She was already in show business then and had made a lot of money, even at her early age. She had a great big, white limousine and let Mother and I use it to go shopping. Ginger's real name was also Virginia, like me, and I believe that Rogers was her stepfather's name. Of course, I followed her career and knew that she won an Academy Award. She had quite a social life. She supposedly had an affair with Jimmy Stewart and was engaged to Howard Hughes, but they never got married. I watched most of her movies that she made with Fred Astaire, but I never saw, or heard from her, after those times we were together in New York.

Ginger Rogers went on to even greater fame and fortune after Virginia's days with her in New York. Not only did she win the Academy Award in 1941 (ironically not for one of her nine RKO's musicals with Fred Astaire), but also numerous other awards. When she and Virginia were together in New York, Rogers was making over $1000/week – a remarkable sum for a teenager in the Depression. In 1942 she was officially the highest paid female performer in Hollywood, making well over $100,000 a year. When

Virginia recalled Ginger's well-publicized affairs and love life, she had the number of marriages at four, but Rogers was actually married five times, and none lasted over ten years. Number four was a Frenchman and 16 years her junior who apparently indulged her new-found passion of sleeping outside every night while they were in Arizona. She was also rumored to have had an ongoing affair with Astaire, but both routinely denied it over the years. Rogers' obsession with ice cream, which so amused Virginia, apparently continued throughout her career; several sources claim that she had an ice cream soda fountain installed in her home. In her later years Ginger Rogers had several strokes and was, as Virginia alluded, considerably overweight at her death, just a few weeks before our interview.

The young man whom Virginia dated while in Panama, Dorrance Brown, died tragically in Lakewood, New Jersey at age 30 due to a broken neck when he dived from a boat into a shallow part of Barnegat Bay near Toms River in 1936, less than five years following being sent off in New York by Virginia and Ginger Rogers. Either Virginia had lost track of Dorrance following her marriage to John, or she simply failed to mention his early death to me. Brown never married and was buried in Louisville, Kentucky, less than 200 miles south of Virginia's home in Goshen.

Virginia now shifted to her days in Baltimore.

My mom and I stayed in New York for a while, and then went back to Baltimore. I began secretarial school in 1931 and then got a job as a secretary to an Episcopal priest at a church downtown, Grace and Saint Peters. I was living at home. At first, they paid me $8 a week, then I got a raise to $10. The pastor was Father Chalmers, and he had two assistant priests – one of them was named Garlic. I don't remember how to spell it, but I think that I would have changed my name if I was him. I was not an Episcopalian, but my father was. Mother was Methodist, so that's what I was. We were living in a part of town called Roland Park which was near Johns Hopkins. I still have two friends who live out there in Towson. I had to take a streetcar from our home to work, and it cost a nickel, I think. My grandfather had an apartment just two blocks from the church so I would walk over there every day and have lunch with him.

I don't remember exactly what many things cost then because I didn't buy the groceries. My family was not affected much by the Depression because my dad got a raise when we moved from Cleveland to Baltimore. He worked for the B&O all his life and was General Manager of the railroad while there in Baltimore. Before, when he was in Cleveland, he was General Superintendent of Transportation, and that's when he got his own private railcar to use when he traveled. People who knew this thought that we had a lot of money, which we never did, but we always had that private car.

I don't know if you know this, but the B&O went to Lake Wawasee in Indiana, which is a summer resort. Our family would get a cottage there for July and August, and Dad would come up for the Fourth of July in that railcar of his and he would put it on a siding there. He would invite his friends to stay there and it was next to a golf course, so they played a lot of golf.

I worked for the church in Baltimore for about a year and a half, but when I was out at Wawasee in 1934 I met John Hawkes at WACO, which was a dance hall. No one now knows what WACO stood for, but it was Wawasee Amusement Company. John was 10 years older than me. His family had a hard time of it in the early days of the Depression, and he didn't have much money. Men couldn't get married young then because they had no money. John had graduated from the University of Illinois, and he got his first job with a Spaulding sporting goods store in Chicago, before they transferred him to Toledo. While he was in Chicago, he met Al Capone several times when he came into John's store. He never told me much about Capone, just that he would come into the store. While he was in Toledo, his father died, and John came back to live with his mother here in Goshen in 1933. He got a job as a salesman for Western Rubber. He always worked on a commission and started with nothing.

Because I could travel on the train anytime I wanted, I often came out to Goshen to see John. We were engaged in February of 1935, and I wanted to get married in June, but he said we had to wait until September because he didn't have enough money. Anyway, we were married on September 28th in Baltimore at the Methodist church in Roland Park.

It was a big wedding, and we drove to Tryon, North Carolina in John's car for our honeymoon. He had a car because he needed it for sales. Because of Dad, I always had a pass to travel on the railroad.

We returned to here in Goshen and lived in a small apartment on Madison Street until we had enough money to get a loan to buy a house. We ended up purchasing this house in 1938, for as I told you, $4200. Our first boy, Johnny, was born in Memorial Hospital in South Bend. I was in bed for two weeks when I delivered him – that was not unusual at the time to have to stay in the hospital that long for childbirth. Our other two boys, Harvey and Frank, were born in the hospital here….it is now a parking lot. I myself had been born at home back there in New Haven. Those three boys were a handful!

John had to do a lot of traveling selling a lot of rubber things that go into cars. He was gone most of every week selling in Ohio and Indiana. Our streets were paved here in town. One of the fellows who John worked with at Spalding went into the CCC [Civilian Conservation Corps], but not too many others that we knew of. We had a lot of businesses that were open, like the Goshen Lightning Rod Company and IXL, which made furniture. Most people seemed to have jobs here then.

There were always a lot of Amish people in this area. When I had Johnny, I had this Amish girl, Fannie, work for me for $5 a week. She would stay here every day but would go home only on every other Sunday. She basically moved in. It was really easy to get help. She had to give her money to her father. She was young, probably about 21. Funny thing happened. First time she was here, she had the table set for three. I wasn't used to that…my mother always had colored help, and they did not eat with us. So, I thought about it and finally went out into the kitchen and said, "Fannie, Mr. Hawkes and I don't have too much time together because he is gone a lot." So that was that. She never said anything about it, but I can understand how she thought she should eat with us. Fannie worked for us for about a year, and then she got pregnant, and had to leave. Fannie is still around, and she is just the same, except her hair is gray. I see her every once in a while, usually at a funeral for someone we knew. But she never married and raised that *boy by herself; she was a nice person. I don't remember anyone else who worked for us. Once the war began, they all got jobs in factories; during the Depression they couldn't get jobs there.*

President Roosevelt was an unfavorite around here in our house. We were always staunch Republicans. First time I voted, I voted for Hoover. My husband and my brother-in-law didn't approve of a lot of the things that Roosevelt did. But as far as I am concerned, I think that it turned out fine having Roosevelt....I like that Social Security. And he got the country back on track.

Life here in Goshen in the 30's was very social. We had to entertain a lot. We belonged to the Tippecanoe Country Club, and we had parties there. We went to the First Presbyterian Church, where John was first an elder and then a deacon. We went down to the Kentucky Derby several times. I have a cup here where some fellow made mint juleps for us. It was quite an experience; our friend had a box there. Those were good times.

When I finished my interview with Virginia, she stopped me on the way out and asked, "Hey, can you guess what Kitty's full name is?" When I told her that I had no idea, she gave a hearty laugh, and said, "Kitty Hawkes! Get it?" I shared the laugh.

Driving away from Virginia's home, I understood why she was so popular with many of the other women her age in Goshen. She was exceptionally sweet, and totally unpretentious. While we discussed her life and times, Virginia patiently related each event in her life in a friendly, but somewhat patrician, manner. Although her family was not extravagantly wealthy, her early life was essentially privileged and removed from the day to day lives of so many other Americans during the Depression years. After her marriage, she lived comfortably, but frugally, in the same small northern Indiana town, following many of the same living patterns of other Americans. She was a joy to interview.

"The Yankee"
Eleanor Bowen Fader

New Bedford, MA
Interviewed Dec 28, 1998

1938, age 20

E LEANOR WAS THE MOTHER-IN-LAW OF a close Navy friend. I was fortunate to meet her when she was in Virginia visiting her daughter, Ronalee, and her family for the Christmas holidays. She spoke with a firm voice and frequently laughed during our talk. She had excellent recall of events from her early years. Before we began talking, Eleanor said, "My life was not remarkable....I'm not sure what we can talk about." She began by telling me about her birth:

I was born in my grandmother's home on Mount Vernon Street in New Bedford, Massachusetts on October 2, 1918 during that terrible influenza epidemic. Our family doctor had suggested that they move my mother to Grandmother Bowen's home to keep her isolated from my father who was going to work every day. They wanted to keep her separate from anyone who might be bringing that flu germ home. I'm not sure how far along she was in her pregnancy when she was moved there. I don't know anyone in our immediate family who got the flu, but I was later told that many in New Bedford were infected and that a large number died. The doctor who delivered me, Doctor Lord - that was his name - was a cousin of my mother. He lived just around the corner from us. If we had any medical problems, Mother would always just send us over to see Dr. Lord. The good news was that my birth went well. I don't know how long my mother and I remained at Grandmother's home after I came into this world.

My parents, Mary Elizabeth Wood and Earle Preston Bowen, both had British blood. My mother's ancestors came from England and my father's family came to the U.S. from England in 1632. The connection to Wales was on my father's mother's side; one of her ancestors, Jonathan Briggs, arrived here on a ship named "The Blessing." He was a young single man but wasn't an indentured servant. I have a family tree going back that far, so we have very deep New England roots. New Bedford was originally a whaling town and later became a mill town. My father was a machinist; he worked with engines on the fishing fleet boats. I had a younger brother who passed away several years ago. He was seriously injured in WW II and later became an executive with New England Telephone. My older sister now lives in North Carolina.

I believe that Eleanor was incorrect on the year her ancestor Briggs came to America. I found an online record showing that a John Briggs, Sr. (1609-1690) arrived on *The Blessing* in 1635, not 1632, as part of "The Great Migration." This mass movement of 20,000 people from England to America took place from 1620 to 1640. Several books have been written about this migration; some have extensive listings of the names and origins of each person. This John Briggs was born in Darrington, a small village in the West Yorkshire area of England. In 1640 at age 20 he was deeded 7 1/2 acres of land in Sandwich, MA. He was listed as "a follower of Anne Hutchinson," a Quaker leader, who had been banished from Massachusetts in 1637 (she, and six of her ten children, were scalped by Siwonoy Indians in 1643). Finding little tolerance for their religious beliefs in the Massachusetts Colony, Briggs' group purchased Aquidneck Island from other Indians in what is now Rhode Island. This area, at the time, was a haven for "Puritans who were not so Puritan." In 1662 Briggs purchased 140 acres in Dartmouth, MA, but later moved back to Rhode Island where he was buried. Of course, it is possible that Eleanor was referring to an earlier Briggs, but Dartmouth is located awfully close to her birthplace in New Bedford. Eleanor continued:

My parents owned our home; we lived on the first floor and rented the second to Mr. and Mrs. Gallagan. He was a fireman and had two daughters who were older and no longer lived with them. That home is still in our family; one of my nieces now lives there. My grandfather Bowen was retired and dabbled in gladiolus. He cross-bred them and named each new one for one of his grandchildren. He had a special bed out back of his house down behind the tool shed where he grew those flowers. We learned never to go near them!

In retrospect, we were spoiled. My mother's sister lived near us. She was married but had no children, so she was always giving us things. Also, the Gallagan's above us treated us just like their own kids. So, we had it pretty good growing up. One of my earliest memories was having a tea party with my sister behind our house. Mother took snapshots of us sitting at a small table drinking "Cambric tea" - that's milk and water. We were never allowed, of course, to have tea. We were in cute dresses; that's all girls wore then.

Cambric tea (sometimes called "nursery tea") was, as Eleanor described it, simply a mixture of hot water and milk. Sometimes sugar was added and, occasionally, a dash of tea. Mothers often gave this drink to children, not only so that they could pretend to drink tea like grownups, but also to provide energy. It got its name from a white and thin fabric called Cambric which allegedly got its name from the textile town of Cambrai in France. Laura Ingalls Wilder mentions cambric tea in her book, *The Long Winter*.

I went to grade school at Clark Street School - kindergarten through third grade. Miss Knight was my kindergarten teacher....I can still see her beautiful teeth. She played the piano for us and we sang songs. In the first half of the year we went to school in the morning, then for the next half went in the afternoon. That way they could have more of us in kindergarten without building another school. For the rest of grade school, 4th through 8th grades, we went to Mount Pleasant School. They let me skip 5th grade because I was doing so well - probably because having been born in December, I was older than the other students. I then went to New Bedford High School and graduated in 1935. I had a mix of courses - shorthand, typing, math, but no foreign languages. We had to bring our own lunches because there was no cafeteria. Our city was short on money then and couldn't afford to build any more schools, so we had double sessions. Some of us went part of the day - for me it was 8 to 1, with an hour for lunch - and others went 1 to 5.

I dated in high school and was always invited to the "Cotton Ball" in the spring. The girls all wore cotton dresses - that was the theme. We had bands at the dances - often with some of our own students doing the music. There was a junior ROTC [Reserve Officer Training Corps] at our school. It was extremely popular with the boys because they got to wear uniforms. Each year they had a ball in the armory called the "Semi-ann" - no idea why it had that name because it was not held semi-annually....just once a year. The cadets would wear their uniforms and march around the armory. We would all fall behind the flag bearers in the Honor Guard and march behind them. It was quite a thing. One of our school counselors knew Rudy Vallee and he brought his band to come to play for us one year. That was incredibly exciting because he was so famous! I was invited to the Semi-ann each of my last three years in high school. I was a sophomore the first time I went, and my date's father drove us to the ball. I had a different date each year. I had a good social life in high school. We often double-dated and went bowling or swimming at Horse Neck Beach or to the ocean over at Cape Cod. All the girls' bathing suits were one-piece, of course. My parents were pretty liberal and knew who I was going with. Whenever we went swimming at a pond, we would be in a group, so the boys would change in the woods and the girls changed in the cars. We were totally innocent.

Rudy Vallee was a wildly popular teen idol at the time of Eleanor's school dance. His performing at a high school dance would have been comparable to Elvis performing at your school dance during the height of his popularity. Vallee, whose real first name was Hubert, was from Vermont. As a teen he formed a band called *The Connecticut Yankees* which played around New England. As a youngster he also spent considerable time in Maine. During the mid-20's he played clarinet and saxophone with a band at a hotel in London. He then returned to the U.S. and obtained a degree in Philosophy from Yale before resuming his musical career. He formed a new band, changed his name to Rudy (after a famous sax player) and began to develop a following among young women who were attracted to his good looks and sweet ballads. Soon he had a recording contract, made several movies, and had his own radio show. Screaming young females greeted him at every appearance. Vallee was not a one-hit wonder; his career lasted well into the 1970's with over 40 movies and numerous television appearances. Interestingly, Vallee asked Louis Armstrong to guest host his radio show in 1937; this was the first time that a Black performer hosted a national radio show. I cannot imagine the thrill Eleanor and her classmates experienced when Vallee showed up at their dance.

Horse Neck Beach is in a Massachusetts State Park near Westport. Eleanor and her friends had several choices for beaches; New Bedford was nearly equidistant from Cape Cod and Horse Neck. She resumed talking about her high school days:

Football was the big sport in our high school and my brother played on the varsity team. I was in the marching band and played trumpet. We had uniforms and looked very smart. Our family was very musical. My mother and sister played piano and my brother played the trombone. We would often play together for my father. Our band director was very imposing. No one fooled around in that band. We once took the train to Boston to play with several other bands under the direction of a guest conductor, Mr. Goldman, who was a contemporary of John Philip Sousa. We girls had gym every day and we had to wear "gym bloomers" with white blouses. They made us do rope climbs in those outfits and I hated that. After we took showers, I remember I was always "racing like 69" to get to class. The school had a swimming pool, but there was no water because the city couldn't afford to keep it up.

Edwin Franko Goldman was one of the most important band composers of the 20th century. He composed over 150 works, but he is most famous for his marches. Goldman established the American Bandmasters Association. He was a native of Kentucky, but his father passed away when Edwin was just eight years old, and his mother, who was a professional pianist, moved to New York City. He studied music under top teachers and was soon playing trumpet for the Metropolitan Opera. Goldman later formed his own band and became nationally known for his work with young bands such as Eleanor's. He was also, as Eleanor recalled, a close friend of John Philip Sousa.

New Bedford was sort of a divided town. We had a large Portuguese population in the south end and the French Canadians lived in the north end. Most of these children were fairly good at English, but the French Canadians did have some strange ways of saying things. However, I never noticed any problems with ethnic groups. Everyone ran with your own crowd - you know, the people in your own neighborhoods. When I was in school most of us envied the Jewish kids because they got all the holidays off - theirs and ours! Our family belonged to the North Baptist Church....it was near our home and we went to services every Sunday morning. As far as I can remember, we had no Portuguese or Canadians in our church.

My father always had his job during the Depression working for Hathaway Machinery Company doing work on the fishing fleet. Dad had invented a device to allow work on marine engines without having to take the engine apart. He traveled all over the East Coast showing other people how to use this equipment. We were by no means rich, but we always pretty much had everything we needed. Mother was a homemaker.... there were not many working moms in our neighborhood at that time. Most of the kids at my school were dressed well, and I didn't see many people near us who were in a bad way. We were always a frugal family. My mother always said, "Use it up, wear it out, or do without!"

Our family generally socialized with neighbors and friends and we would go on vacations in the summer. Often, we would drive to Lake Winnipesaukee up in New Hampshire on these vacations. I remember once going up to Maine. When I was small, we would go in an Oakland Touring Car which my father had. I remember that when it rained you had to button up the windows which had some black material with a piece of glass in them. Later he had a Whippet Sedan for a few years, then a Chevrolet 4-door sedan, then a Mercury. He didn't have a lot of brand loyalty in cars!

The Oakland Motor Car Company was one of early brands of automobiles. It was named for Oakland County, Michigan where it was built. The owners joined General Motors Corporation in 1909 and sold 5000 Oakland cars in 1912. Oaklands were noted for their attractiveness, including brass headlamps and radiator. Most models originally sold for $1600 and were considerably pricier than Model T Fords, but by the 1920's the price was reduced to under $1100 - still far more than the Fords. One of the sales gimmicks during the 1920's was painting the cars a bright blue and calling them "True Blue Oakland." Oaklands were produced until 1931 when the line was dropped in favor of GM's Pontiac brand. The Whippet was built in Toledo, Ohio by the Willys-Overland Corporation in the late 1920's. It was small and quick - hence the name. The cost was low - ranging between $525 and $850. The car was an instant hit; over 100,000 were produced in 1926. By 1931, Whippet's popularity had plummeted, and production was ceased. The company went on to make its mark as the producer of WW II Jeeps.

During the Depression we often had men knocking at our back door asking if Mother could spare any food because their families were hungry. She always gave them something. This happened frequently. They would always come but only to the back door because at that time that is the only door tradesmen were allowed to use. No one asking for food knocked at the front door. Occasionally a "rag man" would come down our street shouting, "Rags, rags, buying rags!" Mother always kept a bag of rags from old clothes in the basement to sell to him. He would also buy used tin foil from us. I also saw a lot of food lines because my father would take us to a different part of town to show us how good we had it. After its whaling days, New Bedford had been a cotton mill town and the mill workers had been on strike for over a year. Finally, the mill owners just closed the mills and moved south leaving all those people unemployed. The ones in the food lines were mostly men and the lines were long. I remember my dad telling us, "Those people are hungry."

My father hated President Roosevelt. He always said that Roosevelt had sent our country down the road to ruin. He believed that everything would have worked itself out if Roosevelt had not put in all those welfare programs. Whenever the talk would come up at dinner about the CCC or WPA [Civilian Conservation Corps and Works Progress Administration, two public works programs which were part of Roosevelt's New Deal], he would yell, "All those people, they're all leaning on their shovels. It's no wonder that they're all going to vote for Roosevelt." My mother would then try to calm him down. There were no Democrats in our house! All of us true Yankees were Republicans; all those "others" were Democrats. We voted at the firehouse and I always voted Republican. Later us original Yankees were outnumbered by all the immigrants and the area became Democratic. I knew no one near us who was in the CCC or WPA. I had no problem with the immigrants who were Portuguese. Many of them had come many years ago on whaling ships from the Azores. In fact, one of the three people I later worked with was Hilda whose folks were from the Azores. She would collect clothes to send back to relatives there.

I did not get the impression that Eleanor was anti-immigrant or racist when I spoke with her. She was, however, very proud of her "Yankee" heritage and frankly shared with me how she felt at the time. Like many children of her era, she readily adopted her parents' beliefs and political leanings. The Portuguese community was still very much in evidence when I was living in the region near Eleanor's home in the mid-1960's.

After high school, my boyfriend, Raymond Daniels, taught me how to drive in a Model A Ford Roadster. It was his own car. I had met him during high school. All the boys I dated in high school are now dead. Before I graduated, I was offered a job at a local insurance office, Wefer and Parker, and I took it. Mr. Parker had contacted one of the high school *teachers and asked if they could recommend a student. I was selected to go to the interview and got the job. I took a trolley to the office and was paid $15 a week. I was happy with that because I felt very lucky to have any job during the Depression. I was living at home and stayed with that job until WW II.*

One of my strongest memories of the late 1930's was the big hurricane that hit us. It didn't even have a name! It came ashore without warning down on Long Island and then came up the Sound and went through us. There were trees down everywhere and many homes were seriously damaged. We had some problems - no power for a long time, but our house had only minor damage. We were lucky because many people were killed, but no one we knew. I remember it well....it was on September 21, 1938. There was flooding everywhere, and some people were left homeless. It's one of those things that you remember forever.

The hurricane of 1938 has often been called "The Great New England Hurricane" or, because of its speed, "The Long Island Express," "The Yankee Clipper," or just "The Big One." It came with little advance warning because the hurricane had stayed off the coast over the warm waters of the Gulf Stream and had not seriously affected the east coast. Also New Englanders had become complacent with respect to hurricanes. No significant storm had hit the area since 1815. This hurricane was moving at an unusually high speed (estimated at nearly 50 mph) and, accordingly, had highly destructive winds in its "dangerous semi-circle." Hurricanes are low pressure weather systems with winds which rotate counterclockwise in the northern hemisphere. If the hurricane itself has internal winds of 120 mph, the effect on the eastern side of the storm moving at that speed is 170 mph winds. Church steeples were sheared off, the storm surge of 15 feet flooded coastal areas, and wind gusts of 186 mph were recorded. Close to 600 people lost their lives and property damage exceeded $600 million ($40 billion in current dollars). Over 20,000 miles of power lines were knocked down, so it is not surprising that Eleanor's family was without electricity and phone for a long period after the storm. It is estimated that two billion trees throughout New England were lost. It is understandable that the storm and its aftermath were seared in Eleanor's memory.

The insurance company I worked for was associated with Liberty Mutual. We sold all types of insurance. Auto insurance was paid annually - usually about $40. The life insurance company we used was Northwestern Mutual. Mr. Parker was an interesting fellow. He never married and had a summer home on Mount Desert Island in Maine. He was wealthy and did golf trips to Pinehurst down in North Carolina. Mr. Parker would give us a Christmas bonus of $25. He had quite a few racehorses and raced them at Narragansett Racetrack in nearby Providence [Rhode Island]. If one of his horses won, there would be an envelope on each of our desks the next Monday with the amount of money a $2 bet paid. We ourselves never bet of course....it was just his way of sharing what he got when his horse won. He once took us to the track to watch the races. We always had Wednesday afternoon off so that's when we went. After I had worked there for a while, I got a raise to $20 a week, and by 1940 I was making $25 a week.

When the war began in late 1941, my younger brother was in a prep school after he had graduated from high school. Immediately after Pearl Harbor, he enlisted and was later seriously injured in the Battle of the Bulge. Most of the boys in my high school class also joined the services and served in the war. I got involved myself, because in early 1942 the Insurance company, Liberty Mutual, asked several of us women around the country who were working for them if we wanted to go to Hawaii to work out there. There were three of us who said yes. We took the train to San Francisco and then a ship to Honolulu where my older sister was a nurse for the Red Cross. In 1939 she had been working at a hospital in Providence, Rhode Island and had volunteered to do nursing for a year for the Red Cross in San Francisco. She got there just two months before Pearl Harbor and so, after the war began, she stayed with the Red Cross and moved to Honolulu. That's how I met my husband. I was working for Liberty Mutual there and living with my sister. He was an Army officer and had been seated on a plane next to my sister flying back from the big island [the big island in the Hawaiian Island chain is named Hawaii; Honolulu is on the island of Oahu] and invited him to dinner with us. His name was Fred Fader. He must have liked either the food or me, because he started coming to our house frequently for dinner. We were married

on December 4, 1943 but didn't get to spend much time together after that because he was sent to the South Pacific. He fought at Iwo Jima in the 147th regiment. He survived that battle and the rest of the war. My husband was a genuinely nice man, and we had a wonderful marriage: two children and many years together.

I was not aware that U.S. Army troops had participated in the Iwo Jima battle. While I was attending the Naval Academy, I had learned much about the important role which the Navy and the Marine Corps had played in this ferocious battle in early 1945. Although the Navy's Fifth Fleet and three Marine divisions were the primary U.S. forces, there was aerial support by the Seventh Air Force and the 147th Army Infantry Regiment. It was a bloody battle and was one of the only Pacific War battles where total American casualties exceeded those of the Japanese. Because Eleanor did not mention Fred being injured, I assume that he was one of the fortunate ones who survived the battle unharmed.

Although Eleanor had stated in the beginning of our talk that her life "was not remarkable," I found her memories to provide an insight into aspects of the Great Depression that were markedly different from people I interviewed in other regions of the U.S. Her family was certainly not wealthy, but because her father had steady employment and their family owned their home, she did not face the economic challenges endured by many others. To gain a broad understanding of that era, it is important to know that, like her father, not everyone was in love with President Roosevelt and his New Deal programs. In fact, there was considerable opposition both in Congress and in many parts of the country where traditional values were dominant. Some argue that Roosevelt's policies would have led to a total economic collapse if it had not been for the beginning of WW II providing a massive boost in employment and manufacturing.

I found it interesting that as a young woman, Eleanor, a very proud "Yankee," chose to leave her comfortable living in Massachusetts and travel alone not only across the country, but to then go on to Hawaii during the war. At that time, it was not certain that the U.S. would win the war or that it was safe to be in Hawaii. It certainly turned out to be a good decision, because she met her future husband there and created a lasting marriage and family.

"The Ballplayer"
Bill and Louise Curry

Ludlow, KY
Interviewed Feb 2, 1996

WHILE VISITING FRIENDS FROM MY days growing up in the northern Kentucky region, I inquired if they knew anyone in the area who had been involved with the Depression-era programs, the CCC (Civilian Conservation Corps) or the WPA (Work Progress Administration). A parent of one of my buddies quickly offered, "I know someone who did both. You need to talk to Bill Curry." He then added a teaser, "I think that you will find some of his other activities from that time very interesting."

When I phoned Bill's number, my call was answered on the first ring by a woman who identified herself as "Mrs. Curry." I explained that I wanted to talk to her husband about their life during the 1930's. She enthusiastically replied, "He's a talker. I'm certain he would love for you to hear his stories. I'll be out for the next hour, but if you're coming now, I can fill in some blanks that he may forget when I get back. I'm Louise. Come on over."

I easily located their modest home on an older residential street in Ludlow. There had been a light snow overnight, and their street had not yet been plowed. It is rare to have snowfalls greater than six inches in this region, so it is equally rare to see a snowplow. One of our jokes at that time was that most of the snow removal equipment in northern Kentucky is solar powered.

Bill warmly greeted me at the door. He was tall and lean and was wearing a long sleeve shirt buttoned at the collar. Before he closed the door, he pointed down the street to show me the house, only a few doors down the street, where he was born in 1912. I knew from growing up in the area that Ludlow is, and has always been, a working-class neighborhood. It sits on the southern bank of the Ohio River directly across from the western suburbs of Cincinnati, Ohio. While offering me coffee (it was a very cold February morning), Bill mentioned that he and Louise were married in a local Catholic church in 1938, one year after meeting on a blind date at a dance sponsored by the "Junior Order," a youth group sponsored by The Order of the Knights of Pythias. Bill could not remember much about the group other than they put on dances at a hall where "The Lodge" met. I later learned that the Knights still exist as a non-sectarian fraternity. They were founded in 1864 under a charter by Congress, and, according to their website, only "after careful review by President Lincoln." Apparently, two Ancient Greek characters, Damon and Pythias, both students of the famed mathematician, Pythagoras, were steadfast friends and were known for helping others. The fraternal organization remains alive and well today - one of the local lodges in New York just made a large donation during the COVID-19 pandemic for hot meals for seniors. Regardless of the history of the organization, Bill and Louise getting together at that Depression-era dance produced a long-lived marriage.

Once Bill and I began our conversation about the early days of his life, his first words were....

You know, we were as poor as church mice. I was born at St. Elizabeth Hospital over in Covington on December 10, 1912. Dad was a boilermaker for the C&O railroad. He worked at the roundhouse out on Madison, and as I was growing up, it seemed like they were always on strike, especially around Christmas. Mom was a homemaker....not many women had jobs then. I went to St. Ann's Catholic grade school and then Holmes, the public high school in Covington because we couldn't afford the tuition at the Catholic high school. I had to quit school in the 11th grade when my father got laid off to go to work to help support our family.

In late 1928 I got a job with the Cassini Tile Company across the river in Cincinnati. My job was to get the tile ready for the setters. I got $12 a week, which I had to give to my Mom. My older brother, George, was two years older than me and got me the job....he was one of the tile setters. We were both living at home and had to walk five miles across the Suspension Bridge to get to work. I didn't like that job, so I quit after two years, but told my Mom that I got laid off. I never told her the truth on this.

We were now in the Depression, but I was able to get some jobs shoveling coal - not the small pebbles, but the big lumps. I also had two younger sisters, Katherine and Dorothy, so we just never had much money. My mother was always scrambling trying to make ends meet. When the stock markets crashed and the banks closed, we were lucky because we had no money to lose. When Roosevelt came into office in early 1933, he had this 100-day program to put people back to work. One of those programs was the CCC, and I immediately enlisted for six months. It was sort of like the Army. They sent us down to Fort Knox, south of Louisville, where we had a two-week initiation, which was like a boot camp. When that was over, they shuttled us off to work camps. We didn't have a choice where we were sent. Some went out west, but I got trucked to a place called Wooten down in the mountains in eastern Kentucky....not sure that town is still there. It was real small. Our job was to help local farmers tear down trees and put in some erosion gullies. We stayed in tents, but didn't wear uniforms, just coveralls. We had reveille at 6 AM and worked until 4 in the afternoon. Then we had different athletic events, like baseball, boxing, or running contests. There were about 125 of us fellows, all between 16 and 25. An Army 2nd Lieutenant was in charge. We didn't have any electricity and no hot water. Our parents got paid something like $22 a month, and we got something smaller for ourselves, maybe 7 or 8 dollars. But we had cooks and ate good. I went *back home after my six months were up. I didn't want to be there during the winter.*

During my interviews with several men who had worked with the Civilian Conservation Corps (CCC), I heard different numbers concerning the pay, but generally the figure was in the vicinity of $30 a month (which was the official number). What was certain that about $25 was mandated to be sent home to the parents, while the young men could keep approximately $5. That $30 wage is equivalent to about $600 today. A side benefit of the CCC was an increased appreciation of outdoor recreational activities because many of the projects involved building or improving state and national parks. For example, much of the infrastructure of the Shenandoah National Park was built by the CCC. Sixty years later the high school cross country team which I was coaching stayed in cabins built by the CCC during pre-season training at Cacapon State Park in West Virginia.

Bill continued his memories of the mid-1930's:

There still was no steady work available, but I got on with the WPA in 1935. I worked three days a week with them for the next couple of years. These jobs were local, in the area around here. I lived at home with my parents. We did a lot of work loading rocks into trucks on jobs up in Goebel Park and in Devoe Park, both here in Covington. We also built two high schools, Simon Kenton and Dixie Heights. I was paid 35 cents an hour and usually worked 8 hours a day. Our bosses were older construction guys or WW I veterans, and they made more - not sure how much more. I brought all my money home to my parents except for a few dollars.

I never got to play sports in high school because I had come from that Catholic grade school....the public school wouldn't let me on any of their teams. But I was a pretty good at baseball and hit left-handed. In 1935 that skill got me a full-time job with the gas company, Union Light and Power because I got recruited to play for the company fast pitch softball team. They gave me a job as a laborer digging ditches for the next 10 months. I was paid 35 cents an hour, but really, I got the job because I could hit. Next year we got a raise of 2 1/2 cents an hour and I became a pipefitter putting in black iron gas manifolds for houses that were getting gas. Even though the company fought it, the union, which was part of the CIO, organized us in 1936, and we got a dollar an hour raise. I worked for the gas company up to the war and ended up driving my own truck.

I don't remember needing to get a driver's license then. I had saved up some money and bought a car in 1937, a black Ford V-8....I paid $714 for it and financed it at $24 a month. Gas was 15 cents a gallon so I could get around. I was still living at home.

At this time Louise came home and joined our conversation. She was 6 years younger than Bill, and considerably shorter. She was wearing a long-sleeved rugby style shirt emblazoned with the logo of the University of Kentucky. She repeated what Bill told me, that they were married in 1938, a year after they had met at the dance. For most of their first year of marriage, they lived with her parents before moving into a 3-room apartment above a grocery store. Bill turned to Louise and asked her to tell me about their first years together:

We were paying $22.50 a month for that apartment, but it included heat and water. We had to pay for the electricity. Bill probably didn't tell you, but after we met at that dance, we dated about once a week. We were married by a priest, Father Ennis, up at St. Ann's where we both had gone to church. We lived in that 3-room rented apartment up on Parkway until after the war when we bought this house here in 1946. Our first child, William, Jr., was born on August 5, 1939 at St. Elizabeth Hospital. Everything went OK, but they kept me in the hospital for 10 days....that was pretty much normal then. The bill for the hospital and the doctor was less than $100 - do you believe that? Those were real hard times for us. We ate OK, but there was no money for much else. Our other child, James, was also born at St. E's after the war, but I didn't have to stay as long, and it cost more. As I was coming in, I heard you ask Bill if he voted. He always told me that in 1932 he voted for Hoover, but learned his lesson, and then always voted for Roosevelt. I just never voted back at that time in my life....in fact, I can't remember when I first voted.

Bill worked all during the first part of the war, but we still had it bad. He finally got inducted in 1943 and was first getting $50 a month, but due to having construction experience, he got into the Seabees which paid better...I think it was $96/month. They also gave us $50/month for our first child and when he got shipped over to the South Pacific, he got 20% extra for overseas duty. I did odd jobs during the war, always being real careful with our money. I bet that Bill didn't tell you much about his ball playing days....he was real good and played all over the place before the war. Tell him about it, Bill.

At this point, Bill sort of shuffled in his chair as if slightly embarrassed and mildly annoyed at Louise for bringing it up. But he quickly perked up and told me of his sporting adventures with great enthusiasm.

Well, I told you how I got on with the gas company because they wanted someone for their fast pitch softball team who could hit and was left-handed. I was also on a semi-pro baseball team called the Kentucky Colonels. We played those games over at the Northside ballpark - pretty sure it's no longer there. Next year I played every Sunday on a baseball team put together by Jake Martz out at Martz playground in Ross. I'm sure that you are familiar with that place....it had a big picnic area, a swimming pool, and a real nice baseball field. The only one of us players who got paid each game was the pitcher. At the end of the season, Mr. Martz would divide up some money to give to each of the rest of us....I got 75 dollars one year. There were some pretty good ball players on those teams. That Hall of Famer, Jim Bunning, pitched out there as a teenager when he was in school at Xavier before he went pro. I guess you know that he pitched a perfect game for the Phillies back in '64. After he retired from baseball, he became a politician. He moved up the ranks and is now our Congressman.

During our conversation on his sporting career, Bill went back and forth discussing baseball and softball. When he used the term "baseball" he was referring to the game played by Major League Baseball teams, such as his beloved Cincinnati Reds, using a "hard ball" which is 9 inches in circumference and weighs approximately 5 ounces. The core is cork and is wrapped in yarn covered in two strips of leather sewn together to make a sphere. It is played today by male high school and college teams, but there are few remaining "semi-pro" baseball teams. There are two variants of softball: fast pitch, which Bill played, and which is currently played by female high school and college teams, and slow pitch, which is generally the variety played recreationally (for example, in church leagues). Interestingly, there are several different size softballs, depending on which type of game is being played. Fast pitch softballs are larger than baseballs and are generally 11 inches in diameter. Some slow pitch leagues use larger balls with diameters up to 16 inches. All softballs have the same type of core as a hardball but are not wound with yarn. During Bill's era, many cities and small towns all had fast pitch softball leagues, but the sport has died out in many places, except for the women's teams mentioned above.

At that time fast pitch softball was also real big around here. We had the Cincinnati baseball team, the Reds, of course, but there was a lot more fast pitch softball being played in local leagues here than baseball. A lot of saloons had teams that they sponsored. I got onto Polher's Cafe team in 1939 and played centerfield for them. We had a real good team and won the Cincinnati area title and then went to Chicago where we won the national championship. The next three years that team was sponsored by Nick Carr who had a cafe and was a real softball nut. We traveled all over the country by train: Chicago, St. Louis, Little Rock, and places in Michigan. We even went to Phoenix where we again won the national championship. Carr paid us all our travel expenses. We were all local boys - no ringers. Everybody knew about us. Other teams were always trying to steal our best players. This team up in Fort Wayne, the Zoelner Pistons, finally stole our pitcher and catcher by giving them jobs on the side where they didn't have to work. Fans didn't have to pay admission to any of these local games, but sometimes they passed the hat. If you were a real good pitcher, you could make big bucks playing fast pitch softball. There was a fellow here named Cannonball Bailey who in the early 30's made $25 a game pitching because you couldn't hit him. You might get lucky and get one hit, but that was all. Cannonball pitched two games a night, seven days a week - all at $25 a game. You can add it up....that was incredible money during the Depression! After the war, we also had Eddie Feigner come to town to play our local *all-star team. I got to play one time against his team, the King and his Court, and never touched any of his pitches. He only had three other players on that team, and they beat the socks off us. Most of us struck out....I heard more of his pitches than I saw!*

I was getting their feeling that Bill could talk about both baseball and softball for the rest of the afternoon, but Louise interrupted him saying, "Bill, Mr. Linz has been here over two hours. We need to let him go." When I requested a photo, Louise suggested that it be taken in front of a cabinet holding glassware that they obtained when they were married.

One of the things which struck me on the way back to my friend's home was the precision with which both Bill and Louise recalled the exact amounts of their pay and expenses from fifty plus years ago. Those figures, always small, were indelibly etched in their memories. The fact that Louise remembered those numbers, but not when she first voted, is telling. Every cent obviously counted to most members of this generation. There was no room for non-essential spending.

Two of Bill's baseball and softball stories hit close to home for me. I grew up in the same area, although 30 years later, and had spent many Sunday afternoons watching baseball games at that Martz playground. The quality of play was indeed very good, and once our family paid admission to enter the park, everything inside was free. The baseball field provided a close-up view of the game because the stands were behind a screen no more than 10 feet from the catcher. It was at one of these games that I first saw a successful "suicide squeeze" to end a game - a memory which has stuck with me throughout my life. The baseball All-Star and Congressman Bill mentioned, Jim Bunning, went on to become a U.S. Senator, the only one from our part of the state in recent memory. He still holds the distinction of being the only person to have been a member of both the U.S. Senate and the Baseball Hall of Fame.

Bill's discussion of Eddie Feigner also brought back memories. I had the good fortune to see The King and His Court on several occasions, both in Kentucky, and on military bases in Virginia and Connecticut. Feigner had been in the Marines during the war and during his tours always ensured that they played exhibitions against local all-star military teams both in the U.S. and on bases overseas. He always donated all the proceeds from these games to military charities, such such as the USO (United Service Organizations). Throughout his career he kept meticulous records of the greater than 10,000 games he pitched. Of those, he won 9743 with 930 no-hitters and 238 perfect (no hits, no walks) games. In addition to being a superb athlete, he was the consummate showman. In every game he would pitch blindfolded to one batter, from second base to another, and from behind his back or between his legs. He sometimes even pitched from center field. He began his barnstorming tour around the U.S and the world (all 50 states and 98 foreign countries) in 1946. At age 41, in a 1967 exhibition game at Dodger Stadium in Los Angeles, he struck out six future Hall of Fame baseball players in succession, including Willie Mays and Roberto Clemente. No one to date has surpassed his timed speed pitching a softball. What was remarkable about Feigner's team was that it consisted of only 4 players: Feigner pitching, a catcher, shortstop and first baseman. If someone was lucky enough to hit the ball to the outfield (an exceedingly rare event), the shortstop chased it down. Feigner suffered several strokes later in life, but still traveled with his team providing colorful stories for those in attendance. He died in 2007. Both Bill and I had big smiles while we were talking about this man who was indeed a legend in his own time.

President Roosevelt's New Deal programs, the CCC and WPA, certainly played a significant role in Bill's and his family's life. Without that additional income, their lives would have been considerably more challenging - as would many of the millions who participated in those work opportunities. One of Bill's comments was, "Everybody I knew joined the CCC."

Although the CCC and WPA were terminated when WW II broke out, many of the programs initiated in the New Deal remain today, such as Social Security, the Federal Deposit Insurance Corporation (FDIC), the Security and Exchange Commission (SEC), the Federal Housing Administration (FHA) and the National Labor Relations Board (NLRB). Most of these programs did not have an immediate effect on 1930's citizens like Bill and Louise but did help to establish stability in those financially desperate times. The CCC ultimately employed over 3 million young men (ages 18-25 were initially eligible but was later broadened to 17-28). Only 300,000 were eligible at one time, and many, like Bill, served only 6-12 months. During its 9-year existence, members of the CCC planted over three billion trees and constructed trails and shelters in over 800 parks. Roosevelt used the Army to transport many of these young men from their homes in the east to work camps throughout the U.S. Although Bill did not mention it, many of the illiterate members of the CCC received basic educational training and learned to read and write. There were even provisions for providing work for Native Americans; 88,000 were employed, mostly doing work on reservations. Not everything was positive about the CCC. In addition to prohibiting women, all African-American members were assigned to segregated camps where they had to live and work among themselves. Segregation was a disturbing part of America during the 1930's.

Bill obviously was in the right place at the right time for both the CCC and the WPA. He was able to obtain work with the WPA shortly after it began by Presidential Executive Order early in 1935. The unemployment level was at 20% nationally, and by 1938, nearly five million Americans had been employed by the WPA. Although the work was not necessarily full-time, it did provide much needed assistance not only for laborers, such as Bill, but also for artists, actors, writers, and musicians in a program called Project Number One. This program was started, allegedly, due to the lobbying of First Lady Eleanor Roosevelt. At its height there were over 5000 artists working. As opposed to the CCC, women were allowed to work for the WPA, and roughly 15% of the overall WPA workforce were African-American. Obviously, there was both praise and criticism of these and other New Deal programs. Many considered the CCC and WPA to be wasteful, inefficient, and simply pointless. Unions complained because the wages were far below those of their members. Others even coined the term "boondoggle" to ridicule many of the projects which occasionally cost many times what the same private work would run. What I do know is that Bill and his family were among the millions who benefited greatly.

"The Farm Girl"
Doris Pentecost

Moss Creek, MO
Interviewed July 15, 1997

I WAS IN PRESCOTT, ARIZONA, VISITING a college friend who was the Chief Flight Instructor at Embry-Riddle Aeronautical University, located north of town just past the Willow Creek Reservoir. His advice was, "While you are in the area, you need to visit this place in Prescott where a lot of older folks live. You are certain to find some good stories there."

I had no problem finding "the place." It was an old, stately brick and wooden structure which sits on a granite hill overlooking the Prescott town square. Directly above two flights of stairs with multiple handrails leading to the entrance a set of black, block letters on white horizontal boarding proclaimed, "ARIZONA PIONEERS' HOME". Six tall white cylindrical columns supported a balcony overlooking the entire main building. There was an additional wing to the left of the same brick architecture which obviously had been added at a later date. After entering and talking to a receptionist, I learned that this complex is a continuing care retirement home built in 1910 as a resting place for some of the original settlers who had come to Arizona to help populate the area. At the time, Arizona was still a territory (statehood came in 1912). The home was originally funded by the Arizona Territorial Legislature and was built on donated land. Interestingly, the architect was a local woman, W.S. Elliott, who had designed several other large buildings in Prescott in the early 1900's. The original criterion was that the occupants should be destitute men, who had been living in Arizona at least 25 years. Roughly ten years later, private money was used to add a wing for women. Near the end of the 1920's disabled miners were allowed entry.

One of the more famous residents of the Pioneers' Home original women's wing was "Big Nose Kate" (Mary Katherine Horony), a notorious madam of an Arizona brothel. She was a Hungarian immigrant whose life story rivals the most outrageous novel. She has been described as being "very beautiful, but with a large nose." One of Kate's accomplishments was that she was the common law wife of Doc Holliday, the famous gunslinger, gambler, and....dentist! Apparently, Holliday worked as a dentist during the day and gambled in Prescott at night, while Kate "worked" upstairs. It was here in Prescott that they met up with the Earp brothers. Later all were involved in the famous "Gunfight at OK Corral" in the silver mining town of Tombstone near the Mexican border. Kate always alleged that she watched that action from the safety of a boarding house where she was staying with Holliday. In her later years she petitioned to be admitted to the Pioneers' Home, but was initially denied because she had not been born in the U.S. After many attempts to gain admittance, Kate was granted entry by the Arizona governor, whom she described as "a long-time friend." Her admission was greatly to the benefit of the home, if only due to her notorious (and entertaining) stories which she gleefully shared with fellow residents.

The Pioneers' Home has been expanded over the years; when I visited, it had a capacity of just over 150. Most of the costs are still paid by the state, although some residents now pay a portion of their expenses. After explaining to the receptionist my purpose for visiting, I spotted several residents in a sitting room and approached an older attractive woman wearing a sleeveless white blouse embroidered with bunch of grapes on the left side. She was wearing shorts and had dark hair in what appeared to be a curly perm. She smiled when I introduced myself and told her of my goal of interviewing people who had memories from the Great Depression.

"You know, I'm a Notch Kid." This was how Doris Mildred Pentecost introduced herself.

I'm not sure you know what that means. See, that's what they call all of us born between 1917 and 1921. We were notched out. I call it "screwed." The government messed up with our cost-of-living calculations for our Social Security back in the 70's, and they made it up to us. So, we are Notch Kids...some call us Notch Babies....no matter what they call it, we didn't get what was coming to us. It still costs me around $300 a month.

I was born on a farm on February 2, 1918 in Carroll County, Missouri in the township of Moss Creek. That's closer to Kansas City to the west than St. Louis to the east. It was real country. My parents were mostly German. I had one full-blooded brother and three half-brothers - they were all older than me. My mother - her name was Opal - died right after I was born due to that Spanish flu that was getting everyone. It settled in her heart. I was always told that she was over six feet tall, but, go figure, I'm only 5'2".

We were poor dirt farmers. Right after mother died, we went to live with my grandmother nearby, and Dad - his name was Fred Boone Herbert - grew wheat and corn on the farm as cash crops. We raised just about everything we needed. Dad used draft horses to farm...he liked only the real big horses. My dad remarried when I was almost five. My stepmother, Frances Katherine Macumbrie, was Irish. That was a BIG wedding. She told me that they were chivareed. It went on for 4 or 5 nights, people banging pots and pans and shooting guns in the air. They took her to the wedding in a wheelbarrow. There was supposed to be no moonshine or whiskey drinking, but two cousins lived for two days on whiskey and water and then died! They didn't even need to get embalmed.

Doris told me this last part of the wedding story without cracking a smile. I could not tell if she was joking or if these deaths actually happened. I learned during my time with Doris that she had a very dry sense of humor. I was not familiar with the term "chivaree" (which Doris spelled for me). I later learned that there are many different forms of spelling for the word. When I later looked up its meaning and origin, I found that it was a folk custom typically consisting of a mock parade with discordant music, often made with pots and pans. The intention was to make as much noise as possible. Doris did not mention whether or not the purpose of this chivaree was to express approval, or disapproval, of her father remarrying. In many instances, this type of event took place because the community disapproved of a widower remarrying too soon or taking a younger bride. I wish that I had asked her more on this. I do know that as a child in Kentucky every wedding that I attended involved metal objects being tied to the bumper of the newlywed's car so that they would have a noisy departure from the church.

My stepmother was good to me, but she was not a loving person. I called her Mom, but our relationship was more functional than warm. She had three children with Dad, but I mostly became their mother. They even called me Mommy. These were real hard times for us then. I had two dresses. I would wear one for a week, and the other the next week. We used a #3 wash tub for bathing, which we did once a week. After we would heat the water from a dug well on a coal stove and pour it into the tub, we would start with the baby and work our way up to the oldest in that same water. I never wore shoes in the summer, but I do remember drinking a lot of "cold tea" - that's what we called it....no ice, of course....we never had any during the summers...just used cold water. Every Christmas our grandfather in Arkansas would send us a gunny sack of raw peanuts which we would roast and eat with some popcorn during evenings after supper. We grew our own popcorn.

We ate ok, and never went hungry. We just didn't have much else. There was no electricity out there and no phones, of course. We raised chickens, pigs, horses, and cows. Dad would butcher a hog, but never any beef....I don't know why not...in fact, no one I knew back there ever butchered a cow. Everyone just ate pork and chicken. On Sundays we always ate fried chicken, and my mother would always give each of us our favorite piece. She ate the liver, and Dad ate the gizzard. That made me curious and I always wanted to see what they tasted like. I finally did much later, and I liked both. Whenever we had visitors, like our preacher, or men from the thrashing crew helping to harvest the wheat, all us children had to wait to eat second. Kids were never allowed to drink coffee like the adults. Because of the cows, we always had plenty of milk. It was raw milk, of course, and we kept it in the cellar where it was always cool. Mother made our own butter and sold cream and eggs to buy sugar and flour.

One year, just before harvest time for the wheat, we had a big hailstorm which pretty much destroyed the entire crop. Our farm had to contend with grasshoppers, locusts, and drought, and in 1932 we lost the farm. Dad had borrowed money from the bank for seeds and couldn't pay it back, so the bank took the farm. We lost everything. That's when we moved to Sugar Tree...not too far away....I always described it as a wider spot in the road. It had a blacksmith shop, a grocery store, and maybe seven homes. We moved into a 2-story white house but didn't use most of it because we had so little furniture. The Gilead Baptist Church was up on the hill...that's where mama was buried.

I was raised very religiously. We were "hard-skilled Baptists." We went to church on Wednesday nights and twice on Sundays. The first one in the morning included Sunday school. Then everyone would go together to someone's house to eat lunch together with the preacher - he was single and lived up in Norborne, about 20 miles away - and then we would all come back for an afternoon service where he preached for about an hour. We had an old Model A to go to church during the summers and fall, but in the winter and spring, it was so muddy on those dirt roads that we had to go by a horse pulling a wagon with us in it. We called the mud in those roads "gumbo" cuz it was like glue. There was no way to drive a car in that stuff. In the winter when it was so cold, dad would put down a layer of straw on the bottom of the wagon, and my mom *would put some warm bricks that she had heated on the stove on top of the straw and she and us kids would lay down on top of this and cover ourselves with blankets to keep warm.*

Every summer the folks in our area would hold an outdoor revival. It would go every night for two weeks. I was nine years old when I gave my heart to God. That event was held in a church, not during one of those revivals. We had to go up to Norborne to get baptized because our church had no baptismal pit where you were dunked. We did not baptize babies.

I didn't have any girls my age to play with, so I had to play boy games with my older brother and his buddies. They were mostly mean to me and wouldn't let me join the games unless I stole matches for them to use smoking corn silk and grape leaves. We would sail tin dishes and play catchers and stuff like that. I became pretty much a tomboy. One Christmas my parents gave me a dumb doll and I was so mad because I wanted a pocketknife. My dad smoked, but not my mom. He had a corn pipe and used to smoke Prince Albert tobacco or RJR, which we used to call "Run Johnny, Run."

I went to 7th grade twice. When we lived out there on that farm, I had to walk three miles each way to school. It was a one-room schoolhouse for grades one through seven. There was one teacher - her name was Marie Ault. She taught grades 1 through 7 one year and then 6 through 8 the next. In winter, there was not much farming in the fields, so Dad would walk in front of us to slush the snow out of the path. When we got to the schoolhouse, he would start the fire to get the room warm for us. When we moved up to Sugar Tree after losing the farm, I was 13 and I went to 7th grade again. There wasn't a high school there.

Like I said, those winters were real cold. We had wool blankets and even a comforter which my mom made with cotton batting. We slept on a feather bed, which meant that we had a layer of feathers inside sheets made of old flour sacks. That was on top of straw ticking, also inside sacks, which sat on top of some springs sitting on wooden slats. A lot of our material came from those flour sacks, even our underwear, men and women's. My mom would use Fels-Naptha soap to get rid of the dye markings on those sacks before she sewed them into things. We also used that Fels-Naptha for mosquito and chiggers bites.

We went on welfare, so that Dad would be eligible for a job with the WPA [the Works Progress Administration, a Depression-era public works program]. His job with them was over in Waverly on the other side of the Missouri River. He would leave home every Sunday night and come back the following Friday night. Then he heard about a strike up in Omaha, Nebraska at the Street Railway Company, so we moved up there where he got a job as a scab [the derogatory term used to describe a strike-breaker hired to do the work of those on strike]. When we moved to Omaha I could go to high school, but that was the first time I was exposed to Black people. [Here Doris freely used the "n-word" to describe this encounter and several other incidents whenever Blacks were mentioned. She told me near the end of our conversation that she no longer uses the term, but that is how she spoke then...."everyone around me did]. When I told Dad that I would not stay in school with these people, he told me that if I could find a place that would let me live there and work for them in return for room and board, I could do so. So, I did. I went out to Bellevue, a suburb of Omaha where there were no Blacks...in fact, they had signs on both ends of the town saying really bad things about what would happen to a Black if they were in the town after sunset. Anyway, I found a nice lady named Mrs. Maude Frazier who took me in. I did her wash, ironing, and housecleaning and provided her company. She became the loving mother I never had.

There is a funny, but terrible story about Mrs. Frazier. She was a very homely lady...not good looking, and she knew it. She told me that some of her cousins would make fun of her saying, "She was so ugly that she would stop a clock when she walked through the door." Well, according to Mrs. Frazier, this actually happened one time when she walked into their house and the clock stopped. Everyone, including her, thought it was hilarious. Can you imagine? The poor lady. They must have rigged that somehow. But I loved her and am still grateful.

I attended Bellevue High School and graduated in 1936. My girlfriends *and I dated some, but never serious. I did some babysitting for 25 cents for an evening, and 35 cents for all night. During the summer I also worked on a dairy for 10 cents an hour doing 10-12 hours a day. I always gave almost all this money to my mom so she could make me and my stepbrothers clothes and get me one new pair of shoes each year to begin school. I had to buy some pencils and paper for school because Nebraska didn't give them to students like they did in Missouri.*

There were 18 of us in our high school graduating class. We had no sports teams or clubs....just classes. During this time, I would ride the street cars in Omaha to get places....you paid with a token, and you could get three for a quarter. Dad was still working for the streetcar company in one of their boiler rooms, but that didn't get us a discount. Right after graduation I looked all over in the Omaha area for a job. I walked the streets lookin' but couldn't get a job doing nothing. Like I said, it was 1936, and there was hardly any jobs for women. So, I got married instead. His name was Rex Rogers. I met him through my girlfriend, Thelma Suess. He was her brother and was 19; I was 18. We got married in the latter part of 1936 down in Moberly, Missouri where he had family. It was maybe 50 miles east of where I grew up. I wore my graduation dress for my wedding dress. It was white in a whirlpool design and was made of taffeta.

Rex went to work for a poultry company pulling the big feathers out of the chickens as they passed in an assembly line. The chicken had been dipped first in hot water and after Rex did his job, the chickens went down the line to someone else. I couldn't get a job, and I got pregnant. We were first living down there with his parents. Our first child was born in 1937 at their home and was delivered by Doctor Griffiths. It cost $25 and my husband went out to his farm and worked for him until he paid off that $25. Rex's hands got so bad from pulling those feathers that he had to quit. We went on welfare to qualify for one of those WPA jobs building streets there in Moberly. It was a big railroad town....you know, the Wabash Cannonball came through there on the Rock Island Line... you know the train they sung that song about. Once we got our own house...it was very little and near the train tracks....the bums riding the rail cars would often come over and ask us for food. We always shared *food with them, and some of them would put a mark on your house so that other bums coming through would know where they could get food. We grew a lot of rabbits and I would fry them and grind them up to can.*

Here Doris gave me a lengthy tutorial on canning not only rabbits, but vegetables and fruits. She went into great detail, including drawing an annotated sketch in my notebook providing how much salt is to be added to the ground-up fried rabbit, and explicit instructions on the water bath which she used to preserve the jar and contents. She told me that in a typical year she would can over 1000 jars which would be used by her family throughout the following 12 months. During the past two summers at our "camp" (what cabins are called here in the woods of Northwest Maine), I have found canning jam to be one of my favorite hobbies. Many of the tips I received from Doris have come in handy, although I am certain that no matter how much jam I make, I will always remain in the novice division compared to her. My canning is a hobby; for Doris it was a necessary way of life. When I told Doris of my own experiences raising rabbits to eat and sell as a teen in Kentucky, I sensed that we had really bonded!

After considerably more discussion on canning and an awfully long explanation of how to make sauerkraut, Doris told me more about her marriages:

I had five kids in 12 years with Rex, the first three were born at home in Missouri, and the other two at a hospital in Omaha where we lived during the war. Rex was not a Christian like me. I suppose it was because his grandfather always called God a bastard. The wedding I told you about, it was not in a church, but before a Justice of the Peace. I think that it cost us $2.00. I know that I did not go to church while we were married....at first it was because I didn't have any decent clothes to wear. Rex had a heart attack in 1950 and died, leaving me with five kids. One thing I taught my kids was to always eat what's on your plate. That's what I learned during the Depression: clean up what's on your plate. You never know for sure where or when the next meal is coming.

I stayed in Omaha and met Bob Tilling at a dance. He was a year younger than me and had worked as a groom at the horse racing track in Omaha.

We got married and eventually moved out here to Arizona where he worked for the Salt River Power Company. But his lungs gave out, and he died. Then I met Tommy Pentecost while we were both in Phoenix. He was originally from Shaw, Mississippi, but had lived in Arizona a long time. He was 11 years younger than me, but when he retired, that is how we got eligible to live in this Arizona retirement place. He passed away just over a year ago on July 4th. That is why I didn't like all the fireworks less than two weeks ago because it reminded me of his death. That was the happiest of my three marriages.

Doris probably could have gone on with more stories....she had mentioned her own children, but it was lunchtime, and the residents were beginning to file into the dining hall. She readily agreed to photographs in several locations at the Pioneers' Home. She told me that if she didn't get to lunch it was "no problem, cuz they feed us way too much here."

We did have a long discussion of chiggers and blackberry picking that certainly brought back memories. In July of 1952, my family took a one-week vacation to visit Uncle Vance, one of my mother's brothers, who had a farm in West Plains, Missouri. We were riding in what was supposedly a "brand-new" Greyhound bus. Somewhere on one of the two-lane highways in the Missouri countryside, the bus broke down. It was an extremely hot day, so all the passengers got off the bus to sit alongside the road because we knew it was going to be a long wait. The next day my 7-year-old crotch was on fire - I had been attacked by chiggers while sitting in the grass alongside the road. The chiggers, I soon learned, are the larval stage of tiny red mites in the Trombiculidae family. Although they are in the same family as ticks, they do not burrow into the skin, but, after crawling into a moist area of your body, they use their claws to make tiny holes. Then they inject a fluid which turns body cells into a mushy substance which they eat for the next several days. I can attest that the resulting itch is ferocious and long-lasting. If you see a photo of someone's leg which has been attacked by chiggers, I guarantee that you will want to look away. During the week on my uncle's farm in Missouri, the women and the children picked blackberries every day for canning. I can confirm Doris' comments on the black snakes in the brambles - there were lots of them, but we did not see any poisonous snakes. We left Missouri with a suitcase full of blackberry jam....and many chigger welts.

I found that I admired Doris because she reminded me of my own mother. She spoke with a country accent, had a superb memory, and was brutally frank. Doris minced no words. If I was unsure how to spell one of the towns she mentioned, she immediately spelled it for me. In her life she had faced adversity from her earliest days, beginning with the loss of her mother. As the only girl in the family, she learned how to stand up to boys and to do whatever it took to get by. When she spoke of her inability to get work after high school, she nearly floored me with her matter-of-fact statement, "I couldn't get a job doing nothing, so I got married instead." In a way, Doris was somewhat akin to her famous predecessor at the Pioneers' Home, Fat Nose Kate. Both were rugged individualists with little time for sentiment. I got the impression that both Doris and Kate, who lived in male-dominated cultures, were comfortable doing whatever was necessary to survive. I am certain that they would be thriving and productive members of "modern society."

"The Republican Daughter"
Margaret Graves

West Union, OH
Interviewed March 5, 1996

WHEN SHE OPENED THE DOOR to her apartment in Washington, D.C., the handsome woman greeted me with, "Please call me 'Meg'." She was wearing a long-sleeved white blouse with ruffles around the neck and down the front. Her long skirt was cinched with a belt. Margaret Ellison Robuck Graves certainly was a very youthful-looking 82.

I had obtained Meg's name from Pat Graves, one of my wife's friends who was a neighbor in our Virginia suburb of D.C. "You have to meet my mother-in-law! She has some interesting stories about her life in Ohio during the Depression. She's Mike's stepmother." (Mike was Pat's husband). I found Meg's apartment on the 4th floor in a Northwest D.C. high-rise called the Quebec House which looks out on Rock Creek Park. When she learned during our interview that I had been in the Navy, she immediately took me to a framed photograph of one of her sisters, Roseanna Jane, who had been a Lieutenant Commander in the Navy. I quickly learned that Meg was a fast talker - so much so that I occasionally had to interrupt her to catch up with my notes. She was very sweet, but feisty....if that is a possible combination. Several times we stopped for lengthy laughs together over stories that we shared. Meg began telling me about the city of her birth:

I was born at home in West Union, Ohio on April 19, 1913. It is in southern Ohio, not too far from Portsmouth and the Ohio River. I was the seventh of eight children - four boys and four girls. I'm now the only one left. My father, Carey Ellison Robuck, was a "self-taught" lawyer - he never went to law school, but became a very respected, and successful, attorney there in Adams County. My mother, Clara Rebecca Brodt, had her hands full raising all eight of us. She was a saint! Father was always heavily immersed in Republican politics. Because he was deeply involved in local, state, and national politics, he was well known. He spent considerable effort promoting the political career of his fellow Ohioan, Warren G. Harding. Although he had helped Harding in his State Senate, Lieutenant Governor, and U.S. Senate campaigns, my father was particularly proud of the part he played in his successful 1920 campaign for President. He always said, "You know, I helped get Harding elected President." Father did run for office one time himself - it was for Common Pleas Judge - but lost by 13 votes. He always said, "If only I had had $100 more."

You asked me how big of a city West Union was....honey, it wasn't a city! It was a little village of a thousand people. We lived in a white frame house; what I remember most is that we had three big, beautiful maple trees in front. With eight kids, we had two bedrooms for us - one for the boys and one for the girls. We also had something you don't see that much anymore. You went across the back porch outside into "the summer kitchen." It's just a building that had an extra stove out where Mom cooked in summer and she stored all her canned goods on shelves. We didn't have a basement. We didn't use the summer kitchen in winter.

A summer kitchen is a small building or shed usually near, or attached to, the house. It is used during the summer months to lessen the cooking heat in the home. Most of these had a large fireplace and/or a stone bake oven and were designed to be used by servants or slaves to keep the cooks and their assistants separate from the main house. These date from 1632. Sometimes these kitchens were elaborate one or two-story barns which were also used for entertaining. Meg didn't mention any entertaining in their summer kitchen. I suspect that cooking for a family of ten made its use totally functional.

One of my early memories was everyone in West Union going out in early 1919 to greet about ten boys coming home after serving in World War I. They came on the N&W train to Peebles, and then all of them came into town in the back of a big truck. They were all heroes to us. Some mothers were crying.

The "N&W" was the Norfolk and Western railroad. It was founded in 1870 through mergers but had its beginnings in 1838. Its headquarters were in Roanoke, Virginia and it was the largest railroad used by the Confederates during the Civil War. It was one of the few railroads to manufacture its own locomotives, as well as its own coal hopper cars. Because it transported so much coal out of West Virginia and Kentucky, one of its nicknames was "King Coal." As a child who lived next to the train tracks, I always found the distinctive N&W logo on its cars to be the best. The company ceased operations in 1982 when it was merged with Southern Railway and was renamed Norfolk Southern Railway. The returning soldiers probably came to Peebles on trains named *The Powhatan Arrow, The Pocahontas,* or *The Cavalier.* All were passenger trains regularly running from Norfolk, Virginia (where many ships returned with soldiers from Europe) to Cincinnati, Ohio. In retrospect, I find it interesting that Meg did not mention anything about the 1918-19 flu epidemic which was sweeping the nation, especially because so many returning servicemen were afflicted. After trading train stories, Meg began telling me about her education:

I went to West Union Elementary and then to West Union High School. All my brothers and sisters were much smarter than me - I've always said this because it's true! Three of my brothers became lawyers and my sisters all finished college. My oldest sister, Rosanna Jane, taught me math all four years in high school. I liked having her as a teacher, *but she hated teaching because the Superintendent of Schools was like a bad guy in a Charles Dickens novel. That's why she eventually went into the Waves [the Women's branch of the Navy established by the U.S. Congress in 1942.] She did not marry until she met a Navy Captain while both were stationed in D.C.; she was forty then. Some of my brothers had interesting names: the oldest was Benjamin Franklin Robuck and my third brother was Ralph Waldo Emerson Robuck....he hated that name, so we all called him "Dode." Benjamin had become the Postmaster in West Union and most of us in the family worked there at one time or other. Everyone in town was mad (or jealous) at us about this because it paid $50 a month, which was big money in those days.*

I never dated in high school - I guess because none of them liked me. The big entertainment in West Union in the summer was for all of us girls to walk around the Court House square in the evening when all the farmer boys would come into town and drive around the square. We would also go swimming in the summers at a local quarry. There were no lifeguards, of course, and our mothers were scared to death that we would drown out there. The biggest thrill for me as a teen was in 1926 when my oldest brother, Ben, gave me an old 1922 Chevy touring car. I was only 13, but there was no such thing as drivers licenses then - at least in our area. Mother told me not to drive it anywhere out of town, but, of course, that's just what I did. I took several of my girlfriends up to Peebles which was about 14 miles away. Well, we ran out of gas on the way back and I had to walk to a nearby house to call my brother to come get us. Mother was furious when I got home. She was even madder the next day when we went up there to get the car and found that it had been stripped overnight. Everything was gone: tires, battery....if you could carry it, they took it. So that was the end of my having a car. One other funny thing about that car....one day I was with some of my friends and we stopped at the gas station and asked the fellow to pump us 13 cents of gas. He was so mad that he kept the gas cap....he never did give it back to us.

Things were pretty good for our family until my father had a stroke in 1925. He had it during the night, and his entire right side was paralyzed. He could speak some, but it wasn't very intelligible. He was so frustrated because speaking had been his life as a lawyer. He was only 49 when this took place. We had no insurance of any kind. Since Dad could no longer work, my older brother became the sole supporter for our family. Fortunately, as long as he was Postmaster, we were okay. We ate a lot of potatoes and fried apples then. Occasionally we could have some meat - usually round steak or ham. We never went hungry. I don't know anyone in West Union who did, even during the depths of the Depression.

I graduated from high school in 1930 but didn't have enough money to go to college. So, I worked in the Post Office for a year. Stamps were two cents and penny post cards were....a penny! I generally liked the job, because I had a job, but one day, a local woman named Mrs. Branson, came in and wanted 75 stamps for invitations for a party. She asked me to help licking the stamps, but I soon found out that she meant for me to lick all 75. I had a glue taste in my mouth for over a day! After that year, I had enough money to start school in 1931 at Denison College up in Granville, just northeast of Columbus. I believe that tuition and all other costs came to $600 a year. It was a Baptist school and most people from West Union who went to college went there. I wanted to be a newspaper reporter and loved my English and Speech classes. I joined a sorority, Alpha Omicron Pi, but we all lived in regular dorm rooms. It was not too strict a place. We had to go to chapel three times a week, and could not smoke, drink, or stay out late, but we had a fairly good social life. My roommate, Marjorie Lore, and I lived on the second floor; our house mother, Miss Helen Bloomer, lived on the first floor. She was what we called "a young old maid." All of us girls were in love with our English teacher, a young man about 28, named Don Wilder.

I spent the next summer working with my brother in the Post Office and then went back to Denison. When Roosevelt won the Presidency in the 1932 elections, my brother lost his Postmaster job immediately the day after the new President, a Democrat, came into office in early 1933. That's when our money ran out, and I had to quit school. I came home to help our mother because everyone in our family was now out of work except my sister who was still teaching. We were all living off her salary. My older brother, Ralph Waldo, was in the process of trying to work his way through law school in Detroit and was working as a Prohibition agent to make some money up there. What I remember most about this period was that we ate a lot of baloney. We were always running up a grocery bill and had trouble paying. I remember seeing a lot of men sleeping on the ground near the Courthouse during the summers.

When I came home from college, my brother introduced me to a fellow named Hoobler from Portsmouth who had become the editor of our local newspaper. I thought he was great and quickly married him. That was a real mistake because he was an alcoholic. It was a disaster and lasted only a year until I got divorced. The only good part of that marriage was that we had a baby boy. So, I was living at home with my mom, my dad, two nieces, and my baby son, Jerome Ellison Hoobler.

When my dad died in 1935, things were pretty desperate for us, so in the summer of 1936 we sold our home in West Union and moved to a small rental house in Columbus near Ohio State University. I needed a job badly and went down to the state capital building. I was scared because the only work experience I had was at the Post Office. I walked around the state house twice trying to get up enough nerve to go in and ask for a job. Finally, I went inside and went into the State Auditor's office and blurted out, "I'm one of Carey Robuck's daughters and I need a job!" A man named - believe it or not - Howard Hughes....not the Hollywood one....took me into his office and gave me a job working from four in the afternoon to midnight addressing envelopes for Old Age Pension checks. I was being paid $4 a day! Mother of God, I felt like a millionaire!!! I worked there only from October 1936 to May of 1937 when I got fired. I didn't do anything wrong....we all got fired, because the Democrats won big and all us Republicans were sent packing.

I had saved a little money but needed work badly. A family friend got me a job working downtown in the tap room at the Deshler-Wallick hotel as a cashier. I was now making only $10 a week working from 6 P.M. to 2 A.M. At first, I had no idea what I was doing and one of the night watchmen, a fellow named Bruce, helped me. I had to take the OWL - that was the name of the streetcar - to and from work. At night it ran only once an hour, so if I missed it, that was a big problem. All this was a new experience for me because I was now "help" and "the help" had to

*use only the back door to come and go. We were warned that we would
be fired if we used the front door.*

The Deshler, as it was known, was indeed a high-end hotel in downtown
Columbus at 1-11 North High Street. It was built in 1916 and was 12
stories high. It had a red brick facade with the exterior ornately decorated
on the top floors. It later was acquired by Hilton Hotels before being
demolished in 1970.

*I did the hotel job for a year, but in the fall of 1938 a Republican
governor was elected in Ohio. Again, because of my dad, I was able to
get a government job working as a receptionist for the State Board of
Cosmetology. This paid pretty well....$80 a month. I had no social life
with men during all this time. I was a working single mother before
my time.*

*Being in Columbus I did have the opportunity to get together occasionally
with members of my sorority from college. Most were a bunch of rich
girls, but it did give me a chance to mix with people other than my family.
Using my Republican connections, I invited a woman named Marion
Martin, who was the Assistant Chairman of the Republican National
Committee, to come to Columbus to talk to our "A-O-Pie" group. Not
only did she accept, but she also stayed in contact with me during the
war. In 1944 she sent me a telegram urging me to come to D.C. to work
for the Republican National Committee. I left my son with Mom and
went to D.C. to work on the 1944 Presidential election. When I arrived,
I must have looked like a total hillbilly. I had on leg makeup and a dress
that was too short. Marion took me under her wing and taught me how
to dress professionally. I stayed there two years but missed my little boy,
so I went back to Ohio.*

*In 1948 I came back to D.C. - ironically on the day of Truman's
inauguration - and worked on "the hill" [Capitol Hill] for three Republican
U.S. senators and one Senate official. My main job was to work in the
offices and answer phones. My son and I were now living here in this
same apartment building where I now live. In 1952 I was involved in
the Presidential election working to help elect Eisenhower. They sent*

me to New York City and put me up in a hotel just down the hall from where Nelson Rockefeller was staying. He was a wonderful man and had dinner with me one night. We talked for over an hour. My son had been living with me in D.C. and he came up on the train to visit me on most weekends.

After that election, I came back to D.C. and continued working on the hill. I met a widower, Mr. Edward Charlton Graves, at a party in this very building on February 3, 1957. I married him less than three weeks later. He had five children, so I became not only a mother, but a stepmother. I moved to his home in McLean, Virginia in an 11-room house on 4-acres with two dogs and a cat. He worked for the FBI and was a wonderful husband.

Meg and I talked for over two hours, mostly about politics. It was obvious that this was one of her favorite topics. She told me that her favorite recent President was Nixon "because he was so well qualified and smart," followed by Reagan. After our interview, I decided to learn more about the political career of Warren Harding, "the man whom my father helped get elected." I knew little about Harding other than having heard of "The Teapot Dome Scandal" which occurred during his time as President.

I found that Warren G. Harding was an interesting life-long politician. When he announced, as a first-term senator, that he was going to be a candidate for the Republican nomination for President in 1920, no one gave him a chance because there were several other more well-known and highly considered candidates. During the Republican nominating convention in Chicago, none of the leading figures could amass a majority. Due to the deadlock, a long series of ballots ensued with Harding slowly gaining strength in each ballot. Finally, on the 10th ballot (unimaginable these days), he won the nomination. Instead of doing national campaigning, Harding chose to do a "front porch campaign" having reporters come to his home in Marion (Ohio). Apparently, Americans were so angry with President Wilson that Harding's theme of "a return to pre-war normalcy" was an effective option because he won in a landslide over his Democratic opponent, James M. Cox (also from Ohio who was nominated on the 44th ballot!) and his Socialist opponent, Eugene Debs (who was in prison at the time!!). Much of this makes our current political shenanigans seem tame! How quickly we forget.

As President, Harding was hugely popular. He installed several well-known and highly regarded individuals to Cabinet positions, such as Andrew Mellon as Treasury Secretary, Herbert Hoover as Commerce Secretary, and former Supreme Court Justice Charles Evans as Secretary of State. His downfall came with the appointment of his Senate friend, Albert Bacon Fall, to be Secretary of the Interior. In 1922 Fall received bribes of over $200,000 to grant oil leases without competitive bidding - one in Navy Petroleum Reserves in the Teapot Dome region of Wyoming and others in California. When Fall's role became known, he was found guilty, but was imprisoned only nine months. Harding was never implicated, but the scandal remained as the defining incident of his presidency.

Despite declining health, Harding embarked on a long tour of the nation in the summer of 1923 with stops and speeches throughout the western U.S. and even in Alaska and Canada. During one of these large public speeches (in Seattle) he predicted that Alaska would become a state. After this speech he fell ill but continued by train to San Francisco where he died at age 57 from a heart attack while his wife, Florence, was reading a book to him. He was buried in his hometown of Marion, Ohio.

After Meg's husband died and their children were grown, she moved back to the Quebec House in Washington where I interviewed her. Her face would absolutely glow when talking about her 14 grandchildren and 6 great-grandchildren. In retrospect, Meg's life personified the ups and downs that so many Americans encountered during the Depression years. She had been fortunate to be raised in a comfortable family setting in rural Ohio at a time when most of their eight children, including the girls, were expected to attend college.

However, after the death of her father, followed by the perils of being raised in a family whose livelihood depended on the patronage politics of the day, Meg found herself in a precarious financial situation in the midst of the Depression. I found myself picturing this young single mother circling the statehouse trying to screw up sufficient courage to go inside to ask for a job. Then, when this new position evaporated with a change in politics, she was again desperately seeking *any* employment to feed her child and her mother. Although she became "the help" who was forced to use the back door, Meg persevered through these difficult days and eventually found herself working in D.C. with the political elite. Hers was a classic example of the perils of trying to navigate between the perks and the pitfalls of a politically dependent life.

It is difficult to get a feel for someone in a short interview such as the one I had with Meg. However, I do know one of her stepsons and his family very well, and they have always had nothing but praise and love for Meg. I know that my impression was one of total admiration for her courage and fighting spirit.

"Walt's Pickups"
Walt Blumhagen

Spokane, WA
Interviewed June 21, 1996

W HILE VISITING A GOOD FRIEND here in Spokane, Washington he told me, "You've gotta talk to Walt....he is one of a kind. I'm not sure he'll talk to you....he's....different."

Hearing this caveat, I was totally intrigued by what to expect when my buddy dropped me off in front of signage proclaiming:

Walt's Used Pickups
1510 E Sprague Ave. KE 4-9245

The above sign was on the side of the adjacent building and appeared to have been painted over another. The lettering was uneven, obviously not professionally painted. A row of very used pickup trucks was neatly parked awfully close to each other with the front bumpers actually sticking out over the sidewalk. I was happy to see that my friend had parked his car and was coming to introduce me to this Walt fellow. He stayed with me throughout the interview.

It turned out that Walt was in his office. It was a tiny wooden structure covered with hand-written signs all over the one front window. Each sign started with "**LOOK**." Above the door was a signboard saying "Business Office" with a horseshoe nailed directly below it. The walls inside the office were totally covered with notes, newspaper clippings, small tools, a very old "pinup" calendar showing cleavage, an angry-looking skeleton with a hand-written faded sign above it (which I tried, but could not read), plus an array of "other stuff." This fellow was obviously a serious collector of "stuff."

Walt did not get up from his chair to greet us, but rather grumpily ignored me and looked at my friend before saying, after a pause, "Hello, Aaron." My friend ran a local "shopper newspaper" at the time and had gotten to know Walt from business dealings. He always described Walt as "the most difficult customer I have ever had to deal with....but he pays cash."

Walt gave me an expressionless look as Aaron introduced me. When I reached out my hand to shake his, he did return the gesture, but his expression did not change. He was stocky, but not heavy, and had a full head of gray hair which was brushed back. His furtive look was that of a slick trial lawyer, suspicious of my every move. As we began to talk about the hot weather, Walt appeared to relax, warmed up, and became somewhat friendlier. He spoke in a gruff, loud voice and occasionally motioned with his arms. Walt seemed to have an unlimited variety of profanities. He was wearing a long-sleeve plaid shirt open at the neck. Both front pockets were full. The left one had a pen and a case for the glasses he was wearing. They had silver rims which were the type that automatically become sunglasses when outside. The right-side shirt pocket had four more pens and a small notebook. Before I could start my usual beginning questions, Walt started to loudly expound:

I can tell you the problem in America with one word....BENEFITS! I never had any goddamned benefits. The last wages I had, where I drew a check, was 1946. Since then I lived by my wits. A guy said that's a gamble...I said I gambled all my life, and I never played a game of cards. Every guy out there condemns a car dealer, but every guy has to live.... operate....exist and to prepare yourself for when you retire. I can put you in my car and take you around town right now and show you a hundred guys that's doing the same thing I'm doing without a license, without paperwork....but they can't make a living doing it, because they got another job. This is all I do, and I'm makin' a livin'.

Walt then began a lengthy harangue about a "dealer investigator" who had stopped by his business to ask him some questions. The investigator was from "Olympia" (the state capital). It was unclear what happened during that conversation, but Walt apparently chastised the fellow for having a "kiss-ass job" and, sin of all sins, driving a foreign-made car. "I told him, I get my Social Security from back East, not from Tokyo, so how come you're driving that Toyota piece of shit?" I sensed that my talk with Walt might last most of the afternoon, but then he smoothly transitioned into telling me about his personal history.

I was born on April 12, 1918 in Annamoose, North Dakota. We had four boys and one girl...she was older than me. All of us were born at home. When I was two, we moved to Milton Freewater, Oregon, which is actually two cities....that's where I was raised...it's south of Walla Walla. My dad was a truck farmer. We had 15 acres and that was a lot of work plowing and working that land with a horse. He looked a horse in the ass for a long time. That's what pisses me off about sports today. After school, these kids play sports. We never got to do that. When our school ended, we walked home, got a peanut butter sandwich, and worked til dark. We didn't have any time for sports. When some other kids would come by to do some fishin' in the crick, my dad would say, "Nah, we got work to do....you can go fishin' tomorrow."

The winters were cold down there. We had no car, no electric lights, no telephone. We cooked on a wood stove. You know what we used for toilet paper? Apple wrappers....those are that thin paper all the companies used to wrap apples in....each company would change to a different decal on them three or four times a year, and they would give the old ones to us, boxes full of the old wrappers that they had left over.

I never seen toilet paper then. People say you can't trust a car dealer cuz they're all bullshitters...sure I bullshit, but I don't lie...I couldn't stay in business if I did.

I got glasses when I was in the 5th grade. My older sister bought 'em for me...cost $14. I paid her back later when I was a teen and was working in the orchards pickin' cherries and apples and also did some peas. I had one weak eye, and when I got out of the Army in late '44, I had 20/500 in it, but I got it mostly back by exercising it using information I got from some guy in Montana. Now I can read that license plate on that truck over there.

At this point Walt spent the next several minutes demonstrating for me some of his eye exercises which seemed to me to consist of simply looking at an object with one eye closed and then the other. He was obviously pleased that he had used this technique to regain most of his vision.

By the way, I've never hired a lawyer. Oh, I've been to court, but I was always my own lawyer. I've won 11 cases without an attorney, never lost one.

Walt now went directly into another rant about sports and how much money current professional ball players were making.

Sports now are nothing more than a pumped-up racket. We used to ride my bicycle on Sunday afternoons down to another school to play pickup games of baseball. You ever heard of The King and His Court? You know, Eddie Feigner....the one that played fast pitch softball with only three other players....he was my cousin's kid. My brother, the one that's dead now, used to board at Eddie's mother's place. Not many people know this, but, Eddie, he's an illegitimate kid. He's younger than me. His real name wasn't Feigner....he changed it. He got a cousin here who's still alive... he looked just like Eddie. He could pitch a ball faster underhand than these pitchers now pitch overhand. He made a lot of money, but he blew it....he drank a lot and had a lot of women. These modern ball players....Babe Ruth would laugh at these guys today....he could hit a hundred home runs with the ball they use now.

I did not interrupt Walt to tell him that I had recently interviewed a fellow in Kentucky who had played against Feigner and who had an entirely different take. Walt did say that he had seen Feigner play with his "Court" and had followed his career, undoubtedly with some combination of pride and envy. Because of his family connection with "The King," Walt had access to many of Feigner's family secrets which he almost gleefully shared with me. Walt then quickly changed the direction of our conversation back to his experiences during the Depression.

I left home sometime in 1933 when I was 15. I worked as a carpenter and lived with my sister, then went down to California and worked in a sawmill just across the border from Klamath Falls [Oregon]. I got paid $4.50 for 8 hours. It wasn't bad pay. Most guys lived in company houses, but I stayed at a house with another guy. I also bought and sold some cars while I was there. Then I went up to Yakima in Washington where I picked hops and pears. I was making 15 cents an hour....it was bad. My mother was getting 17 and a half cents an hour then planting tomatoes. They didn't even pay me; it was paid directly to my dad. We were German, and my dad had a saying in German, "Until you're 21, what is yours is mine, and what is mine is none of your goddamned business." It even rhymes in German! That's what we spoke at home, so I had to learn English when I went to school. My dad said, "I don't care how old you are, when you're in my house, you speak German." My parents actually came out of Romania but spoke German. Never asked why.

I met my wife when we were both working nights at the cannery near my parents' home in Oregon. Her name was Leatha Penry....we're still married....over 50 years now. We both worked nights, and then during the days we worked in the orchards....felt like you had to work 24 hours a day to get by. That was around 1940. It was still real bad around here. She lived nine miles south of where I was living which was five and a half miles south of the Washington state border. We dated for a few years and got married in '42. Leatha was four years younger than me.

I started selling cars before that; it was back in 1936...I was only 18 or 19. I'd find a car and buy it for $20, clean it up, and sell it for $30. In '37 I rented a small piece of land and put 4 or 5 cars on it. Gas was cheap then....I could get five gallons of gas and a quart of oil for a buck. I would hitchhike up to Colfax [WA] and buy a car and drive it back down here to

Oregon and sell it. Most of the local guys wouldn't buy a local used car cuz they didn't want people here to see them riding around in somebody else's old car. So, they would pay me more for a car nobody had seen. I could sometimes easily sell a car for $40 that I bought up there for $20. Every once in a while, one of my brothers and I would paint 'em before we sold them. Sometimes I would get cash, and other times they would pay me later. One time I took in a horse for part of the payment, thinking that I could sell it easy for $10, but it died before I could sell the damn thing. I ended up losing on that one! I never took back a car once I sold it. Whenever anyone came looking at one of my cars, I always asked, "What do you want to pay for it?" If it was near my price, I would take it. That way, if he brought it back to me, I would say to him, "You told me what you thought the car was worth, so that's what you got." So, I never "sold" anything in my life....I just took what they wanted to give me.

Walt had a hearty laugh over this philosophical tidbit. I laughed with him while thinking of him telling me earlier about never losing a court case. I was guessing that some of his court issues revolved around interpretations of his sales tactics. He then continued to ramble on over a variety of topics.

We were German Baptists, but I wasn't very religious. My buddies and I had a prayer [here Walt quickly recited a rhyming sentence in German, which he then translated for me] "Thank me Heavenly Father, here we are; tomorrow morning we haul manure." That's when I got away from religion. We had twelve churches in town and three of them were German Baptist. Here's how I looked at it. You got 50 different churches all lined up in a row with a preacher in front of each one, and they're all different. So, I figure that 49 of them are wrong, and one is maybe right, but I couldn't know which one it was. My wife is still sort of a religious Bible thumper....not me.

One time back in the late 30's I was working over in Yakima - that's there in Washington where they grow all the hops - and a fellow comes into town with an airplane - one of those open cockpit types. He would take us up for a flight with him for a penny a pound. If you weighed 130 pounds, it cost you a buck thirty. I went up with him and we flew across Pippen Ball Field and back.

They had the WPA and CCC back here then, but I was not qualified because my Dad had his own fruit farm. We had a pig, canned all our vegetables and my mom baked our bread. The other guys, the ones who didn't work hard or who drank too much, their families qualified. That's what's wrong with these government programs. Their kids could get on with these programs, cutting down trees, building roads....they got $30 a month plus room and board - 25 went to the family, and 5 to the kid. Some of my buddies went into these. I talked to one guy in a WPA truck. He said he had 9 in his crew. But I didn't see anyone but him. He said to me, "Well, two are shittin', two are mowing, two are coming, two are going, and I'm boss." I think that they were getting about a dollar and a half a day for this shit.

While these guys were doing this, I was pickin' apples. I got 2 1/2 cents a box, and an extra 1/4 a cent a box if you stayed for the whole season. I could make $4.50 a day picking apples. The trick to making good money like this was knowing where to put the ladder to get to the most apples. Most orchards didn't pick on Sundays, so while most guys would be drinking beer or playing cards, I could make a bunch of money picking on Sundays. I bought a 1917 Indian motorcycle for $11 and rode it all over those orchards....I sold it for $14. We had guys picking apples from Chicago who had never seen a horse....they would walk miles to see a friggin' horse! We would sleep in tents or in the barns. One year I saved up $75 and bought me a gray Oxford suit for $19. Corduroy pants cost 98 cents, work shirts 29 cents.

Walt then talked for at least the next 15 minutes about cars that he had bought and sold over the years. Each story was peppered with nearly constant profanities; he twice went back to the '28 Dodge on which he lost money due to the horse dying. In addition to the numerous old pickup trucks on the lot, he kept mentioning more and more types of cars that he had "around," including a 1917 Ford Model T which he remembered cost $361 if you bought it new. "I never buy any new cars anymore....my newest rig is a '73 Impala.

As we were getting ready to take some photos, Walt went into another tirade about not being able to get anybody to do any decent work on cars. He also proudly told me about his son who at age 16 went into the carnival business. He bought his first amusement ride which he operated around the country at fairs after hauling it there in one of Walt's pickup trucks. Walt bragged that his son then went on to spend 20 years in that business and did well.

As I took photos of Walt in front of several of the pickup trucks on his lot, he beamed with obvious pleasure while giving me a brief history of how he obtained each one. One old Chevy truck had lettering hand-painted on the hood saying, "BUY THIS FOR YOUR WIFE. (SORRY) I HAVE (ONE)." Frankly, I was afraid to ask Walt the thought process behind this strange marketing ploy.

Walt was a challenging interview. He was far more profane than I have reported here and reminded me of several "old salts" whom I encountered during my time in the Navy. He was truly a rugged entrepreneur with no patience for the increasing government bureaucracy which he viewed with obvious disdain. He had survived the Depression, served honorably during WW II, and raised a family. Because he had worked essentially his entire life in jobs many now would avoid, he had zero empathy for others who might need assistance. He was proud of his truck lot business and certainly appeared to be pleased with all that he had achieved. I liked Walt, but he was way too sharp for me if I was looking to buy a pickup!

"The Girls"
Ida Lee, Mary, Bessie, and Ophelia

Dayton, Kentucky
Interviewed February 2, 1996

Ida Lee Reitz, Mary Munster, Bessie Busse, and Ophelia Boeh.

C LARICE NELLO HOGAN, MY MOTHER, completed nursing training at Speers Hospital in Dayton, Kentucky in 1936. After passing the State Board of Nursing examination in Louisville, she became a R.N. (Registered Nurse....someone who has completed nursing training and passed the state examination). During her nursing training, Mom made several lasting friendships. Among these close friends was a group of fellow nurses whom she always called "The Girls."

The Girls was how my mother referred to members of "The '38 Club." It was founded by several nurses who graduated in 1938 from the Speers Hospital nursing program. Membership in the club was by invitation only.

Some of the founding members invited a few of their friends from the Classes of 1936 and 1937 to join. By 1939 the membership was mostly set with approximately 14 members. Meetings were held in members' homes on a rotating basis. As far as I (and surviving members can recall), the ladies rarely missed a monthly meeting from 1939 to at least 1991. There was one inviolate rule in the '38 Club: no men were allowed at the meetings. This was generally interpreted as NONE....NEVER. I can personally vouch for the steadfastness of this rule: from my earliest memories until I left home for college, no men were ever present at a '38 Club meeting. When it was my mom's turn to host the meeting, my father would take me elsewhere - sometimes as a toddler to the local corner saloon.

Mom passed away in 1991 following a horrific single-car accident near her home in Kentucky. Her three passengers were all members of The Girls. In addition to my mother, one of the other passengers died. Just prior to the accident, I had been diagnosed with a rare, life-threatening heart disease and was given two years to live. The year 1991 was difficult for our family. One of my great regrets was never sitting down with either of my parents to talk about their childhoods and what they did up to my first memories. I do know more about my mother than my father, but there are significant gaps. This void became the genesis of this book. Following my life-saving heart transplant operation in 1994, I began to collect remembrances from others comparable in age to my parents so that I could understand the Depression era and the surrounding decades.

In early 1996 I returned to northern Kentucky to meet with four of The Girls to listen to their stories. For me it was a casual gathering of old friends because each Club member had a detailed knowledge of the others' children and immediate family after so many years of sharing stories with each other. Although I had been gone from the region for most of the past four decades, I immediately recognized each of the four ladies and knew the names of each of their spouses and most of their children. The order in which they discussed their lives was Bessie Busse, Mary Munster, Ida Lee Reitz, and Ophelia Boeh. I suggested that each tell me about their early lives in Kentucky and how they ended up as students at Speers Hospital. Then we could talk as a group about their nursing training.

All except Ida Lee had white hair, and each appeared to have had recent perms. Bessie was wearing a long, beaded necklace over a long-sleeved white blouse. She began by discussing her childhood:

I was born in Torrent, Kentucky in Wolfe County on December 22, 1915. It was really just a little railroad siding not far from Natural Bridge. We were on the L&N railroad which comes out of Winchester and goes up into the mining area to bring coal and lumber out of the mountains. There weren't mines in our immediate area; the railroad ran up there near Hazard - that's where the mines, and the jobs, were. My father was Millard Fillmore Profitt and my mother was Anna Pence Profitt. Dad was a farmer. I had four brothers and three sisters. I was born at home - no one there was born in a hospital. I used to joke about it when I was in nursing training saying that where I was from, we didn't even know the word "hospital." It was very rural.

Torrent, Kentucky remains a small town. Its only apparent current attraction is a large waterfall for which the town was named. Both its post office and railroad station closed in the 1930's. The L. Park Hotel, an enormous structure, was built near the falls in 1890 and was a significant tourist attraction. It featured a suspended stage, an orchestra, and a large dance floor. It burned to the ground in 1927; fires were a constant hazard in remote areas such as this. Bessie did not mention the hotel. The falls are now privately owned, but there is free public access and hiking is allowed, but strictly controlled.

Being named after a President was not unusual when Bessie's father was born in the late 1800's. Millard Fillmore was Vice President when President Zachary Taylor died in office in mid-1850. Fillmore was interesting in that during his career he changed political affiliation from the Anti-Masonic Party, to the Whig Party, to the Know Nothing Party, and finally ended up in the Democratic Party. He is one of the few Presidents not to gain nomination for re-election from his own party (Whigs). I did not ask Bessie why her father was named for Fillmore, who (as far as I can determine) was from the Finger Lakes region of New York and never had a relationship with Kentucky.

Bessie resumed by telling me about her education:

I went to grades one through six in a Presbyterian church boarding school in Guerrant, Kentucky - that's in Breathitt County, near Jackson. To get there we had to go on the train and then walk five miles to get to the school. My older brothers didn't go to high school or even finish eighth grade. They left home and went up to the coal fields near Hazard and found work in the mines and got married and had children and so on. So, for 7th and 8th grades I was living with a brother in Jeff, Kentucky. That's in Prairie County near Hazard. Then for high school I came back home and went to Pine Ridge High School, which is a Methodist boarding school. It was about five miles from home. I was exposed to a lot of different religions growing up.

Guerrant, Kentucky is even smaller than Torrent. The boarding school was probably founded by Edward O. Guerrant, a Confederate Captain who rode with Morgan's Raiders. He wrote a 736-page diary of his wartime experiences and later became a traveling Presbyterian minister and physician. Bessie did not explain why she always attended boarding schools and spent two years living with her brother. It is unclear if there were any schools in the vicinity of her home at that time, but what is certain is that her parents were in a very remote area in the hills of southeastern Kentucky. Jeff, Kentucky is also a very small town up the Kentucky River from Hazard in the heart of what was then coal mining country. Many television viewers may confuse Hazard, Kentucky with the popular series, *Dukes of Hazzard,* which ran for seven seasons beginning in 1979, if only because moonshine (and "hillbillies) are associated with both. Hazzard was a fictional county in Georgia, far from Kentucky. Pine Ridge High School no longer exists, but there is a Methodist boarding school, now named Oakdale Academy, in the same immediate area described by Bessie.

She then told me about how she ended up at Speers Hospital:

When I graduated from high school in 1934, I wanted to be a teacher, but I didn't have the funds so I thought maybe I could become a nurse. My sister, Edna, who was two years older than me, had finished the 8th grade, but waited until I came back from Hazard so she could go to high school with me. After we graduated, she came up here to northern Kentucky to look for a job. You see, in those days, girls like us from the country would come up to the Cincinnati [Ohio] area to work in wealthy homes for two dollars a week. One of the homes in northern Kentucky was owned by a doctor who was working at Speers Hospital and he told Edna about it. So, she went over and talked to them and decided she wanted to become a nurse there. I had been accepted for training at Good Samaritan Hospital in Lexington [Kentucky], but when Edna told me she was going to go to Speers, I gave up my idea of going to school in Lexington and joined her here. So, we began training together at Speers on August 1, 1934 - right in the middle of the Depression.

I was surprised to hear all four women use the term "go into training" instead of saying "attend nursing school." Most nursing training prior to World War II involved three-year programs associated with hospitals. There was not nearly as much "book work" as in current nursing courses at universities, but far more practical training. I would learn much more about this as our conversations continued. Mary Munster spoke next. She was also wearing a long sleeve white blouse with dark pants.

I was born on January 24, 1916 in my maternal grandmother's home in Squiresville, Kentucky. My father, Arvin Thomas Morgan, was teaching in Boonesville so he had brought my mother, Virginia Reeve, to her mother's home for her to have me delivered there. Not long later my grandfather died, so Dad had to come home to take over his farm because widows were not left alone in those days. But Dad was not a farmer, so he opened a feed store in Owenton. He got sick with appendicitis and was taken to a hospital where the first thing they said was, "Give him an enema." He died quickly, leaving my mom with us five kids. I went to six years of grade school in a one-room schoolhouse in Squiresville. Then we moved to Owenton and I went to high school there. Our house had no inside john and no running water. We never had hardly any money after Dad died.

Because I was raised by a nurse of this vintage, I was very familiar with the term "enema" (an injection of fluid into the lower bowel by way of the rectum). Mom had her own "enema bag" at our home to use on me at what seemed to be far too frequent intervals. It is a sign of the times that the word "enema" is now not recognized by Word software. Mom also kept penicillin in the fridge and a trusty syringe (she would boil the needle) to plunge into my bottom whenever I so much as sneezed. One of my bodily parts was very relieved when I left home to go to college.

I was interested in going into training at the Baptist hospital in Louisville, but they had a requirement that you had to have a year of college first. Well, that wasn't going to happen with me. Not long afterwards I happened to be talking to a local fellow, Mr. Creo, who repaired watches. He told me about his niece who was in training at Speers Hospital in Dayton, Kentucky and that she loved it. I had never heard of it or Dayton, but I wrote a letter there and was accepted. It turned out that his niece was "Tate" who is, as you know, a member of our Club. So, I started in September of '33 with Hogan, that's what we called your Mom. I didn't have any money, but my grandmother gave me a check for 15 bucks. That paid for the tuition, books, and your uniform. My uncle gave me a ride up there. We weren't paid during the first four months; that was our probation period. Then we got our cap and started getting paid $8 a month, and that's what we lived on. We got our nursing tools when we got our caps.

Squiresville is another very small Kentucky town. It is approximately halfway between Louisville and northern Kentucky, where Speers Hospital was located. Owenton was not much larger than Squiresville and was a short distance to the east.

The "cap" that Mary mentioned was a particularly important part of nursing training. It originated from head coverings worn in early Christian times by women called "deaconesses." Its functional purpose in medicine was to keep the nurse's hair in place, but it became an important symbol that you were now a serious candidate to become a nurse. It is said that Florence Nightingale wore a white cap in the 1800's. In the late 1800's many nursing schools designed unique caps to signify graduates of that school. I recall visiting my mother during her days working in a hospital and her pointing out to me the different caps worn by her colleagues which indicated where they had gone for training. By the mid-1960's many U.S. programs no longer required nurses to wear caps or any head covering, perhaps because of the increasing number of men becoming nurses. I still have a miniature replica of my mother's cap from Speers Hospital.

Ida Lee was the next to speak. She was wearing a bright, wildly decorated blouse covered with a patchwork of quilt designs.

I was born at home on August 4, 1916 in California, Kentucky on 12th Avenue. The doctor took a train up to deliver me, but I was already born. We had a fireplace and a drum stove in that house. My dad, John Burns Youtsey, had a grocery store – actually, general merchandise - and sold everything from soup to nuts. It was in Alexandria, so we soon moved there. I went to grade school and high school at Campbell County schools in Alexandria. Of course, being from the area, I had heard about Speers and the training program there. The reason I wanted to become a nurse was that my father had a R.N. taking care of my mother when she passed away at age 35 from diabetes. Also, we had a R.N. private duty nurse when my grandmother passed away from pneumonia. It just stuck with me and I always wanted to be a nurse. So, I showed up the same time as Bessie on August first, 1934....early in the morning.

California was another extremely small Kentucky town. It was situated on the southern banks of the Ohio River and was regularly flooded. In 1952 my mother purchased a small house in California as an investment at a county courthouse auction (sold to recover unpaid property taxes). Her bid of $1700 was accepted. When we drove there to see what Mom had bought, we found a family of squatters living in it. They had cut a hole in the kitchen floor and dumped all their garbage down into the basement below. It turned out not to be a particularly successful investment.

The nurses Ida Lee mentioned were "private duty nurses." Many nurses at the time did not work in hospitals but took short-term jobs in homes caring for ill patients or those recovering from hospitalization. My mother did this type of work for many years. It was a common practice in the U.S. until the 1960's. Medicare does not currently pay for private duty nurses.

Ophelia spoke last. Like Ida Lee, she was also wearing a rather fancy blouse and had a small, golden chain around her neck. Both she and Ida Lee were married to physicians they had met while in training at Speers.

You don't want to hear my story. I was born on May 30, 1912 in Fort Henry, Tennessee. It's near Dover about 20 miles from Clarksville which is about 15 miles from Fort Henry. My father was Fred Gardner, and my mother was Kelly Hodges. I had just one brother and one sister. When I was about five years old, my father had TB and was in bed for as long as I can remember. I think he fished or farmed....not sure....my mother was doing most of the work on the farm. When I was five, I moved to Tobacco, Kentucky....I'm not kidding. It's near Murray [Kentucky] and for the first two years I went to Tobacco School. My dad died when I was seven, so we moved to live with my grandmother out in the country. It was a farm about 15 miles from Murray. Not too long later my mother married again. When I was living out there, I went to Martin's Chapel one-room country school through the 6th grade. Then we moved to Murray and I went to high school there. It was four years before I came into training. I went to college almost a year at Murray State. Then I worked in a dime store as a telephone operator for the next three years. One of my friends had gone to Speers and liked it so a friend of mine, Helen Ezell, came up with me and we began training on August 5, 1935.

Fort Henry, and the neighboring towns in Tennessee which Ophelia mentioned are on the Tennessee River close to the Kentucky border. It is now on the eastern shore of Kentucky Lake. I can find no mention anywhere of Tobacco, Kentucky - at least none with a population over 250. The area surrounding Murray, Kentucky is now called "The Land Between the Two Lakes" due to its location near Kentucky Lake and Barkley Lake, both man-made. Kentucky Lake was formed in 1944 by the TVA (Tennessee Valley Authority) with a dam on the Tennessee River. It is the largest artificial lake east of the Mississippi River. Barkley Lake is smaller and newer, having been created in 1966. Tobacco, Kentucky is probably now underwater.

The four ladies now began to reminisce about their days in training. This was a rapid-fire conversation with each "girl" adding new thoughts to the memories being discussed. I smiled when they used each other's maiden names when referring to one another, just as my mother had done when talking about "the girls." Ophelia continued her story:

That $15 tuition that Mary mentioned went up to $25 in 1934. We each received three blue dresses with white aprons to wear on duty. Our uniform also had white stockings and white shoes which we had to keep clean and white with polish. Every morning before we could go over to the hospital from the Nurses Home, we were inspected head to toe by Miss Fry or Miss Wiggs, both R.N.'s. They also inspected our little box of instruments which we had to carry. It had two thermometers, bandage scissors and surgical scissors, tweezers, a probe, and a hypodermic syringe - we boiled the needles in a teaspoon. When you went on duty you put your syringe in alcohol and looked at the number on yours to pull it out. We did the same thing with dressings - after taking them off we just put them back into the alcohol and used them again. But you know, we didn't seem to have that many infections then.

You didn't get your white bib until you got your cap. During our three months' probation period all we did was make beds, give baths, and empty bedpans. We learned how to make beds with "Miss Chase." She was a doll dummy. First, we had to learn how to make an empty bed without a patient in it, then how to make the bed with Miss Chase in it. Miss Steinhauer - Sophie Steinhauer - was in charge of the hospital. We were all terrified of her, but, boy, could she run a hospital. She was also on the State Board of Nursing and would always travel to Louisville when we took our boards to become R.N.'s. She died in 1938 after we were all finished. She was a big and powerful woman - very imposing and very intimidating with a loud, gruff voice. She was in charge of everything.

Miss Wiggs was our teacher in charge of our classroom training. Miss Fry ran the operating room. "Ma" Kenny was the housekeeper in charge of our nursing residence. None of us knew her real first name. The night supervisor was Miss Evans. On a typical day, once we got our caps, we worked from 7 to 1, then class from 1 to 4, then worked again from 4 to 7, and then another class from 7 to 8. It was a long day. When we had to do the night shift, we worked from 7 P.M. to 7 A.M., and still had to do the daytime classes! We weren't sleeping anyhow. But you did get two days off when you ended night shift. Basically, we were always working six days a week. We didn't have classes during June, July, and August and had three weeks' vacation, but had to work at the hospital the rest of the time. We got paid $8 a month, but if you broke a thermometer, they'd take 50 cents out of your pay. If you broke two, they took out a dollar. We didn't have a stethoscope or take blood pressures; they didn't do that until World War II time.

In our second year, you would be in charge of a station. In your third year, when you were "a senior nurse." You basically ran the hospital. We learned to mix drugs in the pharmacy. When a patient needed morphine, we would either go to the pharmacy and get some, or catch up with Miss Fry, because she always carried "a quarter" in her pocket. That was what we called a fourth of a grain of morphine.

We were not always at Speers. We went to Louisville Children's Free Hospital for pediatrics for three months and had lectures on psychiatry at Longview State Hospital over in Cincinnati.

At this point, Ophelia's husband, Dr. Boeh, passed through and told us a joke. (I never once heard any of "the girls," including Ophelia, refer to Dr. Boeh, by his first name, or anything other than "Dr. Boeh." This generation of nurses were always respectful of physicians, even if they did not care for them). Ophelia then mentioned that if you thought $15 was a bargain for getting into nursing training, her husband paid only $200 for all of med school. Mary interjected, "Money meant more then." The ladies then returned to talking about life in the nursing home where they lived for three years.

When we were in the nursing home, we had to be in by 9 P.M. through the week, with 10:30 P.M. on one weekend night and midnight on the other. We lived in an 8-person dorm room about the size of a closet our first year, then got up to be in a double room, then a single room in your third year. They locked the doors when the curfew came. We didn't have that much time off, but we would sometimes walk down to Newport (about four miles to the west, directly south across the river from Cincinnati). There were streetcars to go there, but they cost a nickel each way. We ate all our meals on the fourth floor of the hospital. Everyone ate there, doctors, nurses, and students. There was no selection. You ate what was served. But the doctors and the nurses had a separate room and a tablecloth.

There were public wards on the third floor - the men on one side and the women on the other. The city of Newport and the County paid the hospital $2.50 a day for these patients, but that covered everything - care, food, and medicines. And those patients got just as good care as the patients out in the private rooms. There were five private rooms on the first floor, and the C&O railroad had their own rooms for their employees on the second floor.

We had dances - just not often enough. At one of them one of the doctors spiked the punch. Miss Steinhauer caught him, but he did it again. She must have liked him because she didn't say anything. Someone had a boat on the river and some of us would go down there. There was a dance hall called Horseshoe Gardens in Bellevue (a city of comparable size to Dayton, also across the river from Cincinnati), but that place got wrecked in the '37 flood.

Here Ida Lee interrupted:

Before your Mom met your Dad, he took me out to Pompilleo's (a bar in

Dayton) for a date. He was so broke that he was scared to death that I was going to order another Coke. I think I met him when all the boys would see us sitting on the porch of the Nursing Home and would come up to talk. I only dated him once, then handed him off to your Mom. It must have worked out, because here you are talking to us!

Mary Munster chimed in:

I was in a saloon in Dayton called the Silver Bar and met a guy named Frank. He said, "I have a date for you and your friend. So, he flipped a coin, and said "Heads you get me, tails you get Doug. It came up tails, so I met my husband, Doug, on a coin toss. Mostly we went on dates to movies. They cost a quarter and sometimes just a dime if you went in before six o'clock. I never went out on a date for dinner.

Ida Lee interrupted and said she went out to dinner a lot, but it was mostly at Dixie Chili in Newport where you could get a "coney" for a nickel. A "coney" refers to a small hot dog which was called a "wiener" and is served with "Cincinnati chili," mustard, onions, and grated sharp cheese on a roll. This type of chili is a specialty allegedly seasoned with cinnamon. It remains available primarily in the region around Cincinnati and is served in "chili parlors." Dixie Chili is still in Newport, but its coneys now cost over a dollar. They have several competitors who have far more parlors in the region. Whenever I return to Kentucky, I *always* visit Dixie Chili. It's the best!

Mary continued with more of her memories:

We had rules that you couldn't graduate until you're 21, so some of us had to wait after we finished training to graduate. They also had a height requirement that you had to be at least five feet tall. Delphia Weber was real short. One day in her first year, Miss Steinhauer asked her in that gruff voice of hers, "How tall are you?" Delphia told her that she was 4 foot 9. So, Miss Steinhauer pulled her application, but Delphia had listed her height in inches and Miss Steinhauer had not bothered to convert it. She looked very angry, but said, in that same voice, "Alright, you got me. You can stay." They had that height requirement so that you were tall enough to reach across the beds with a patient in it.

Ophelia now provided background on how the '38 Club came into existence:

I graduated in 1938. There were four of us still around the local area. We decided that each of us would invite someone to join a club with us. We met over at Vida's place across from the hospital. Pretty soon by 1940 we had 16 people in the Club. Once each year we would go to some special place, like Beverly Hills Country Club or the Latin Quarter. By 1950 we seemed to settle on about 13 members and met nearly every month. We may have missed some during the war. Your mom even came when she had her teeth pulled one day.

Bessie now entered the conversation discussing life at the hospital:

There was not much messing around between the interns and the nursing students. A lot of us ended up eloping and getting married by a J.P. [Justice of the Peace]. Tate and Younts ran off and got married secretly. Your mom and dad went down to Lawrenceville, Indiana and were married by a J.P. In those days, most of us had no money for a big wedding, or even a small wedding. So, you went over to Indiana and found a willing J.P.

Ida Lee wanted to tell me about a "funny story" and then segued into a lengthy discussion joined by all the others:

The biggest thing for most of us was the 1937 flood. The river came up so high that it was in the basement of the hospital. That's where we had the morgue. Well, I was working the switchboard; in our last year we took turns working that too. Someone called in and wanted to know the condition of one of the patients. I looked up his name and told them that he had expired. They threw a fit because no one had called them. I called Miss Fry over at the Nursing Home and she came over and found the corpse floating around in the basement. She had forgot to call the family. So, they had to force the door open and go in there in a boat to get the corpse. Mrs. Fry made us swear that we wouldn't tell anyone.

The flood water kept coming up, so they moved the patients and everyone up the hill to Dayton High School for the next two weeks. They did operations and delivered babies in that high school. They would not let anyone leave Dayton; they had barricades up keeping everyone in town. Everyone who had boats used them to ferry people around. The flood lasted nearly a month and was during January and February, so it was also terribly cold. We couldn't get back into the hospital or the Nursing Home until they got everything dried out afterwards. They brought in wood stoves because they couldn't get the furnaces running right away. Clean water was a problem. Each one of us was given one basin of water a day. You would wash yourself in it, then wash your hose and underwear. All the water came from a truck which came around once a day. You could use the toilets only certain times each day, so we would use bedpans for ourselves and flush them during the designated times. We even gave patients enemas so that we could flush them at the right time.

The Ohio River flood of 1937 was permanently seared into the minds of everyone who lived through it - at least that was my impression. This flood was the frequent topic of conversation everywhere in the Cincinnati region, even as late as the 1950's. Major damage occurred along most of the length of the river from Pennsylvania to Illinois. Nearly 400 people died, and property damage exceeded $500 million - close to nine billion dollars using current values. Nearly every family that I knew growing up had photographs and saved newspaper articles about the flood. The river level in Cincinnati 80 feet above flood stage remains a record....by far. It was truly a defining experience for everyone involved. The Girls brought it up and talked excitedly about the flood for over 20 minutes.

Now the topic turned back to social life. Mom's classmate, Mary Munster, resumed the discussion:

Your mom had a private room on the first floor of the Nursing Home away from Ma Kenny. When the girls would come in late, they would tap on Hogan's window. She would get up and put a chair out the window so that they could climb in. That was what we called the auxiliary door.

We had a fun time then in training, but we had to work really hard. Nurses now have to do a lot of things which we couldn't do. For example, we didn't do IV's [intravenous lines]. But we did direct blood transfusions

- one patient on a stretcher giving blood to a patient on the next. They also did one of the first C-sections in our area while we were there. The doctor that did that got barred from the hospital for that even though the mother and the baby lived. We didn't have pediatricians then. GP's [General Practitioner physicians] did most everything. Surgeons did all types of surgery - everything, including bones. We had a friend who was operated on her kitchen table in her home....that wasn't that unusual. No one had insurance. Many of us said at the time that medical insurance would be the downfall of medicine.

The Girls and I continued talking about our families for the next hour. One interesting fact mentioned was that none of the members of The Club had divorced - apparently surviving Miss Steinhauer was a solid preparation to endure any future family issues! I came away from my session understanding how immensely proud they were of their time as nurses and the life-long friendships which resulted from their days together "in training." Because my wife was also a nurse, but educated in a 4-year program at a state university (my daughter-in-law is also a nurse and now my granddaughter is studying nursing at a university), I have seen first-hand the pros and cons of different approaches to educating nurses. Sometimes I even had to officiate some heated family discussions. But no matter the changes which have taken place in the nursing profession, the ladies who were trained at Speers Hospital during the depths of the Depression were dedicated professionals who learned how to care for patients, mostly through on-the-job training. I did not realize how many of the hospitals of that era were manned with so few doctors and nurses with most of the care being provided by young women who were still learning the "ropes."

Speers Hospital was closed in 1973 following over 75 years of service to the northern Kentucky region. The hospital had been established as the result of the will of Elizabeth L. Speers, who had been treated by a local physician before she passed away in 1894. Her will left $200,000 (now equivalent to over $6 million today) "to build a non-profit hospital" to be named after her husband (he had apparently become very wealthy growing cotton in Texas). The original hospital had four wards and 15 rooms, and after two additions, had five wards and 38 rooms with a capacity of 100 beds - much as The Girls had remembered. Following the '37 Flood the hospital was completely renovated and refurbished. It was the only hospital in Campbell County until a Catholic Hospital was built (using government funds!) in the mid-50's. When Speers was torn down in 1973, a senior citizen complex was built on its site. I have been unable to determine when the Speers nursing training began or ended.

My other dominant thought was how so many of these nursing students in Kentucky came from the smallest and poorest sections of the state. My mother's background was similar to that of three of the ladies I interviewed: growing up in a small, rural town where struggling to make ends meet was the way of life. In my mom's case, it was Cleaton, Kentucky - a nearly obscure town in the little-known coalfields of the western part of the state. For many of these young women, the only professional choices were teaching and nursing, often far from their homes and families. While in "training" they had essentially volunteered to become indentured servants working for room, board, and a few precious dollars each month. But for many of the young women on the farms and in the "hollers" of the Kentucky hills, there were few other options beyond finding a coal miner or a farmer and starting a family in those incredibly hard times. To make the decision to go forth on your own to forge a new life with little money or family support was an indication of the courage, persistence, and determination of these women.

Final Thoughts

"We didn't have much money, but we didn't care."
"Use it up, wear it out, or be without."
"You know, we were poor as church mice."
"I walked the streets lookin' but couldn't get a job doing nothing."
"One more mouth to feed was apparently one too many."
"I couldn't get a job, so I got married instead."
"Clean up what's on your plate.....
You never know for sure where or when the next meal is coming"
"We were poor, but clean."
"We lost everything."

THESE WERE JUST A FEW of the defining comments provided by the 22 Americans interviewed for this oral history of the Great Depression. It was a grave, challenging period for our nation, but, as demonstrated in the stories of these survivors, it was also an opportunity to adjust, judge, create, and discover determination to move irresistibly forward.

Transportation themes ran throughout their memories. One of the most common involved the types and models of cars. Perhaps the novelty of a first car has now lost its prominence because current youngsters have grown up with grandparents, parents, and friends having cars. In fact, some teenagers in our neighborhood have no interest in getting a car and have even deferred getting a driver's license. However, for those Depression survivors I interviewed, that first car was a *very* special memory. Because their parents had been born before the automobile had been invented, their first cars were viewed as far more than simple transportation. They were a pathway to personal freedom, adventure, and a new avenue to move far beyond the locale in which they were born. I could almost feel the nostalgia oozing from these folks as they recalled their cars: all the Model T's and Model A's, Thelma's '29 Chevy, Arden's Hupmobile, and Walt's too-numerous-to-mention vehicles. And whenever they talked about their cars, they inevitably remembered the price of gas – always less than 30 cents a gallon.

Natural disasters made indelible imprints. Both Bill Curry and The Girls wanted me to know how much the "37 Flood" of the Ohio River affected lives all along the swollen river. They brought out photos and shared recollections. Diana told me her vivid memories living through the 1933 Long Beach earthquake. Eleanor remembered the devastating damage of the 1938 "Great New England Hurricane." Willie matter-of-factly reminisced how hurricanes frequently hampered his livelihood fishing off the North Carolina coast. For each of those living in the "Dust Bowl" in the Midwest, it was not a single natural event, but a prolonged disaster, exemplified by Doris recalling the horrors of "grasshoppers, locusts, and drought." Weather has always been a convenient topic to begin conversations, and extreme weather events seem to become permanent talking points. It is easy to understand why talks of "climate change" or "global warming" find such easy reception today....everyone likes to think that "their" weather has been unique and important. The difference is that the folks I interviewed all had the belief that little could be done by humans, other than prayer, to influence future weather patterns. Many now seem convinced that we can act to avoid weather problems in the decades ahead. Time will tell.

What primarily determined how you fared during the Great Depression was whether you, or your family members, had a job. Scant governmental social assistance was available then, and losing a job was a catastrophic blow because the odds of finding new employment were low. I still have vivid recall of Ken sharing memories of those mornings when he and his mother "would pray that the phone would ring" in the hope that his mother could get a substitute teaching job for the day. And Meg walking around the state capital building in Ohio trying to screw up enough courage to go inside to beg for a job. My father often told me about losing his job in the early 1930's and his desperate attempts to earn any small amount of money by moving back into his parent's home (in his 30's) and trying to sell cars for a friend's Dodge dealership. It surprised me during my talk with J.C., a Black man in segregated Georgia, when he proudly told me that he "always had a job" whenever he wanted to work. It may have been in the turpentine forests, but he was working. Of course, those who lived on farms automatically had employment – and a lot of it - but your good fortune lasted only so long as weather was good, or the bank did not repossess your land.

A few occupations seemed to always provide employment - teaching and nursing. Although the pay was low in both fields, country schoolteachers such as Mary Jeanette and nurses such as The Girls always had jobs and were reasonably secure. They were by no means wealthy, but they had sufficient means to avoid being homeless or hungry. Even if one family member had a way of earning money, whether it was Richard, whose Mormon family was kept in work by a successful brother who owned a store, or Meg, whose postmaster brother provided jobs for most of the family, they were never in danger of starving. Because hard times were so widespread during the Depression with so many out of work, families often shared food and belongings with others who were suffering. Several of those with whom I spoke proudly recalled providing food to neighbors or anyone who came to their back door in need.

I heard many common memories of the suffering generated by the global pandemic in the final years of the second decade of the 1900's. In some cases, immediate family members did not survive this devastating "Spanish" virus, yet each family managed to discover means to push ahead. Few mentioned to me immediate economic issues associated with that pandemic unless the breadwinner passed away, possibly because those I interviewed were young at the time, or because their family was already in a challenging financial situation. Certainly, no government checks were dispensed to every American, nor was federal aid targeted to businesses. Another distinction from today, as far as I can determine, was that there were no mandated shutdowns of businesses during that pandemic except for theaters and funerals. Some cities closed schools and churches and banned large gatherings, but none closed "non-essential" businesses or issued stay-at-home orders.

Obviously, the COVID-19 pandemic has occurred in a totally different era with medical expertise and information at a far higher level of sophistication and quantity; it will be fascinating, once this ongoing pandemic has run its course, to study both the immediate and the long-term effects of the differing public policy responses. What is certain is that the COVID pandemic has placed many Americans in challenging, and in some cases, extremely difficult, economic circumstances, comparable to the darker days of the 1930's. Instead of federal work programs, such as the CCC and WPA, which directly aided millions of struggling families, the current national response has been to directly dispense money to essentially all families, whether needy or not. Some of those I interviewed spoke openly about the feeling of satisfaction of having a job during the 1930's, as opposed to simply receiving what they termed "a handout." Others saw the New Deal jobs as men leaning on shovels rather than performing meaningful work, Those I spoke to who had these jobs certainly did not see them in that light. As with so many political issues, the lens through which the action is viewed colors the evaluation.

These people did not feel sorry for themselves. They continually tried to find work. Even the children contributed. Quite a few teens (e.g., Pat and Clair) found jobs as caddies on nearby golf courses and were able to parlay this work into future jobs due to contacts made on the golf course. Except in professional and elite golf, today's caddies have been replaced by golf carts. Teens now make money on the side by mowing lawns and other jobs, but it is doubtful that they turn this cash over to their parents. Many Depression girls, such as Mary Jeanette and Tillie, did babysitting to assist their families. Although many youngsters still do babysitting, I doubt that this money is given to their parents. And frugality is not a common trait among the teens I know.

I was also surprised that several young women were literally taken to the air by suitors flying airplanes. Both Diana and Mary Jeanette found husbands via serendipitous encounters with early aviators who took them on plane rides. I doubt that many current young women have had this experience!

One key fact pervaded my interviews: the Depression generation was not a "throw-away" culture. As Doris recalled, many families made their own clothes and handed them down to younger siblings. Used flour sacks were a valuable commodity to convert into sheets and clothing. Appliances, cars, and other equipment were not replaced, but repaired or converted. Clair told me with obvious pride how he turned his 1923 Model T into a truck to haul rocks and then into a farm tractor. When shortages of many goods began to occur during WW II, these depression survivors with frugal habits were prepared. Indeed, they were ***the generation who never threw anything away***.

Timeline of the Great Depression

ANY "TIMELINE" DESCRIBING A DECADE-LONG event is necessarily incomplete because of the subjective decisions made as to the relative importance of events. The information below has been drawn from multiple sources in an attempt to present some of the major events.

1920's

The "Roaring '20's" were not without significant economic problems. During the decade, an average of 600 banks failed each year out of just under an average of 26,000. Agricultural, energy, and coal mining sectors were continually depressed. The value of farmland fell nearly 40% between 1920 and 1929. Union participation declined; the United Mine Workers, for example, saw its membership fall from 500,000 in 1920 to 75,000 in 1928. By 1929 less than 200 large corporations controlled half of American industry. Income inequality was extreme; by 1929 the richest 1 percent owned 40% of the nation's wealth (as opposed to 38.5% in 2017).

The stock market began its spectacular rise in 1924, but the increases did not reflect most of the economy. Between May 1928 and September 1929, the average price of stocks rose 40%. Trading of securities during this period increased from an average of 2.5 million shares a day to over 5 million. At the same time, public consumption of products fell significantly, while business inventories grew three times larger. Automobile sales, for example, declined by nearly a third in the first 9 months of 1929. A significant recession began in August 1929, two months before the major stock market crash which is often cited as the beginning of the Depression.

1929

The stock market reaches a peak on September 3 and begins a slow decline. It starts to crash on October 24, initially called "Black Thursday," but larger drops on October 28 and 29 become known as known as "Black Monday" and "Black Tuesday." Investor losses during this month exceed $16 billion – comparable to nearly $250 billion in current dollars. The stock market bottoms with the Dow Jones average at 46 on November 23 and will not recover to that September high for the next 25 years. Unemployment levels are not immediately affected and are still only slightly over 3 percent.

1930

The Federal Reserve cuts the prime interest rate from 6 to 4 percent. Treasury Secretary Andrew Mellon states that the Fed will "stand by as the market works itself out."

The Smoot-Hawley Tariff is signed into law by President Hoover on June 17 increasing tariffs on over 20,000 imported goods. Foreign trading partners retaliate reducing American exports and imports over 60% during the following years.

A summer drought hits farmers in the nation's mid-section, the first of many over the next few years causing conditions subsequently labeled "The Dust Bowl Drought."

Gross National Product (GNP) falls nearly 10% from 1929 and unemployment rises from 3.2 to 8.7 percent.

Bank failures become a significant factor. When the Bank of Tennessee fails on November 7, a daisy-chain sequence leads to the failure of other banks, primarily throughout the Southeast. The nation's 4th largest bank, the Bank of New York, fails on December 11 creating even more banking panic throughout the entire U.S. By the end of the year, Gross National Product (GNP) decreases 9.4% from the previous year.

1931

No major legislation is passed in Congress addressing the ongoing Depression. In February food riots break out in Minneapolis.

A second banking panic takes place throughout much of the U.S. in the spring.

The economy continues to shrink. Prices, which had begun to decline in 1930, now fall another 9.3%.

The unemployment rate increases to 15.9%. Many Americans are now feeling severe economic effects.

1932

In January Congress passes legislation to create the Reconstruction Finance Corporation to lend $2 billion to financial institutions; in the summer states are authorized to receive some of this funding. Nonetheless, the economic decline continues. GNP for the year falls over 13% - a record. On July 8, the Dow Jones stock average bottoms at 41.22, even lower than at the depth of the crash in 1929 - a 90% decline from its 1929 high. 10,000 banks have now failed, with over $2 billion in deposits lost.

Over 13 million Americans have lost their jobs and farm prices have fallen 53 percent since 1929. The unemployment rate is 23.6% and prices have declined another 10.3%.

Fourteen dust storms hit the Midwest ruining crops and forcing many farmers into insolvency.

The top tax rate is raised from 25 to 63 percent.

Shantytowns of tin and wood begin to appear throughout the nation and quickly become known as "Hoovervilles." Newspapers used as covers by homeless people trying to keep warm become known as "Hoover blankets."

By fall, public opinion turns against President Hoover and the Republican Congress allowing Franklin D. Roosevelt to easily win the election. A Democratic Congress is also elected.

1933

Roosevelt is inaugurated on March 4 and immediately begins his "First 100 Days" of legislative activity directed at ending the Depression.

When another series of bank runs begin, Roosevelt, on the day after he was inaugurated, declares a 4-day "banking holiday." During this period, he introduces the Emergency Banking Act of 1933. On the third day of the banking closure, Roosevelt does his first "fireside chat" to the American people to reassure them that banks will be safe.

Prohibition ends on March 22, much to the glee of many Americans looking for any form of good news.

Congress creates the Agricultural Administration, the Civilian Conservation Corps (CCC), the Farm Credit Administration, The Federal Deposit Insurance Corporation (FDIC), the Federal Relief Administration, the National Recovery Administration, and the Tennessee Valley Authority (TVA). These measures are intended to get America back to work, protect personal savings, and enable industry and agriculture to recover.

In April, President Roosevelt stops a run on gold by having the U.S. abandon the gold standard and orders everyone to exchange any gold privately held for dollars.

48 more dust storms ravage Oklahoma and surrounding states. Farmers slaughter over 5 million hogs in an attempt to raise prices for pork.

The economy continues to shrink, but only by 2%. Unemployment is now at a record 24.9% affecting 12.8 million workers. The Dow Jones average is 84.

1934

The worst dust storm to date occurs across the Great Plains on April 15, dubbed Black Sunday. The hottest temperatures on record occur with 29 consecutive days at or above 100 degrees. By the end of the year, drought is now affecting over ¾ of the country.

With unemployment in Toledo, Ohio at 70%, workers at the Electric Auto-Lite Company go on strike seeking higher wages. An interim settlement is reached, but on May 23 a crowd of over 10,000 picketers are met with tear gas bombs. A melee between the crowd and the police ensues with over 20 people injured. The following day the Governor sends in National Guard troops to restore order. A running battle takes place throughout the day and night. Over the next several days, two strikers are killed, and many others injured by bullets and a bayonet charge from National Guardsmen, many of whom are also injured by objects thrown at them. Roosevelt sends mediators to Toledo, but the strike is not settled until May 28. The incident becomes known as "The Battle of Toledo."

In response to many of the New Deal programs, the economy grows 7.7% and prices rise 1.5%. Unemployment falls but remains well over 20%.

1935

Congress passes the Works Progress Administration (WPA) to hire 8.5 million people.

The National Labor Relations Board (NLRB) and the Rural Electrification Administration are created.

The Social Security Act is passed by Congress to assist the elderly, the disabled, and children in low-income families. It is funded with payroll taxes.

The Supreme Court rules that the National Recovery Administration is unconstitutional.

Farmers are now paid to plant soil-building crops.

The economic recovery continues. GNP increases by another 8.1% and unemployment declines, but only to 20%.

1936

Germany and Sweden are now fully recovered from the Depression, mostly due to deficit spending. Economic recovery continues in the U.S with GNP growth at a record 14.1%. Unemployment decreases to 16.9%.

More record high temperatures occur in many states during June and July. Twenty states experience temperatures above 110 degrees, with Seymour, Texas recording 120 degrees in August. Nearly 1700 die due to heat, and 3500 are reported to drown while attempting to cool off.

The top tax rate is raised to 79%.

President Roosevelt is easily re-elected defeating Governor Alf Landon of Kansas. Roosevelt wins all but 8 electoral votes, losing only Maine and Vermont. In Congress, the Democrats overwhelm the Republicans by winning ¾ of the seats. In the Senate the results are much the same; the Republicans give the Democrats a supermajority by holding only 16 seats.

1937

The Supreme Court declares the National Labor Relations Board to be unconstitutional. Roosevelt seeks to enlarge the court by adding justices more sympathetic to his New Deal programs, but his attempt fails due to public outrage.

At the beginning of his second term, Roosevelt launches more New Deal programs, including state-run housing projects and loans to tenant farmers to buy land.

The President and Congress opt to cut spending in an attempt to reduce the growing national debt, but during the summer the recovery stalls and the economy falls into a steep decline. Despite the recession, the yearly GNP rises by 5.0% and unemployment continues to decline to 14.3%.

1938

In a major legislative victory for Roosevelt, Congress establishes a federal minimum wage of 25 cents per hour. The original goal was 40 cents an hour but was scaled back to secure votes from members of Congress from southern states.

Congress passes the Agricultural Adjustment Act and the Fair Labor Standards Act, but no additional significant New Deal legislation is passed after April due to Roosevelt's weakened political power.

Kate Smith first performs Irving Berlin's song, "God Bless America" on an Armistice Day radio broadcast. Two years later both FDR and the Republican candidate for President, Wendell Wilkie, choose her version for their campaign theme song.

The recession continues and is felt as GNP drops 4.5% for the year and unemployment again rises to 19.0%. Eight million are now unemployed.

Prices fall nearly 3%. Near the end of the year, economic activity begins to pick up. The Dow Jones average is 132.

1939

Drought conditions return to the Southeast. Farmers again suffer.

The U.S. begins to emerge slowly from the Depression as nearly $1 billion is borrowed to build up the Armed Forces.

In September, Hitler invades Poland, starting WW II. American manufacturing begins to increase sending arms to France and Britain beginning in November.

The economy grows 8% but unemployment falls only to 17.2%.

Follow-on Years

Over the next two years, many Americans begin to obtain jobs and the economy grows. By the end of 1941, following the U.S. declaration of war on Japan and Germany, unemployment declines to under 10% and American manufacturing is headed to wartime production levels. With millions of men now in military uniforms there is no longer a shortage of jobs. The Great Depression is over, but the nation is now in a wartime footing with no certainty of victory. It is not until November 23, 1954 that the stock market returned to the level of September 3, 1929.

Some averages prices and numbers during the Depression:

	1929	1933	1938
Average Income	$2062	$1555	$1731
New Car	$450	$550	$860
New House	$7246	$5759	$3900
Loaf of Bread	9 cents	7 cents	9 cents
Gallon of Milk	58 cents	42 cents	50 cents
Gallon of Gas	12 cents	10 cents	10 cents
Dow Jones Average	311	84	132 (1929 is prior to crash)

It is interesting that the price of a new car climbed steadily during the Depression, while houses declined by nearly half. Bread, milk, and gas remained relatively steady, but with average incomes decreasing in the depths of the Depression, affording these necessities became more challenging.

Acknowledgements

To paraphrase the English poet, John Donne: No book is an island. None of the work associated with this collection of remembrances about the Great Depression would have been possible without the life-saving heart donation by the family of my donor, Monica, in September 1994. It was during the recovery from that transplant miracle that I began to regret not having listened to the life-stories told by my parents who both struggled to survive the Depression. Because both had passed away years earlier, I became determined to listen to other parents who, I soon learned, had rich, informative memories of their lives. I am grateful for each interview. I cannot say enough about their warmth and willingness to share memories with, in most cases, a total stranger. Of course, as I mention in the beginning of many chapters, I was the the beneficiary of suggestions by friends and relatives concerning people they knew "with great stories." Without their help, I would have remained on "the island,"

I also had the benefit of several generous reviewers who continually provided feedback and suggestions on the format and content of these chapters. Lynn Mulholland and Betty Ryder in Maine, Bruce and Mary Jane Heater in New Jersey, Mary and Chip Seymour in Maryland, Elizabeth D. Smiley in Arizona, Fred Berthrong in Mexico, Hank Horn in Virginia and my long-time editor and friend, Aaron Spurway, in Washington - all contributed valuable insight. Without their thoughtful assistance, the stack of notes and tapes I gathered in the late 1990's would have remained dormant. I also am grateful to family members of the interviewees who, when contacted over 20 years later, graciously found additional material and provided missing facts about their loved ones. Finally, I must acknowledge the support of my wife, Sharon, and daughter, Emily, who provided constant encouragement during those writing days in Maine when I could have been hiking and kayaking with them.

Of course, I alone am responsible for the final content of this book. Any errors or omissions are totally mine.

Ed Linz
Greenville, Maine

2021

About the Author

E D LINZ GREW UP ON a small farm in Kentucky. He graduated from the U.S. Naval Academy in 1965. His subsequent 20-year career in submarines included an assignment as Commanding Officer, USS KAMEHAMEHA (SSBN642), a nuclear-powered ballistic missile submarine. Following retirement from the Navy he taught Physics and coached cross country in public schools in Virginia for over 25 years. His education includes Master's degrees from Christ Church College, Oxford University in Economics and George Mason University in Secondary Education.

Ed continues to teach Physics to home-schooled students in Virginia and has been a guest lecturer on trips abroad (as shown above). He lectures on the intersection of science and special education and does presentations on organ donation based on being the benefactor of a life-saving heart transplant in 1994.

They Never Threw Anything Away is his fourth book. His interests include hiking; he recently "made it" to 15,000 feet on Mount Kilimanjaro in Tanzania. In addition to his weekly column, **Eyes Right**, he is currently working on another non-fiction book, ***Heart Transplant Hiker,*** and a sequel to his novel, ***Hurtling to the Edge***. Ed encourages you to contact him via email at **edlinz@edlinz.com**, on Facebook or on Twitter **@edlinz65**. His columns and book information can be found at **www.edlinz.com**.